M000310946

THE FLY-FISHER'S COMPANION

The
Fly-Fisher's
Companion
A Fundamental Guide to Tackle, Casting, Presentation, Aquatic Insects, and the Flies that Imitate Them

Darrel Martin

Skyhorse Publishing

Skyhorse Publishing books may be purchased in bulk at special discounts for sales promotion, corporate gifts, fund-raising, or educational purposes. Special editions can also be created to specifications. For details, contact the Special Sales Department, Skyhorse Publishing, 307 West 36th Street, 11th Floor, New York, NY 10018 or info@skyhorsepublishing.com.

Skyhorse® and Skyhorse Publishing® are registered trademarks of Skyhorse Publishing, Inc.®, a Delaware corporation.

Visit our website at www.skyhorsepublishing.com.

10 9 8 7 6 5 4 3 2 1

Library of Congress Cataloging-in-Publication Data is available on file.

Cover design by Brian Peterson
Cover photo credit: Darrel Martin

Print ISBN: 978-1-62914-408-5
Ebook ISBN: 978-1-62914-952-3

Printed in China

CONTENTS

ACKNOWLEDGMENTS

I wish to acknowledge my gratitude to those whose knowledge and generosity have enriched this book. To the various companies and individuals who have generously supported my passion. To Simms Fishing Products, Korkers, and HMH Vises; to the Sage Company for their support and Marc Bale, who keeps fishing my English waters; to Daniel Galhardo and Tenkara USA; to the ever-helpful Tom Rosenbauer and the Orvis Company; to John and Ione Claggett for their friendship and lovely water; to Bill Klyn and Patagonia. And to all my past angling students who still enjoy the bend of the long rod. To Michael, my son, a fishing companion who still tolerates his father. To my wife, Sandra, who knows how much she is part of my life and this book.

INTRODUCTION

This book grew from a desire to consolidate instructions found in my fly-fishing classes. It is a textbook that includes concise and selective commentary on tackle, casting, tying, and other topics. The word "companion" derives from "one with whom we share our bread." After more than fifty years of fly fishing, I would like to sit at the streamside and share these observations. Here is the knowledge and understanding that I wished I had when I began fly fishing. Some sections are twice-told tales. They come from my decades as Contributing Editor to *Fly Rod & Reel* magazine, others from my books, especially *Fly-Tying Methods* (Nick Lyons Books, 1987), *Micropatterns* (Lyons & Burford, 1994), and *The Fly-Fisher's Illustrated Dictionary* (The Lyons Press, 2000). And much here is entirely new.

There is always the challenge of depicting complex actions of casting with static drawings. I have sought the clearest language and images to explain each topic. The detailed photography and drawing should allow the student to follow each reason and wrap in the tying process. Like all text books, this companion works best with an instructor. Fly-fishing instruction is available from certified teachers, numerous websites, informative videos, and countless books. To the casual observer, fly casting may look like a clock hand arcing through the numbers. However, proper fly casting is controlled and natural. And, once understood, fly casting is remarkably simple.

This companion may serve as a foundation or a supplement for fly-fishing instruction that includes casting, presentation, knots, and fly-tying. It may also be a reminder or reference for the more experienced angler. As a retired educator, I recognize that instructors present material in different ways. Instructors may wish to select only those topics that fit their syllabus while omitting others. These instructions and commentary have produced, in my classes, decades of competent fly fishers. We all learn by image, word, and action. Since the sepia days of Walton and Cotton, fly fishing has been an enthralling sport. And, as this companion hopefully makes clear, there is more to fishing than fish. There is pleasure in learning a skill and doing it well.

The Basic Insects is a brief guide to identifying common aquatic insects. It is only a beginning. Matching the hatch is a traditional method of capturing an insect and selecting a fly pattern to match it. It is direct and simple, requiring minimal insect knowledge. In time, however, most anglers want to know more about the insects that trout consume and that tyers imitate. Insect knowledge—what they look like, where they live, and how they move—is a fascinating study that often results in greater angling success. When sampling insects, select the most active and prevalent. Check the aquatic plants, the rocks in the water, the leaves on trees, and bushes along the bank. What flies in the air or floats on the water, and what clings to the leaves? It is certain that when you fly fish, you will eventually come to admire a few selected insects. They are, after all, the exquisite charms of fly fishing.

Here are no apologies for historic references. The early anglers were thoughtful and competent. Though they lacked modern equipment, they were skilled in their tackle and their theories. I have illustrated this text with my personal tackle and trim, but there are countless products on the market from which to choose. I further believe that this textbook can be useful to all anglers, no matter their skill or experience. Let these lessons and experiences, which have matured along the banks for more than fifty years, help you enjoy angling with a fly.

THE TACKLE AND TRIM

W ELCOME TO TACKLE AND TRIM. THIS SECTION describes the basic components of fly fishing. It also illustrates the major features of equipment as well as the proper care. There is an immense variety of rods, reels, lines, and vests available for the modern angler. I include information on wading safety, the backing loop connection, protective clothing, wading boots, and other items of interest. In any case, a novice should be well informed before the purchase and use of tackle.

SELECTING THE FLY ROD

An expensive rod does not make you an accomplished caster. Before selecting a rod, take professional casting instruction if possible and cast various rods. Perhaps the first consideration when selecting a basic fly rod is the line weight. The line weight is determined by, to a significant extent, the water fished, the fish sought, and the fly cast. Here are common line weight preferences:

Line	*Fishing*
0–3 (and smaller)	Ponds and small streams, minimal wind
4–6	Medium to large trout, medium to large rivers
7–9	Large water and large fish, bass, pike, and steelhead
10–15 (and larger)	Big game fresh and saltwater fish

Fly rods are sometimes classified as light weight (0–5 and smaller), medium-weight (6–7), heavy weight (8–9), and big game (10 and larger).

What a medium-weight rod is to one angler may be a light- or heavy weight rod to another. There are varied preferences as to what constitutes the proper rod weight and length for a given water or fish. *At present, there is a trend toward lighter-weight tackle for larger fish.* The most common rod sold in the American West is a 9′ 5-weight or 6-weight rod. These rods can tolerate moderate winds and launch long lines. It has been said that the 3-weight is the first efficient rod weight. Rods under 3-weight may require more effort for less effect, especially against wind. Having said that, some anglers, such as my adult son, find great pleasure in fishing the ultralights—the 00- or 000-weight rods. Note the following elements when purchasing a fly rod.

The Bend

The bend or spring is perhaps the most individual feature of a rod. Facetiously, I tell my students that the greatest expense of a rod is the bend. When you buy a rod, you buy a bend. Select the bend carefully. After the casting stroke, a rod should dampen quickly; there should be negligible bounce, wave, or wiggle that affects accuracy and distance. There are fast tip-flex rods, soft full-flex rods, and many in between. Although not always possible, a rod should be cast before being bought. And cast as many available rods as possible before making a decision. Try the rods of several friends. The more you cast, the more you will know. Rod testing is usually done on land without water tension. Although seldom possible at specialty fly shops, the best test scenario is on water. Just note that a dry cast is not a wet cast. Water expresses more of the rod's character. Remember, too, that a different fly line can make a different rod. If possible, use your own reel and preferred line when rod testing. A rod with a reel attached should feel relatively light in the hand; it should not drag the hand down when held. This rod drag can be tiring after a few hours.

The Rod-Blank Diameter

A large-diameter rod blank pushes more air during the casting stoke thus requiring more effort while generating lower line speeds. Select narrow diameter rods that lessen air drag and sustain line speed during the casting stroke.

The Rod Length

The multi-piece 9′ rod is the most common rod now purchased. It allows line management and manipulation, such as curve casts and reach casts (see Chapters 3 and 4) while limiting total rod weight and air drag. A long rod establishes a high backcast and efficiently mends line. Rods longer than 9′ are appropriate for float-tubing, deep wading, and casting over cattails and other tall vegetation or obstacles. Rods 7½′ to 8½′ long are best for restricted line-mending, limited-length casts, and bushy or canopied streams. The standard trout rod length ranges from 7½′ to 9′ long. Most multi-piece rods, especially 4- and 5-piece rods, fit into checked air baggage; no longer do stiff ferrules create undue rod weight or dead joints. Most modern multi-piece rods bend smoothly when cast.

Quality Cork Handle

Quality cork is expensive with limited production. There is, however, no suitable synthetic material available to replace cork. The handle shape should allow comfort as well as grip security. The ubiquitous, popular, and attractive cigar grip—usually on light trout rods—offers only a modest but adequate placement for the thumb's power. Until recently, all my 4-weights had cigar grips. Lately, a manufacturer produced a new 4-weight with a full-Wells grip. Although I first reacted against a plump full-Wells (which swells at top and bottom) on a 4-weight, I soon discovered that I enjoyed the comfort and power available.

Rod Weight

Keep it light; total rod weight performs a major role in casting ease. Here are the total rod weights of four 4-piece, 4-weight, 9′ quality rods: the Sage One rod is 2½ ounces, the Orvis Helios 2 rod is 2⅜ ounces, the Winston BIIIX rod is 2½ ounces, and the Hardy Zenith Sintrix rod is 2⅘ ounces. These are light and responsive rods that cast with the trajectory of a .30-06 rifle. A light rod usually translates into a fast stroke and fast line speed. A 9′ 10-weight rod with fighting butt may be more than twice that weight. A day of pushing and pulling heavy patterns through jungle heat with a heavy 10-weight can exhaust even the most enthusiastic angler. Manufacturers will continue to make lighter and more responsive rods. Most quality rods have an adequate guarantee against defects and breakage. No matter what the rod length and line weight, the lighter the rod, the greater the casting comfort.

A quality modern fly rod has the muscle to conquer wind, create long casts, and control powerful fish. The 6-weight rod today does the bidding of a 10-weight from ten years ago. Anglers have conquered double-digit fish on 2-weight or lighter rods. I began casting with a heavy telescoping steel fly rod. Needless to say, it took several years and a fiberglass rod before I could call myself a beginner. Not all fly rods are marvelous.

Cosmetics

Care should be evident in the thread wraps, the thread finish, the rod-blank finish, and reel seat. An up-locking reel seat keeps grime and grit farther from the reel mechanics. The attractive gloss of a fly rod blank can reflect sunlight that frightens nearby fish. Although seldom offered by manufacturers, a matte rod finish is preferred by some anglers. Generally, however, long casts keep the flash away from fish. Fish are more likely to be frightened by aerialized line or fleeting shadows. Avoid rods that have a rod section with scratches or scrapes that can grow into something more.

THE DEDICATED FLY ROD

It is only natural that the fly rod, like the modern fly line, has become more specialized. Here are a few dedicated trout fly rods that are available. These specialized rods include a cast from the past (the Tenkara) and focused rods (the Czech Nymph Rod, the Switch Rod, and the Indicator Rod).

The Japanese Tenkara Rod

The modern Japanese Tenkara rod, usually 9′ to 15′ long, is reel-less. A furled thread, silk, or fluorocarbon monofilament, either level or tapered, attaches directly to a soft, fine rod tip. The graphite Tenkara rod telescopes into the handle for convenient transportation and storage. Reversed hackle patterns are traditionally cast. This is elemental angling: simple, Spartan, and minimalistic. There is neither reel nor rod guides—only a rod, a line, and a fly. From its ancient Japanese origin in the fairly peaceful Edo period (1603–1868), the Tenkara was bamboo with a loop at the tip (hence loop rod) for attaching a horsehair line. Such loop rods appear early in angling history. Claudius Aelianus (Aelian), a Roman who dates from 170 to 230 AD, describes a 6′ wooden loop rod and horsehair fly line traditionally fished in Macedonia. Modern materials make the Tenkara rod light, flexible, and pleasant to cast.

The Tenkara is gaining popularity. Casting is intuitive and quickly learned. The *lilian* (a short braided line) secures the fly line to the rod tip. According to Dr. Kevin Kelleher in *Tenkara*, the term derives from "lily yarn," a manufacturing process. Earlier it was called *hebikuchi* or "snake mouth" for its resemblance to the tongue of a snake. The Tenkara is especially appropriate for small streams and waters. There are several casts done with the Tenkara, including the reach cast, the overhead cast, the T-cast, the C-cast, the roll cast, and the horizontal cast. It is often fished by dapping (only the fly touches the water) or with minimal watered line. Like all loop rods, the casting distance is severely limited to rod length, line length, and the extended arm. Daniel Galhardo of Tenkara USA notes that it is possible to cast and fish a 30′ line; however, he recommends a 20′ to 24′ line. Landing a fish requires drawing the fish close before grabbing the line or netting the fish. It requires stream craft and the ability to approach fish. This is intimate angling. The key to tenkaring is water selection. Select water or cover that places the fish within your casting range. The Tenkara is perhaps the easiest entry into fly fishing.

Before using such rods, check all appropriate fishing regulations. Present Washington State fishing regulations require that for fly-only water, an angler must use a "conventional fly line (other line may be used for backing or leader if attached to at least 25 feet of fly line)." The term "conventional fly line" and the "25 feet of fly line" prevent, at present, the use of the Tenkara in fly-only waters. Other waters and selective-gear waters that use single-point, barbless hooks allow Tenkara. The Washington State Fish and Game Department plans to fully address the use of loop rods.

Tenkara rods appear in various configurations from several companies. For example, the Temple Fork Outfitters Soft Hackle 10′6″ Tenkara closes down to 20.5″ and conveniently comes with an extra tip and second section, which are the most likely to suffer damage. The rod bag also has a built-in line holder.

The TFO Soft Hackle 10′6″ Tenkara

The Rhoda from TenkaraUSA

The extendable Tenkara Rhoda is a light rod (2.1 oz.) with a Triple-zoom, 8-segment system that allows fishing at three different lengths: 8′10″, 9′9″, and 10′6″. The rod closes to 21″ and comes with an extra rod plug.

The Czech Nymph Rod

Czech nymphing—a melding of Polish-Czech patterns and techniques—achieved popularity in European fly-fishing competitions during the '80s. Instead of the traditional overhead cast, the angler extends his or her arm and rod to flip the fly upstream, drifting the weighted fly under tension

Sage ESN (European Style
Nymph Rod), 10′, 4-weight,
4-piece

deep in the flow. Its effectiveness was apparent in 1986 when the Czech team won its first gold medal in Belgium. Czech nymphing has expanded in North America. G. Loomis, an American rod company, produces two 4-piece Czech Nymph Rods: a 10′ 3-weight and for larger fish and heavier water, a 10′ 4-weight. These charcoal gray rods with dark plum windings feature fine-diameter grips and soft tips. They taper quickly from light, sensitive tips to firm butts for slinging weighted nymphs on short drifts. The fast taper and spring of these rods also allow for a quick lift and recast.

The Sage Company produces five 4-piece rods for 2- to 5-weight lines. They range from 10′ to 11′ long. The latter rod has a short fighting butt. As Sage notes, the nymphs are bounced among the boulders and debris and "fished under tension on light tippets to systematically dissect these micro-environments." Customarily, Czech nymphing uses two or three varying-weight nymph patterns, which are often tied on round shrimp hooks. It is short-distance, direct-line drifting, usually about a dozen feet, with an extended arm and multiple weighted nymphs. Rod length and an extended arm keep the angler away from the trout. Anglers finely tune the pattern weight to water depth and flow. The short drift usually passes under the rod tip, and in some cases, the fly line does not drift upon the water surface. A long, light leader and heavy nymphs do the work. After each cast, the angler steps upstream for another cast. This repetitive casting requires a light weight rod that places a pattern in every foot of water. A folktale explains the origins: Polish anglers lacked fly lines and thus were forced to use monofilament line only. By necessity, they used heavy nymphs and discarded the overhead cast.

Czech nymphing, however, is not just for short-lining. It is also successful with the more traditional long-line fishing where the patterns are actually cast—upstream, across stream, or downstream—and the fly line lies upon the water. Movement from the line or strike indicator announces any takes. The soft rod tip keeps a struggling fish on the hook. The best Czech nymph rods are long, light, and sensitive. With the extended arm and frequent casting, an angler requires the lightest possible rod. Though these rods can flip a fly a remarkable distance, line tension on the fly should always be present.

Steve Rajeff, an international competitive caster and Loomis's Director of Engineering, notes that Europeans "use either a small level line, such as monofilament, or even straight backing." In the United States, however, fly-fishing regulations may require a conventional fly line and restrict the number of weighted nymphs. "They use weighted nymphs and basically lob-cast one or more upstream and pull the flies through a short drift by leading with the rod tip." Czech nymph indicator fly lines are often floaters with a highly visible thick tip, a short front taper, and an ultra-long head for mending. The Czech method was developed to seduce pressure-sensitive trout in streams.

The Switch Rod

The switch rod is an acknowledged hybrid of the Spey rod (two-handed rod) and the trout rod (one-handed rod). An angler can then switch between two-handed and one-handed casts. The switch rod executes the standard Spey cast as well as the traditional over head cast and mend. To accommodate this, most switch rods are significantly lighter than a Spey rod and somewhat shorter, about 10′ to 12′ long. They commonly have a shortened, isolated upper grip and a short lower grip that looks like an extended fighting butt. Some switch rods have a single protracted upper grip. The rod length and the extra lever with the double grip create greater distance in the casts, longer reach casts (mending), and longer overhead casts. Such rods are used for fishing streamers, nymphs, and dries in rivers and lakes. The melding of Spey and trout produces a light, powerful rod for long casts and multiple flies. Some switch-rod anglers use a heavier line (usually 1-weight heavier) for two-handed Spey casting. The switch rod grew out of the development for ultra light long rods that could be handled with one hand as well as two.

The Indicator Rod

The indicator rod is designed for casting strike indicators, split-shot, heavy nymphs, and multi-fly rigs. In general, the rod tip is usually stiffer than the center section. The rod may load farther down to the softer mid section to widen or open the casting loop. A relatively firm tip ensures that the rod will cast the weight of multi-fly rigging and heavy nymphs. These rods are longer and may aerialize more line than conventional rods. The stiff yet sensitive tip subtly detects strikes and the oversized guides feed line quickly. These rods, developed to handle the often-awkward indicator and nymph systems, offer tangle-free fishing of multi-nymphs and stack-mending tactics where line loops or circles are placed on the water and slowly extend with the current for long drifts.

THE FLY ROD HANDLE

There are several traditional rod handle designs. There are also some unique variations. The cigar-shaped handle is, perhaps, the most common trout design. However, manufacturers may vary this handle shape from a

The Sage Z-Axis (5110-4), a 5-weight, 11′, 4-piece switch rod with extended handle

traditional cigar handle (the classic torpedo shape) to a modified, reversed half-Wells design with a mild flare at the lower end. It all depends upon the degree of the flare. A large flare creates a reversed half-Wells; a small flare creates a cigar handle. Manufacturers often label this handle either way. The lower palm pads (the thenar and hypothenar muscles—the heel of the hand) press against the lower flare for casting power. Greater casting power comes when the thumb presses against a top flare during the forward casting stroke. Flares are found in the half-Wells (upper flare) or full-Wells (upper and lower flares) handle designs. Trout fishing and trout distances, however, usually do not require a power handle with significant flares. Moreover, the gently tapering cigar grip (offering no support for thumb or palm pads) remains remarkably attractive. Some anglers find that a full-Wells handle on a light trout rod appears clubby and gauche. Half-Wells and full-Wells are usually found on the heavier, 8- to 12-weight rods.

There are, of course, departures from the established handle designs. For example, the Gordon handle, vaguely akin to a Ritz with a lower flare, illustrates a possible variation. The Gordon, an early design now rarely found, has a lower flare and an increasing taper toward the top. The lower flare offers a seat for the palm pads, while the top gives width for the thumb. Even when manufacturers make the same handle design, there are usually minor variations in the flare, the taper, the diameter, and the length. Rod grips are commonly made with glued cork rings that are hand-shaped with rasps and sandpapers on a lathe. A template determines the final shape.

No matter what grip is selected, a rod handle should be comfortable. Several hundred (if not a few thousand) casting strokes are made during a single fishing day. The handle diameter must offer a secure grip, neither too narrow nor too wide. Handles should be more than 6″ long to allow hand repositioning, an important factor in comfort. Synthetic handles, which seldom appear on quality rods, lack the comfort and responsiveness of cork. Double AA quality cork is the best and rarest material for handles. Anatomical grips (those with cut-out channels that match the hand shape) are eventually more tiring. They demand that the hand maintain the same position and placement for each cast. Although we get the handle that comes with a rod, it is still of value to consider how handle shape affects casting.

The Ritz: The broad top of the straight-tapered Ritz favors thumb placement and repositioning.

The Full-Wells: The full-Wells, a common grip for heavy-line rods, has flares on each end of the handle. The full-Wells may be the handle shape that most closely follows the contours of the hand and thumb, thus providing a secure and commanding grip.

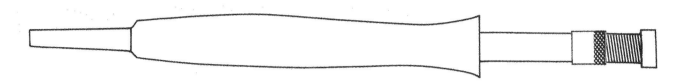

The Reversed Half-Wells: With an understated lower flare, the half-Wells may be labeled a cigar grip. With exaggerated proportions (swelled center and large lower flare), the reversed half-Wells becomes the fishtail grip. This grip can be remarkably subtle and understated, making it traditional and ubiquitous.

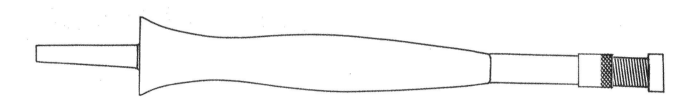

The Half-Wells: The clean and simple half-Wells favors the thumb.

The Cigar: This classic and attractive fusiform cigar handle grip, sometimes identified as the standard or torpedo, appears on many light-line rods.

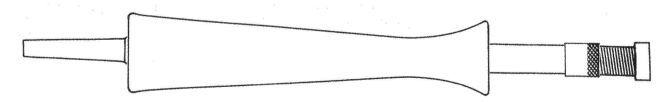

The Gordon: The Gordon grip offers both the hand heel and the thumb sufficient support.

FLY ROD CARE AND MAINTENANCE

To remove slime and grime, carefully clean a rod handle with a mild detergent. Soft Scrub liquid soap or a powder cleanser with bleach can be used on particularly soiled grips. A judicial use of fine sandpaper smooths down rough spots, but take care to avoid reducing the diameter or misshaping the handle. Unless the cork is of the highest quality, a handle usually has rut fillers that can deteriorate with time. These small ruts left behind are readily filled with a mixture of waterproof glue, such as Titebond III Ultimate by Franklin International, and cork dust.

Polish each rod section with carnauba paste wax. Buff each section with a soft cloth. Rub candle wax (void of sticky resins or tack) on the male ferrules for ease of separation. Moreover, candle wax often helps to secure the connections. Candle wax should not be applied in extremely hot or tropical conditions. If rod and line are exposed to salt water, thoroughly wash them with fresh water and dry them before storage. Use desalination products for total care.

THE FLY REEL

The fly reel does three things: to a minor extent it helps balance the fly rod, it holds the line and backing, and it applies resistance when fighting fish. With the modern ultra light reels and rods, balance is far less a factor. Furthermore, depending on the aerialized line length, rod-reel balance constantly changes. All the reel has to do is to make the casting stroke natural and comfortable. A trout fly reel should be narrow (to prevent line stacking on one side of the spool) and have a large diameter (to avoid tight ringlets and tangles in the fly line). If the line stacks on one side of the spool, it may cascade over previous line wraps and bind, breaking off trout. Nearly all modern fly reels are ported or ventilated to reduce weight and dry the fly line and backing. Most trout reels allow switching the handle from one side of the reel to the other. Like many right-handed trout fishermen, I cast with my right hand and reel with my left hand. This allows me to reel in or strip in line without switching hands, which is especially important during a trout skirmish. I can, of course, reel in line faster with my right hand, but seldom is such speed required. I commonly strip small trout in and put large trout on the reel by taking up the line slack. Big game fishing, though, may require the handle on the right side for rapid recovery. Reels machined from solid bar stock aluminum are considered stronger than those cast from an alloy. A less experienced angler should purchase a quality reel with a smooth, strong drag. Such a reel can control fish better.

The Drag

A smooth, durable drag is essential for large aggressive fish. The drag works only for outgoing line and should be adjusted to prevent over spin or backlash when the line is suddenly yanked. Drags are commonly spring and pawl, tooth and gear clicker, caliper compression, or disk. Trout reels frequently have a ratchet drag (spring and pawl) or a disk drag. For fast-running, powerful fish, select reels that have an adequate range of adjustable pressure. Conversely, some trout reels have a simple click drag that merely retards spool movement and prevents overrun that would produce line tangles. Additional fighting-fish drag must be supplied by friction from the fingers or palm to the revolving rim. The more serious disk drag applies pressure against a cork or composite pad between the frame and spool. A smooth, modest startup tension is important. On some reels, it may be best to begin with negligible drag—just enough to prevent overspin. Once a good fish takes, the proper, predetermined tension is then dialed in with the drag knob. The two common drag systems, the click-pawl and the disk drag, are illustrated here.

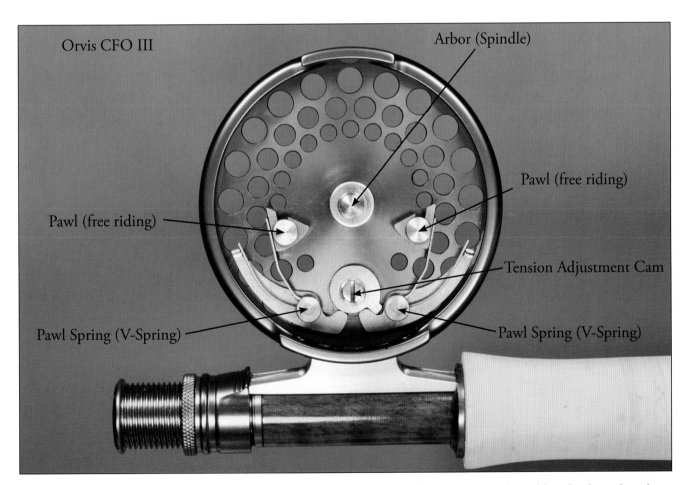

When inserted in the frame, a gear attached to the spool engages the pawls. Pawl tension is adjusted by a knob on the side of the frame that rotates the cam. Both pawls can be adjusted for maximum tension. The pawls are commonly adjusted, however, to click stronger in one direction (extending line) than in the other direction (retrieving line).

This traditional CFO fly reel has an adjustable spring and pawl (click-pawl) system. The spring compression on the pawls determines the drag resistance and may be adjusted by turning the drag knob located on the back of the reel frame. Apply additional resistance by palming the spool rim with the fingers or the palm. To prevent line overrun, adequate drag pressure must be applied when stripping line out or when fighting fish. Overrun is when the spool continues to spin, thereby slackening and loosening the fly line. Overrun can cause line tangles and macramé. When not in use, back off the drag to release all tension. Many reels sold are adjusted for left-hand retrieve for right-handed casters. In this reel, the curved sides of the pawl face the wind side. If the curved pawl sides face right, it is right-hand wind. If they face left, then the reel is left-hand wind. Although this spring and pawl system only retards the spool, many trout fishermen find that the management of line through stripping, releasing, or palming line is part of the pleasure of trout fishing. Most trout anglers appreciate the hand-work of fighting and landing fish.

Adjust a disk drag reel so that the fish requires effort to take line but not so much effort that it breaks the tippet. It is best that a fish take rather than break line. On some reels, additional drag may be applied by the hand or fingers pressing against an exposed revolving rim. Before storage, the drag should be completely backed off and relaxed to prevent compression damage to the disk drag. Single-action reels (one rotation of the handle equals one rotation of the spool and line) are common and simple. Multiplying reels—one rotation of the handle equals two rotations (2:1 ratio) or three

This drag, adjusted with a drag knob on the side of the frame, is typical of other disk-drag systems. When the line extends with the drag set, the spool is forced against the impregnated-cork surface and the pawl is operative. When retrieving line, the side plate revolves. A few turns of the drag knob exerts enormous spool resistance.

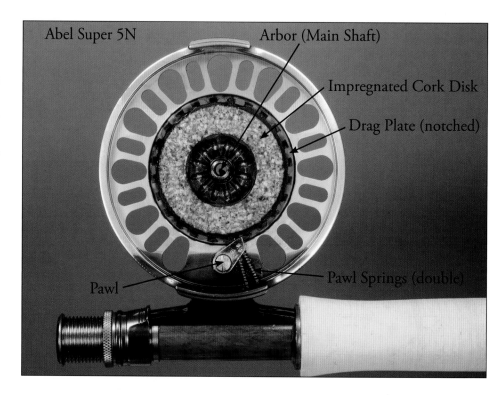

Abel Super 5N — Arbor (Main Shaft) — Impregnated Cork Disk — Drag Plate (notched) — Pawl — Pawl Springs (double)

rotations (3:1 ratio) of the spool—are uncommon in trout fishing, as are automatic reels. When mounted on a rod, a line-loaded reel should balance the rod near the top of the handle or slightly lower at the center of the hand. Although the reel varies its weight as the fly line lengthens or shortens, this balance minimizes fatigue and encourages a more natural casting stroke.

Reel Care

Reels require little care as long as they are kept clean. A periodic fine oil film over the metal and a good wipe is all that is required. Excessive oil will pick up dirt and grit and can cause damage. Cork drag disks can dry and harden; a fine film of neatsfoot oil conditions and preserves cork and leather drag disks. Apply pure neatsfoot oil only if the drag is not smooth. An all-temperature grease should be used on springs and gears. Most center arbors (spindles) occasionally require a light grease or medium oil. Usually, a fine film of grease on the arbor is all that is required. Thoroughly air-dry a reel before storage and protect the reel with a case. Preferred cases cover and protect a reel while connected to the rod. Keep smooth running freshwater trout reels away from dirt, mud, and saltwater. If used in the salt, rinse the reel completely with warm, fresh water and soap or soak it in Salt-X from K. C. Trading Limited, a concentrate for flushing away salt residue and crystals. Thoroughly dry before storage. If screws are present, check them for tension. Some anglers remove all exposed or loose screws and paint their threads with lacquer and reinstall. Loctite Threadlocker may be too aggressive and result in screws impossible to remove when required. For most freshwater reels, periodic disassembly and cleaning (perhaps once a year or after contact with dirt and sand) is all that is required. Use a soft cloth and small brush to wipe away the old oil and grit. Clean the arbor and gears before applying new oil or grease.

THE FLY LINE

Unlike other forms of angling, fly fishing uses a distinctive heavy line. And the fly rod casts the line weight; the feathery fly, which lacks sufficient weight (mass) for casting, merely follows the leader and line. It is the weight of the fly line that makes casting possible. In brief, we cast the weight of the fly line and the distribution of that weight (the taper). The weight and its distribution give a fly line its particular casting characteristics. A fly line has two fundamental components: (1) the central core and (2) the outer coating. The central core presents a foundation for the Polyvinyl Chloride (PVC) or Gel Spun Polyethylene (GSP) coating.

The Anatomy of a Fly Line

THE ANATOMY OF A FLY LINE
[Figurative Illustration]

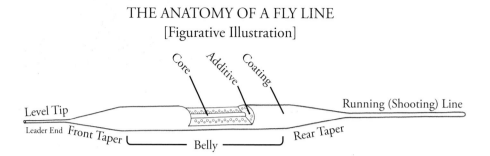

Line Core

Fly lines are further classified according to water temperature: cold water, temperate water, and tropical water. A tropical line placed in cold water becomes stiff and unruly; a cold-water line in the tropics may nearly dissolve, especially if left on a hot metal deck. The core material, which significantly determines the temperature range, establishes the strength, the rigidity (stiffness), and the stretch of the fly line. Various core combinations are used. Tim Pommer, in the Product Development Department for Scientific Anglers, defines the three cores used in their fly lines.

1. Braided Multifilament: Hundreds of tiny nylon filaments are braided around a hollow core that resembles a Chinese finger trap. The result is a limp, high-floating core used mostly for temperate or cold fishing lines. The multifilament core has low memory, high stretch, and moderate shooting characteristics.

2. Single Strand Mono: This moderate-stretch core is simply a single monofilament strand. It is typically found in wet lines since it sinks quickly. It has superior shooting ability as well as high coil memory. Most single-strand monofilament core lines retain reel coil memory. When stripped from the reel, it continues to retain the memory of the reel loops. A firm line stretch purges most loops and tangles.

3. Braided Mono: The braided mono core, the strongest core, has about eight strands of nylon monofilament braided together. An SA proprietary primer makes the line coating stick to the core. The braided mono offers several characteristics of the single strand mono core but with reduced memory and minimal stretch. These features plus its superior shooting ability make it appropriate for tropical saltwater lines.

The Line Coating

The outer coating often includes plasticizers, lubricant, UV inhibiters, Teflon powder, heat stabilizer, and particular additives. Within the coating, various float additives (such as hollow glass microspheres or micro-balloons) or density additives (such as tungsten dust) determine the line's specific gravity. The quantity and location of the additive determine the degree of flotation or sink. The specific gravity of water is 1.0; a specific gravity of 0.9 or less—due to the presence of microspheres, gaseous cells, or other ingredients—produces a floating line. The amount and distribution of the additive determine line composition and casting characteristics. A fly line, such as a sink-tip (S/T) may be both floating and sinking. To improve strike hookups, a density-compensated coating allows a fly line to sink without creating a large, sagging belly. Line length varies from about 80′ to 110′ or more. Most fly lines run around 90′ long.

The Line Loops

For rigging convenience, some manufacturers add welded loops on both ends of a fly line. This creates a strong and nearly seamless connection to leader and backing. Line loops, however, should be small and streamlined to prevent excessive water drag and surface rip during pick up.

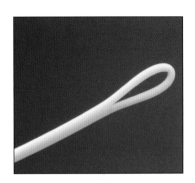

A line loop

Fly-Line Color

Floating lines tend toward bright colors, including various pale shades of yellow, cream, orange, peach, olive, blue, and tan. This allows the angler to see the line, fly placement, and movement even in low light. Sinking lines tend toward the dark side, such as brown, green, willow, and gray. With subsurface, unseen fly patterns, the angler must rely on line tension or sensation, especially when nymphing. Line color changes may indicate the beginning of a wet tip, the line loading point, or the start of the running line. Bright sink lines may be appropriate in low light and shallow nymphing. A dark line against a bright background may spook fish. Even the overhead flash of a bright or dark line can startle them. However, the leader and tippet should address the fish rather than the fly line.

In contrast, there are colorless fly lines. Monic Fly Lines, manufactured by Flo Tek of Colorado, produced (using in-line extrusion) the first clear floating fly lines in 1996. The use of a buoyant polyethylene coat over a monofilament core required no additives, such as micro-balloons, to create a clear floating line. These smooth, fairly firm transparent lines shoot extremely well due to a low coefficient of friction and have become effective in clear tropical saltwater and freshwater. Some Monic lines have a Gel Spun Polyethylene (GSP) core. The fine GSP cores are extremely strong with nil-stretch for instant strike reply. Although a clear line makes tracking the fly rather problematic, the stealth of a transparent line nearly eradicates spooking fish.

Sinking Lines

Fish feed primarily beneath the water surface. Sinking lines allow an angler to offer them a fly. Sink rates range from the intermediate to the deep sinkers. In a sink-tip line (S/T), the first 10′ to 30′ sinks beneath the surface. The remaining running line floats. To break the water tension of the sink tip, a roll-cast pickup is commonly used. As the roll cast lifts the sunken line from the water, an immediate backcast extends the line in the rear.

The Sink Scale

Although line manufacturers may offer different sink rates, the following scale is somewhat representative:

Line Type	Description	Sink Rate (inches per seconds)
Type 1	Slow (Intermediate)	1¼ to 1¾
Type 2	Fast	2½ to 3
Type 3	Extra fast	3½ to 4
Type 4	Super sinker	4¼ to 5
Type 5	Super fast	5¼ to 6
Type 6	Extra super sinker	6¼ to 7

Cortland manufactures a range of sinking lines in different densities or sink rates. The 444 Sinking Lines come in varying shades of brown with the darker shades indicating a faster sink rate than the slower lighter shades. This allows an angler to simply select a sink rate based on the shade of color.

The Intermediate Line

The thin intermediate lines may use just the density of the PVC coat, rather than tungsten powder, for their slow sink. The intermediate fly line (with an approximate density of 1.15, slightly heavier than water's density of 1.0) sinks slowly for shallow running nymphs or emergers. It is especially effective for lake fishing directly above weeds or along shallow lake margins.

The Sink-Tip Line

A sink-tip or dual-density line has approximately 10′ to 30′ of sink tip ahead of a floating belly and running line. This places the fly beneath the surface while offering the angler some control of the floating line. Sink tips come in various sink rates. The water resistance and weight of the sunken tip make pickup and casting more difficult. The roll-cast pickup is often preferred for sink-tip lines.

The Textured Line

In 2006, Airflo created polyurethane Ridge Lines with diminutive longitudinal ridges running the entire length of the line. More recently, Scientific

Anglers has added the Sharkskin, a line imprinted with micro-replicated scales. Unlike the conventional smooth surface, these new textures claim extraordinary performance; they trap air and increase surface area for higher floatation, have a longer shoot distance, eliminate line flash, reduce rod-guide friction, generate less water drag, ease line pickup, lessen spray, and shed more water in the backcast. Golf ball flight research has even suggested diminutive dimples to increase line flight distance. Although the early tex-tured lines were rather noisy through the guides, most modern textured lines have much to offer.

The Fly-Line Weight

In 1961, the American Fishing Tackle Manufacturers Association (AFTMA; now the American Sportsfishing Association, or ASA) established a numeri-cal line-rating scale that replaced the older letter designation system. The older silk line system used letters (such as HCH, a double taper) to indicate line diameter and taper. Due to the uniformity of the material (silk) and manufacturing methods, the line diameter, which ranged from A (0.060″) to I (0.20″), correlated to the weight. With the advent of synthetic lines, however, the letter-diameter designations became meaningless. Equal diam-eters can be unequal weights. The various materials, cores, finishes, and additives created different weights for equal diameters. The AFTMA chose a new standard based on the weight of the first 30′ of fly line (an assumed aerialized line length) exclusive of any tapering or the level tip. This first 30′ of line should load, or bend, the rod but not collapse, or eliminate the spring of the rod. The weight unit is based on grains: 437.5 grains=1 ounce (1 pound avoirdupois=7, 000 grains). The grain designation, one of the old-est and most precise weight units, derives from the weight of a single wheat grain. Fly lines ranged from a 1-weight (60 grains) to a 12-weight (380 grains). After all, a fly rod casts the weight rather than the diameter of a line. Thus any rod that responds to 30′ of 140 grains of line (no matter what the material or taper) is a 5-weight rod.

AFTMA STANDARD FLY-LINE WEIGHTS
(Grains per first 30′ [9.1 m] of line, excluding the short level line tip)

Designation	Weight	Acceptable Range
1-weight	60 grains	54–66 grains
2-weight	80 grains	74–86 grains
3-weight	100 grains	94–106 grains
4-weight	120 grains	114–126 grains
5-weight	140 grains	134–146 grains
6-weight	160 grains	152–168 grains
7-weight	185 grains	177–193 grains

Designation	Weight	Acceptable Range
8-weight	210 grains	202–218 grains
9-weight	240 grains	230–250 grains
10-weight	280 grains	270–290 grains
11-weight	330 grains	318–342 grains
12-weight	380 grains	368–392 grains
13-weight	450 grains	
14-weight	500 grains	
15-weight	550 grains	

Some modern lines do not correspond to the AFTMA scale. These specialty lines are manufactured for particular angling situations or specific fly rods. Moreover, some sinking and shooting lines do not have a traditional numbered weight but rather are designated by the actual grain weight of the first 30', such as a 250-grain sinking line. Line taper, weight, and density are designated by a standard code. For example, WF6F means a weight-forward taper, 6-weight (152–168 grains in the first 30' of fly line), floating fly line. The line code may also indicate a sink rate, such as type 3 sink (3½" to 4" per second). Finally, a few manufacturers have created their own variant line scale.

Although the ultra light ought lines (0–000 weights) and heavy-game lines (13–15 weights) are outside the traditional AFTMA scale, the extrapolated scale extends from the ought lines to the 15-weight. Line weights beyond (and even within the industry standard) may vary according to the manufacturer. Moreover, some special lines are over weighted ¼ to ½ or more standard line weight for fast action rods or special angling conditions. For example, to optimize high-performance rods, Sage's Performance Taper lines and Scientific Angler's GPX lines are ½ line heavier out of specification.

The Ought Scale

Tim Moon, Rio's General Manager, notes that the ought line differences (with few grains of range) are so minute that they are nearly negligible. According to Eric Gewiss, Sage's Marketing Manager, Sage's in-house ought designations lack a range. Sage, in fact, created its own in-house weight scale for their exclusive ultra light rods. Gewiss offers the following ascending scale for the ought-weights:

Ought Designation	Grain Weight
000-weight	40 grains
00-weight	47 grains
0-weight	53 grains

Line Matching

Matching a line to a rod is not absolute; anglers may over- or under-line a particular rod action or casting style. Remember, too, that most modern rods can accommodate more than one line weight. Casters should always select the particular line that matches their ability and circumstances. An over weighted line may actually load the rod shorter for more efficient close casting. For example, the Royal Wulff Ambush Triangle-Taper Fly Line with an abrupt 20′ heavy head and an ultra-thin diameter running line allows close-quarter casts and shooting roll casts. The Ambush Triangle- Taper floating line for a 6-weight rod is 235 grains. The AFTMA, however, rates the standard 6-weight line at only 160 grains. In short, anglers should fine-tune or tweak their tackle.

Under the AFTMA line scale, tolerances are fairly wide. In most cases, the balance of rod and line is a matter of preference. The AFTMA rating assumes that the average caster will aerialize approximately 30′ of line beyond the rod tip. It also assumes that if the rod balances with 30′ of line, then that balance will persist for customary longer and shorter casts. According to Don Green of Sage Rods, the modern fly rod is designed to aerialize 35—36′ of line, not just the AFTMA 30′.

When casting shorter than 30′, a heavier line may match the rod flex better. When casting beyond 30′, a lighter line may match. Although fly lines vary, there is some truth to the statement that *for every five feet of line beyond the taper, the line weight increases by one weight.* For example, a 5-weight line (at 4.9 grains per foot) would require about 4′ to accumulate 20 grains, the AFTMA line weight. A 3-weight (at 3.5 grains per foot) would require about 5.5′ to accumulate 20 grains. As line extends and recovers during casting, it actually becomes many different lines. A good caster accommodates (by timing and energy) the various lines within a line.

Suppleness may be the most significant quality when selecting lines for trout fishing. The suppleness, when rifled by a modern fast rod, produces distance with tight, narrow loops. Throwing deltas, those sharp running wedges at the front of a fast cast, results from flat line trajectory, extreme rod speed, and suppleness of line. A fine-diameter line also fosters penetration and distance when required.

Notice that while line weights are mathematically calculated, rod bend is still an art. The Orvis Company defines rod flex with a label and a numerical scale: tip flex (9.5–12.5), mid flex (6.0–9.0), and full flex (2.5–5.5). Such a system may be valuable for rod comparisons within specific models. Furthermore, a low tip flex for one rod company may be a high mid flex for another. There also remains the persistent problem of determining where a continuous bend starts and where it stops. A longer length of aerialized line would bend deeper into the rod. A 15′ cast with a 3-weight rod would require, according to the AFTMA scale, an 8-weight line. A 15′ cast with a 4-weight rod would require an 11-weight line. The point is simple; the appropriate but short line may not load the rod.

A 6-weight line is only a 6-weight at 30′. At shorter distances, it may be a 3-weight; at longer distances it may be an 8-weight. Some rods tolerate changes in line length better than others. Casting a given line length is one thing. But double-hauling and mending line may be entirely different. Although a rod may not distinguish any difference in loading 30′ of an 8-weight line or 70′ of a 3-weight line, casting and aerializing 70′ of a 3-weight line is different.

Furthermore, fly lines vary within the upper and lower range limits established by the AFTMA. The Cortland 444 Lazer Line 3-weight occurs in DT and WF. The DT, however, appears at 105.63 grains, while the WF appears at 93.26 grains. Both are 3-weights. The average 3-weight is 100 grains, ranging from 94 to 106 grains. As the ranges do not overlap, the light WF is considered to be a 3-weight. Depending upon the rod, these two lines may be significantly different. The heavier DT might prove superior for short casts, while the lighter WF might be better for longer delicate casts. Anglers who regularly cast shorter than 30′ may improve rod performance by increasing the line weight. Even small stream casts to 20′ may not be unusual. Assuming that a 10′ leader-tippet is used, the fisherman will cast only about 10′ of line, less than one-third the established AFTMA rod rating. The first several feet of a fly line, whether a 3-weight or an 8-weight, weighs nearly the same. Line weights only increase substantially when the heavier belly is included. A rod *feels* only the distributed mass of a fly line.

A rod works only when given energy. In the complex interplay of caster, rod, and line, a rod can pass only some energy to the fly line. Even in the simple overhead cast, energy transfer is intricate. First, energy is given to the rod during line pick-up. The rod consumes some energy as it bends when loading. During this time, the caster has loaded the rod to vertical. The rod stops dead and releases some energy throwing the line back. The extending backcast increases rod load. The caster now drifts the rod forward increasing the load. At maximum forward acceleration, the rod stops, passing energy into the extending forward line. Ideally, the fly line extends straight and smooth, exhausting all energy prior to touching the water.

The Coil Memory

Most anglers maximize the backing length by creating a larger diameter of line to increase retrieval speed (by creating a larger diameter of line) and lessen coil memory. Coil memory describes the tendency of a fly line to remain coiled once removed from the fly reel. Coil memory and its resulting tangles are generally considered to be directly related to the stiffness of the line. In contrast, line stiffness increases line shoot. A stiff line shoots through the rod guides with less line slap (when a ricocheting line slaps against the rod while passing through a guide) and less friction, resulting in a longer cast. Stiffness, however, often comes with brittleness and cracking. Additionally, a soft or flexible line swims better on the surface. Suppleness allows a line to drift with less surface drag and creates tighter and sharper casting loops. All line properties, including stiffness and softness, require appropriate balance for proper performance.

The Reel Freebore

Finally, maximizing the backing can create a common reel problem. When mounting a fly line and backing on a reel, one should allow approximately ¼–¾″ of free bore between the line coils and the line guard. Shorten the backing if required. When a fly line loads with firm, full wraps on the reel arbor, the spooled line may swell or expand during stripping and retrieving. This expansion can jam the spool during fishing. Adequate freebore prevents this.

Fly-Line Tapers

The line taper is imparted by the coating. A taper gives the fly line its particular casting characteristics. These tapers, moreover, are often modulated for particular casting conditions. All modern fly lines are variations of the following tapers. Basic line types are double taper (DT), weight forward (WF), sink tip (F/S), intermediate (I), sink (S), level (L), and shooting taper (ST). The shooting taper is also known as a shooting head (SH). Technically, the belly (the thick section of the fly line) and its tapers make up the head. Special lines may incorporate more than one taper profile, creating compound or complex tapers.

The Level Taper

Although designated as a level taper (L), this line lacks a taper; the diameter and commonly the weight are uniform throughout the entire length of the fly line. Fine-diameter level lines are often used as running lines for shooting heads.

The level-taper fly line

The Double Taper

The double-taper (DT) line is thicker and heavier in the midsection. Toward each end beyond the central belly, the diameter and weight is duplicated and decreased. This traditional taper, which loads near the rod tip, excels in close quarters. Generally, it works well for roll casts (as the heavier line extends the lighter line) and small streams. The proposal that a double-taper

(DT) line lasts longer because it reverses when worn is suspect. Reversing a DT line places the worn section across the guides, causing greater friction and abrasion both to line and guides. This reduces the shooting distance. Better to replace a fly line than the rod guides. Like the level line, a leader may attach to either end of a true DT fly line.

The double-taper fly line

The Weight-Forward Taper

The most efficient and popular taper is the weight-forward. This taper concentrates its weight in the front section, usually about 30′ or farther. The remainder of the line, the running line, is narrow and level. This allows the heavier head section to shoot (or pull) the light running line, creating longer casts. The weight forward is especially effective in driving heavy flies against wind. Some dedicated WF lines lengthen or shorten the head for particular angling conditions. When attaching a WF line to the reel, make certain that the heavy head attaches to the leader and that the thinner running line attaches to the backing. Manufacturers produce numerous variations of the WF by changing the belly lengths and taper angles to produce fresh and saltwater lines.

Leader End

The weight-forward taper fly line

The Triangle Taper

The triangle taper (TT), developed by Lee Wulff, excels at moderate distances and roll casts. In the progressive triangle taper, the large-diameter segment turns over the small-diameter segment. This is a continuous straight taper from the rear of the head to the line tip. In this design, a heavy line section continuously unrolls a lighter line section, making this an extremely efficient taper. The triangle taper is a constant taper in the head of the fly line that diminishes at the leader. All along the taper, each line segment continuously turns over the next smaller line segment. In brief, the thicker line continuously advances the thinner line. The light running line follows the taper as if it were a shooting head. The continuous taper offers a delicate presentation because the line narrows as it approaches the leader and fly. The combination of an extended weighted taper and a light running line creates something akin to a shooting head. This is one of the most efficient yet delicate tapers available. Other manufacturers have copied or modified this taper.

Leader End

The triangle-taper fly line

The Shooting-Head Taper

The specialized shooting head (SH) or shooting taper (ST) is designed for maximum distance. The thicker weighted head (the first 20′ or so) pulls out the thin, light running line during a shoot. This permits longer casts than a standard double-taper line or weight-forward taper. The light, thin running line reduces air resistance and line drag. The heavy shooting head, although wanting delicacy, can launch a long line. Although the shooting taper can produce surface splash, such lines are often used for extreme distance and for combatting wind. Thin running lines are usually attached to the sinking or floating shooting heads. Some anglers use a stripping basket to store, retrieve, or shoot the long, thin running lines.

Leader End

The Shooting-Head Taper with level running line

The Weight-Forward Compound Taper

Modern fly lines go beyond the traditional tapers. Modern tapers are often modulated or modified for particular casting conditions. Such lines may incorporate more than one taper profile, creating compound or complex tapers. For example, the following weight-forward compound taper is designed for maximum distance, wind penetration, and bulky fly patterns. This heavy head shoots a long, light, and narrow running line. Compound tapers have two or more tapered segments with dissimilar diameters.

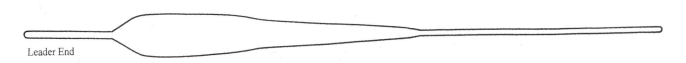

Leader End

The Weight-Forward Compound Taper

RIGGING THE FLY ROD

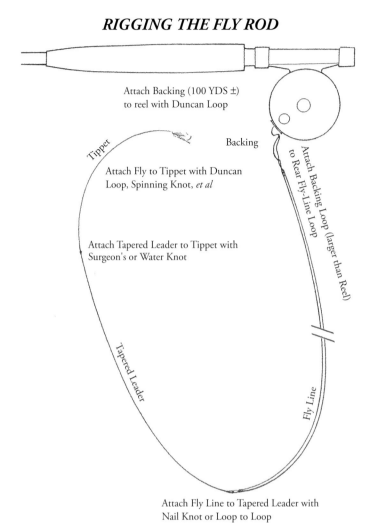

Attach Backing (100 YDS ±)
to reel with Duncan Loop

Backing

Tippet

Attach Fly to Tippet with Duncan
Loop, Spinning Knot, *et al*

Attach Tapered Leader to Tippet with
Surgeon's or Water Knot

Attach Backing Loop (larger than Reel)
to Rear Fly-Line Loop

Tapered Leader

Fly Line

Attach Fly Line to Tapered Leader with
Nail Knot or Loop to Loop

RIGGING THE ROD, REEL, AND LINE

The traditional trout rigging consists of approximately 75 to 125 yards of backing, a 90′ to 110′ tapered fly line, an 8½′ to 12′ tapered leader, and a 20″ to 36″ tippet. A large backing loop (large enough to accept a fly-line spool or detached fly reel) allows convenient fly-line changes. The larger diameter (butt) of the leader, a tapered monofilament, connects to the forward end of the fly line. Some modern fly lines have small, convenient welded loops for connecting the backing and leader. The tippet, a moderately elastic non-tapered monofilament, connects to the fine end (the X-designated end) of the leader. The fly attaches to the end of the tippet. The fine end of the leader is often defined as a tippet and like the tippet section, designated by an X-number. Each fly change snips the tippet back, shortening it. When the tippet becomes too short for the angling conditions, the truncated tippet is removed, and a fresh, full-length tippet section is added. Tippets are less expensive than leaders. If the fly is attached directly to the leader, then the tapered leader would soon become too stiff for a natural float and too thick for the eye of the hook.

The backing, the fly line, the leader, and the tippet are all stored on the fly reel. Most quality fly reels have a variable drag and can convert to either right- or left-handed retrieve. A fly reel is sometimes described as a storage container for fly line; it is, however, as important as the rod or the fly line. A ported reel, a reel with holes in the frame, reduces the weight and accelerates the drying of line and backing. Select a reel that accommodates the chosen line with generous backing. A large-diameter spool and generous backing lessen the small tight line curls. A counter-balance, mounted across from the reel handle, reduces the wobble of a revolving reel. Single-action reels (where one turn of the handle equals one turn of the spool) are popular and traditional. The less popular compound-geared multiplying reel retrieves line faster per handle turn.

An exposed rim, acting like a revolving brake, allows the angler to apply finger or palm pressure to slow a fleeing fish. A quality reel can defeat a strong fish with only negligible help from the rod. Some anglers acquire bragging rights by landing large strong fish on light rods. Such fish are usually battled from the reel rather than with the rod. In any case, we require that our reels do yeoman service. A good reel balances out the casting stroke, provides adequate drag, and stores ample backing.

Although a right-handed angler can usually recover line faster with the right hand, a right-handled reel requires that the rod change hands, which is an awkward maneuver with a struggling fish. A left-handed reel (my right-handed preference) still allows adequate line reeling. Moreover, fleeing fish can be checked with line pressure or landed by stripping in line. Reels with large spool diameters retrieve line quickly. The smaller the diameter of spooled line, the greater the force required to pull out that line. A spooled-line radius of .5 cm (a nearly empty reel) requires seven times the pull force of a spooled-line radius of 3.5 cm (a full reel). This assumes that the torque created by drag (any mechanical resistance) is constant for all rotational speeds. It also assumes no rod or water resistance. Thus, a wide and large-diameter arbor—and consequently a large-diameter spooled line—lessens the pull force and minimizes lost fish.

An adjustable-drag reel and ample backing are essential when combatting large spirited fish. The reel drag should be adjusted to prevent over-spin or backlash, which often traps and tangles spooled fly line. Adjust the drag so that a hard line yank avoids over-spin. During fishing, drag can always be increased or decreased as desired. Remember to release the drag when the reel is stored or unused.

A click pawl on a reel prevents over-spin, rather than applying serious fish-fighting drag. Adequate backing controls fish sprints, increases the line retrieve rate, and mitigates line curls. Powerful fish are usually placed on the reel as quickly as possible. Adding the proper length of backing to a reel can be a challenge with the variety of modern fly lines.

Calculating Backing Yardage

Reel manufacturers often indicate the backing yardage for particular lines. Manufacturer's yardage, however, seldom takes into account the length and diameter of different lines or the backing changes that you may want. The numerous variables in line and backing make these suggestions a guide rather than gospel. I often use heavier backing than recommended; strong fish and ultra fine backing can actually slice fingers. Heavier backing, of course, reduces yardage on the reel.

It may be necessary, though inconvenient, to determine the proper backing yardage for a selected reel. Calculating backing yardage can actually be done with two extra empty spools or reels. Avoid stripping a fly line on the floor; this only creates tangles and twists. Remember to charge the reel with enough backing to create a sizeable diameter for the fly line. Do not, however, maximize the backing so that the fly line catches or rubs against the reel frame or line guard. Line coil diameter changes when stripped (diameter shrinks) or retrieved (diameter swells). Furthermore, fly line is seldom retrieved with the same line pressure. Fly line in an overly-loaded reel may swell and jam against the reel cage. There should be a minimum of ¼" freebore space between the spooled fly line and the reel cage.

Tackle shops usually have knowledge and winding machines that quickly determine the proper amount of backing. Otherwise, the tedious task is to load the spool with fly line and attach the backing in reverse order. Backing is wound on to the proper capacity then cut, leaving an adequate freebore between the backing and the reel frame. Backing and line are then stripped off and reversed. This is done with two extra spools or reels in six steps.

Step One: First, attach with tape the tail end (often with "attach backing here" tag) of the spooled fly line onto the arbor of the selected reel, the reel that will eventually receive this fly line and backing. Spool the fly line on the arbor in smooth touching turns. Note: *This reverses the fly line on the reel with the front end outermost.*

Step Two: Then, attach the spooled backing to this front end of the fly line with an appropriate knot or loop. This connection must be temporary, as the fly line is now reversed.

Next, wind the backing on the selected reel to the proper level, leaving ½" to ¼" freebore. *Note*: Stop when the line and backing are wound on to the proper reel level. This becomes the maximum line and backing yardage for the selected reel. Now, cut the backing at this maximum point.

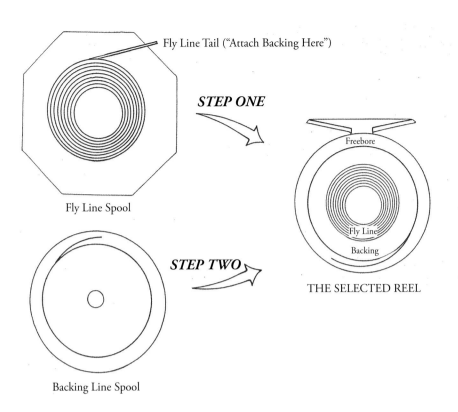

Fly Line Tail ("Attach Backing Here")

Steps One and Two: Transfer Fly Line and Backing to Selected Reel

STEP ONE

Fly Line Spool

Freebore

STEP TWO

Fly Line

Backing

THE SELECTED REEL

Backing Line Spool

Step Three: Now, detach and return the backing only to another reel or spool. At this time, undo the temporary knot at the front end of the fly line.

Step Four: After that, wind the fly line on yet another empty reel or spool. This corrects the fly line reversal so that the tail end is exposed. The fly line is now properly positioned for reattachment to the backing.

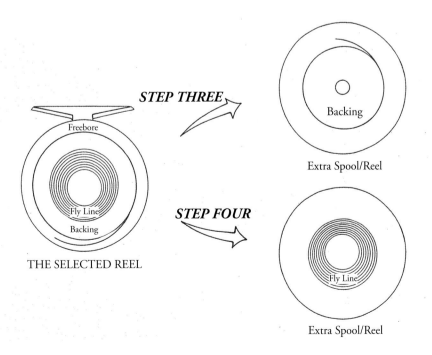

Steps Three and Four: Transfer Backing and Line to Extra Spools or Reels

STEP THREE

Freebore

Backing

Extra Spool/Reel

Fly Line

Backing

THE SELECTED REEL

STEP FOUR

Fly Line

Extra Spool/Reel

Step Five: Next, connect the backing to the selected reel with an appropriate double-lap arbor knot (see Chapter 2). With smooth touching turns, carefully wind the backing onto the selected reel.

Step Six: Lastly, connect the fly line to the backing and wind home. The reel is now loaded with the fly line and maximum backing. If required, further adjustments can be made by removing the fly line and trimming the backing. Quality fly lines with self-loops at each end facilitate line and leader changes.

Steps Five and Six: Transfer Backing and Fly Line to Selected Reel

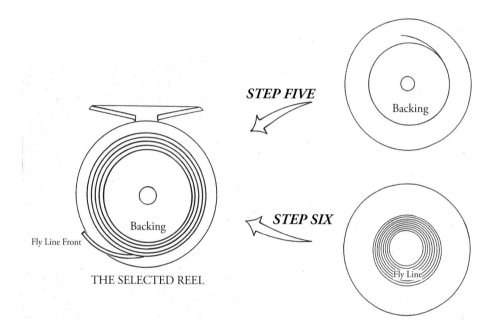

The End of the Line

The End of the Line

For fly fishers, the leader and tippet diameters may be more important than the breaking strength. This is based on matching the relative impedance or flex of each section so that the line energy passes down the leader length to properly extend the fly forward. This is why fly-fishing knots should extend in-line and avoid hinging. Typical leader butt diameters range from .026 (0.660 mm) for an 0X leader to .021 (0.533 mm) for a 7X leader. Standard leaders range from 7.5′ to 12′ (7X to 0X) and tippet spools from 7X to 0X. Some leaders have a straight diminishing taper while others have a variable taper. There are leaders with a 35 percent straight butt taper, a 45 percent mid-taper, and a 20 percent integral straight tippet section. Modern resin coating improves monofilament knotting and durability. With special leaders and angling conditions, an attached tippet may be omitted by mounting the fly directly to the leader tip. Each pattern change, though, increases the diameter of the leader. For example, surface poppers are often tied directly to the end of a tapered leader. This is especially effective in nymph fishing when knots may grab drifting detritus, such as aquatic weeds. Occasionally, straight (level or un-tapered) monofilament leaders are used for salt or fresh-water big-game fishing. Most of my Amazon fishing was done with 8- to 12-weight rods and heavy straight, stiff monofilament leaders lacking tippets; my spring creek fishing was with a 4-weight rod, 9′ leader, and 4X tippet. The pleasure of fly fishing depends on matching the rod, the reel, the line, and the leader to the situation.

Keeping the Natural Arc

We want the energy of the rod to pass down the line, leader, and tippet to the fly itself. As long as there is neither excess energy nor hinging (especially between the line and the leader and between the leader and the tippet), then the energy transfer should be smooth. This is why impedance matching—matching the approximate resistance to flexure—is so necessary in terminal tackle. For a simple impedance test, hold the connected line sections (leader and line or leader and tippet) in a circle. If the connected sections continue the natural curve (described as keeping the arc), then impedance is matched and energy can pass from one section to the other.

Keeping the Natural Arc

BOOTS AND WADING

Fly fishing has advanced with the modern Boa closure system and the breathable wader. The fast and convenient Boa boot closure system, first introduced into snowboarding in 2001, now appears on wading boots. Gary Hammerslag—a Southern California surfer who moved to Steamboat Springs, Colorado—created the Boa system. There are boa boot systems for various athletic and field sports. This proprietary closure system of steel lace, nylon guides, and a mechanical reel achieves a comfortable fit with a convenient turn of the dial. It locks down with a push and releases with a pull of the dial. It creates a smooth closure with no pressure points. At any time, one-handed micro-adjustments are possible. Once used, they tempt you to abandon laces, straps, or hook and loop systems.

The Simms RiverTex wading boots with Boa lacing system

Another exceptional wading boot system is Korker's ten interchangeable soles. In minutes, the soles quickly change according to shifting conditions, including felt for drift boats, studs for mossy rocks, rubber-lugs for marl substrata, and compressed felt with embedded carbide spikes (13 spikes per boot) for slippery shale and granite boulders.

Regrettably, boots, waders, and nets gather some sinister hitchhikers. Precautions should be made to prevent the spread of these invasive species. Check, clean, and dry all equipment that comes in contact with the water, especially waders, wading boots, float tubes, fins, landing nets, boats, and trailers. New Zealand, Alaska, Idaho, Maine, Montana, New Mexico, Oregon, Maryland, South Dakota, and Vermont have banned the use of felt-soled wading boots. At present, six other states are considering a ban. In

The Korker Whitehorse wading boot with the Boa lacing system and Korker's interchangeable sole system

time, more states will continue to ban felt-soled boots. Consequently, it is probably best to avoid felt boots entirely.

Avoid transferring anything wet from water to water. Visually inspect and remove all mud and debris at the water side. When possible, soak and scrub all items in a solution of 2 percent household bleach or detergent. Dry completely before reuse. Perhaps the best solution is not to share equipment; instead, have specific wading equipment for specific waters. In most cases, do contact the local fish and game agency if these invasives are observed.

The Unholy Trinity

Diseases and invasive species claim our clear and clean fishing waters, and they are here to stay. They inflict serious damage to our watersheds, our aquatic insects, and our fish. This unholy trinity includes Didymo, whirling disease, and the New Zealand mudsnail. Even the casual angler should be aware of these dangers.

Didymo (*Didymosphenia geminate*), or rock snot, is a diatom (a single-celled exotic alga) that attaches to rocks, plants, and other submerged surfaces where it produces stalks and massive blooms that resist degradation. It smothers plants and rocks, reducing the available food for aquatic insects and consequently reducing the food available for fish. Didymo creates yellow, tan, beige, or brown mats. It is often described as trailing toilet paper and feels like wet cotton in the stream. The individual diatoms are invisible.

Whirling disease (*Myxobolus cerebralis*) is a parasite that infiltrates the head and spinal column of salmonids, where it multiplies rapidly and causes the fish to swim erratically and, in extreme cases, die. Advanced whirling disease symptoms include erratic circular swimming, blackened tails, and skeletal deformities. This parasite is spread by boaters, anglers, and birds. The parasite, present in mud, spreads naturally throughout the watershed. The *Tubifex tubifex* worm, a ubiquitous worm usually shorter than one-inch long, ingests the spores and releases *Myxobolus cerebralis triactinomyxons* (tams) into the water column. The tams then enter through the fish's skin and travel to the head and cartilage. After several months, fish reveal the symptoms of whirling disease. Mature spores are released by the fish, and the cycle repeats. Found in more than twenty states in the United States, the pernicious spores can be dormant for thirty years, and there is no known cure.

The New Zealand mudsnail (*Potamopyrgus antipodarum*) has spread at alarming rates in Montana, Wyoming, Idaho, Colorado, and California. Without natural predators, the mudsnail devastates rivers by destroying mayflies, stoneflies, caddis, and midges. Unlike typical snails, the mudsnail aggressively explores and readily attaches to boots and waders to hitch a trip to other waters. They are brown or black and can be the size of a sand grain and reach lengths up to ⅛-inch long. Although they are small, they can completely carpet a streambed and destroy the native aquatic insects.

It is a perfect storm. Through cloning, a single snail can create a colony of forty million snails within one year and destroy a new stream. They have no predators. They consume without being consumed. They appear in most Western states, including Washington, Idaho, Montana, Oregon, Wyoming, Nevada, Colorado, California, and Arizona.

Waders

There is a wide range of waders available to the modern angler made from Gore-Tex, neoprene, coated nylon, and coated polypropylene. A popular wader-boot combination is the Gore-Tex chest stocking-foot wader with attachable boots. This is economical, as one damaged component allows further use of the other. The Gore-Tex breathable waders generally made of coated nylon or polyester materials vent moisture and heat while preventing water entry. Moreover, Gore-Tex breathable stocking-foot waders are often light and somewhat soft, much like wearing normal clothing. Breathables are especially appropriate for long treks to water or extended periods of active fishing. Although the cost of a breathable is higher than neoprene waders, the comfort compensates. Colder weather and water usually require neoprene waders with attached boots for warmth and comfort, but neoprene does trap moisture. Heavier boot-foot waders with attached boots are convenient when walking is limited because fishing is nearby. Though the boot-foot wader may limit leg movement, it is often more durable and less expensive than a breathable. Hip-high waders are convenient for long treks, shallow water, and bank fishing. However, there is a caveat; they usually offer false security and a temptation to wade too deeply. The preferred chest-high wader requires a snug wading belt that prevents water entry during a tumble or mishap. Quality waders may have a waterproof zipper for nature's call, a hand-warmer pocket, a zippered chest pocket, belt loops, gravel guards, quick-release suspenders, welded seams, taped seams, anatomical neoprene booties, flip out waterproof pockets, and abrasion-resistant patches. Selecting the proper fit is crucial. If possible, try them on with your socks and wading boots before purchase. Kneeling, squatting, and walking can test the body fit of most waders.

Wading

Seriously consider a life jacket for potentially powerful or deep waters. An adjustable vest or yoke PFD (personal flotation device (PFD)) allows freedom of movement during casting and wading. An uninflated PFD lies relatively flat against the body. The yoke or suspender style passes around the neck and down the front and can be worn over the fishing vest. Wear nothing over an inflatable PFD. Some quality PFD vests activate automatically when submerged and can be blown up manually as well. These auto-inflatable life vests are recommended for deep or swift waters, whether you are in a boat,

The award-winning Simms G3 Guide Stocking-Foot Wader with 25 percent more breathable 5-layer Gore-Tex® Fabric

on the bank, or wading. Fully adjust and secure the life jacket prior to fishing or wading. If submerged in deep water, assume the H.E.L.P. position to conserve body heat: draw legs up to seated position, cross arms in front, and keep head out of water. Hypothermia may claim more lives than drowning alone. If afloat on a river, point your legs downstream as you travel toward the bank. When wading in cold water (60° and colder) a jacket or Type V PFD should be worn. In waters 40° to 50°, exhaustion or unconsciousness occurs within sixty minutes and death within three hours. Avoid rocks, logjams, sweepers, and low-hanging limbs that can trap you. Swimming increases the rate of body heat loss. Do not wade with an unzipped or loose PFD. All PFD vests should fit properly and be approved by the USCG.

Wading deep or swift rivers can present hazards, especially those strewn with boulders. A small-diameter wading staff reduces water drag and vibration. However, it should not be so narrow that it cannot support your body weight during a slip or misstep. A staff also serves to read, or feel, the stream bed as you wade. Staff length is important; select a staff that extends from the ground to the armpit. Many wading staffs are multi-sectional and carried in a holster. These should snap together securely. All staffs should be tethered and, when on the dangle, avoided as a tripping hazard. Finally, when crossing rivers, wade diagonally with the flow and step downstream of rocks that decrease water flow.

I first encountered the four-legged beast in New Zealand. When crossing shallow, swift rivers, lock arms together (not hands) with a companion to create the four-legged beast. Grip both your wrists with your opposing hands to create a carabiner with your arms. A companion then locks his carabiner arms through yours. Wade sideways to the current, establishing one foothold at a time. Avoid wading swift, deep rivers; the power of moving water is extraordinary.

The Angling Hat

An angling hat is essential tackle. The baseball cap is the most popular and inexpensive, but it offers no sun protection for the neck and ears. I admit that I am a modest collector of hats. Once, I bought a leather Western hat that I wore only once; it was too heavy and too hot. I have used a 4X beaver Stetson with 3½" brim for desert creek fishing, a baseball cap for spring creeks, an Irish wool Connemara for winter steelhead, a caped-flats hat for Kiribati bonefish, a soft Italian Borsalino fedora with tether button, and a lightweight Stetson sovereign for travel. For air travel with a stiff Western Stetson, I made a plastic outer shell that shields the crown; I then packed the crown with underwear and socks and put it in checked luggage. An angling hat has essential requirements; a full front brim that cuts glare and, with polarized glasses, allows vision into the water. A back brim screens the neck from the sun, and a side brim may deflect passing patterns. The hat color should be neutral and natural—such as tawny, tan, olive, and brown—and the front bill underside should be dark to reduce water reflections. Full-brimmed hats should have a tether to prevent loss by wind grabs. The light saltwater hats are usually kepi style with a rear drape to protect the neck and a long front bill for tropical sun. A tropical cloth hat is often a pale color that matches the sky and reflects or moderates heat. These hats may be dipped in the water and worn for evaporative cooling. I often carry an extra ultralight cloth cap with neck flap in my fishing vest. No matter which hat is selected, it should be light, comfortable, and securable.

THE FLY-FISHER'S VEST

Stuffed with brave new patterns and the thousand other things that fish and flesh are heir to, the fly-fishing vest celebrates our sport. It is the badge of the fly fisher. A properly charged vest promises independence and success. Yet the fly vest was not always part of fly fishing. Lee Wulff, credited with the creation of the first fly vest in 1931, observed that the vest did not become immediately popular—anglers rejected the idea of wearing equipment outside their clothing until about 1946. Perhaps World War II, with all the harness of combat, turned anglers toward the vest. In any case, one vest cannot serve all masters. With the variety of fish and fishing conditions, several vests may no longer be a luxury. If we select rods and lines for particular applications, perhaps we should select vests in the same fashion. Experienced anglers often conclude that it is best to search for a pattern in a few large pockets or boxes than in numerous smaller ones. A single spacious fly box with dividers can accommodate different patterns. This avoids the chaos of countless small fly boxes and fretful searching.

All anglers have a vested interest in vest design. Although selecting a vest is a personal decision, there are basic considerations. Quality vests typically have felled or enclosed seams. Exposed seams, which avoid labor-intensive workmanship, may indicate other cost-cutting measures. All stitch locks should be tight and uniform and should follow the proper lines. Puckering or irregular stitching will probably not affect the durability but may indicate shoddy detailing. Bar tacking should appear at all the stress points, including the pocket corners. Vest fabrics vary from light cotton shirting to Supplex, polyester, and nylon blends. A stiffer fabric holds the architecture of the pocket for easy entry and exit. Whatever the fabric, it should be strong, yet light enough for drape and ventilation. For deep wading and warm weather, I prefer a light, short vest, fewer than eighteen inches from collar top to bottom seam. The modern resin-treated poly-mesh vest has several advantages: ventilation, it is lightweight, and it is compact for travel. Furthermore, it has minimal water absorption and dries quickly.

Another consideration is how a vest utilizes space. There should be none wasted. Both front panels should have zippered access. Experienced anglers often prefer vests with fewer but larger pockets rather than a labyrinth of smaller ones. Yet most experienced anglers want specialized pockets for pliers, tippet spools, and polarized glasses. Front vertically stacked rib pockets, the pockets most used, avoid the bulk of lower horizontal side pockets that often get in the way of the casting stroke, especially when float tubing or deep wading. Pocket placement and cut, especially of the neckline and armholes, is as important to casting ease as size. Some manufacturers size the vest as standard attire. Others consider the fly vest an overgarment and size it accordingly, making it one-half to one size larger to accommodate underclothing. Try a vest on before purchase.

The collar should be wide cut and broad across the shoulders to distribute the load evenly. A vest should have wide shoulder panels to distribute the load on the shoulders rather than on the neck. A vest should be a neutral color, especially browns, olives, olive-browns, and gray. All Velcro patches should be adequately sized—two inches or longer. All pockets should be face sewn with T-mounted Velcro closures, placing the strips at right angles. Whether the pocket is flat or full, the patches catch and close. When there is more than one back pocket, the zippers should open and close in opposite direction. This avoids the confusion of which pocket when extracting items. And most of all, an empty vest should be lightweight. The trappings and trifles will make it hefty enough. You must be master of your fly vest; it will want to carry more than needed. Finally, a good test is to fill the vest, hold it upside down, and briskly shake it. Nothing should fall out. I often add more Velcro patches if required. To secure all those dangles and tools, I transport and protect my vest in a light zippered nylon bag.

Although less may be more regarding vests, I will list common items often found in an angler's freshwater trout vest. Tackle will differ according to personal preferences and fishing conditions. Not all of the following may be needful; select only those items listed that may be required. Much depends on the quarry and the quest. Retrievers and dangling accessories—such as clippers, floatants, and pliers—should be tethered and mounted either inside the vest or inside a pocket. While still convenient to hand, the tools are less likely to tangle lines or brush and if tethered inside a pocket, even if detached, loss is prevented. Some dangles, such as pliers, can be expensive. A properly charged vest promises independence and self-reliance. The short net vest, illustrated on the next page, has large vertical front pockets that do not interfere with the casting stroke or line management. Although short, this vest holds an adequate amount of tackle. Its minimalism may encourage an intelligent abridgement of tackle and trim. This comfortable and compact traveler allows deep wading and unencumbered movement. Both Simms and Patagonia produce a range of quality vests.

In all vests, whether traditional or not, form should follow function. A vest should accommodate and make accessible our angling tools. A good vest should be familiar and friendly. It holds our hopes. There is a sense of completeness as we wade the waters in full harness. And a vest offers itself up to fondling, an intimate rite of spring. There is pleasure, if not promise, in filling the bowels with trappings and trifles, those precious bagatelles of trouting.

The Patagonia Master Mesh Vest with Trapping. This light polyester mesh vest has vertical pockets, a foam collar for comfort, and a high double-zip back storage system for deep wading. It contains multiple exterior and interior pockets for tippet spools, leader packs, and fly boxes as well as an adjustable front closure.

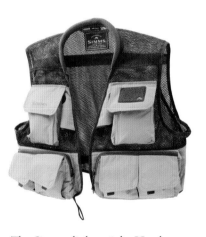

The Patagonia Convertible Vest, shown here with trappings, is light and compact. This minimalist vest, excellent for air travel, has vertical pockets, Hypalon tabs for tool attachment, a plethora of pockets for tippet spools, leaders, fly boxes, and rain gear. For increased capacity, the Convertible attaches to three other Patagonia packs—the Sweet Fish Pack, the Stormfront Roll-Top Pack, and the Stormfront Pack. This polyester mesh and nylon vest weighs only 14.3 oz.

The Simms Greystone Guide Vest has 24 pockets, including 2 large and 2 medium chest pockets, 6 waist pockets, 2 tippet pockets, 8 internal pockets, 1 split back pocket, 1 bellowed back cargo pocket, and 1 dry-shake pocket. The Guide has two built-in retractors for tools and an elastic draw-cord at rear waist for adjustment. The nylon fabric with DWR finish has a breathable. padded collar for cool comfort.

The Simms lightweight Headwaters Mesh Vest for hot weather and protracted exertion has 6 chest pockets, 4 vertical-waist pockets, 8 internal pockets, and a horizontal rear pocket. Additional features include 2 built-in tool retractors, buckle closure, and padded rib knit collar.

There are countless creative vest models available as well as other tackle systems. Other options include lumbar/waist packs, chest packs, backpacks, and sling packs for those trappings. Some packs have an adjustable suspension system, a drop-down work station, a hydration unit, and enough room for lunch, fly boxes, rain gear, and other necessities. Others are minimalistic with just room for flies and tools. Waist packs can be slid in front when wanted or moved behind when not. Some adjustable packs can be worn on the waist, chest, or back. Beyond the vest and pack are the lanyards. There is a Spartan simplicity in the angling lanyard. Some have foam collars that cushion the weight, breakaway connections if snagged, and beads that separate the tool hooks. Lanyards are excellent for the deep jungle and the tropical flats. From my Amazon lanyard hung a stripping glove, sun lotion, cutters/pliers, compact Leatherman tool, tightening tool (to secure fly patterns on heavy monofilament), and a hook release, plus other essentials. No matter what the storage system chosen, careful research is necessary in order to find that perfect tackle and water match.

Dependent upon personal preferences and angling conditions, different items may appear in a trout fly vest or kit. Moreover, all items are not essential for all angling at all times. Nevertheless, a comprehensive fishing checklist can ensure completeness. Here are some items that I may want for trout fishing:

1. Tippet spools—especially 6X to 3X, otherwise 7X to 2X. Always place a date on newly purchased leader packs and tippet spools. Use fresh leaders and tippets each year. Discard nylon leaders and tippets that are more than two years old.
2. Pliers for crimping down barbs or removing hooks, forceps, and hook file.
3. Floatant (silicon paste, silica crystals, or beads), sink paste, and strike indicators.
4. Amadou pad (a desiccating fungus) for drying CDC patterns.
5. Tapered leaders—especially 9′ to 12′, 5X to 2X.
6. Clippers (nippers) for cutting monofilament, compact flashlight, compact scissors. Anglers find the compact Leatherman Micra and Style CS tools with spring-action scissors especially useful.
7. Sinking heads of various lengths and weights.
8. Toilet paper, compact first aid kit, sunscreen, insect repellant, and prescription medicine.
9. Fly boxes and fly patterns (dries, wets, nymphs—weighted and unweighted—terrestrials, streamers, and poppers).
10. Fly line cleaner/dressing, ferrule wax, and cloth tape for field repair.
11. Landing net, wading staff, rain gear, and a hat with tether.
12. Fishing license with waterproof case, map, compass or GPS, small magnifier for insect inspection, pencil, and small notebook.

13. Reel and extra loaded spare spool(s).
14. Extra fly lines—floating, wet tip, intermediate, sinking etc.
15. Camera, waterproof camera bag, extra body and extra lens, digital cards, extra batteries, and lens cleaner.
16. Polarized eyewear and extra prescription eyewear.
17. Light nylon zip bag for transporting the vest. The bag may be stored inside the vest while fishing.
18. Adequate vest sizing so that a hydration unit may be worn beneath the vest in hot weather.

Polarized eyewear is essential for fishing. Its use, however, is not restricted to bright sunlight. An evening rise may compensate for bright, empty summer days. Fall and late summer angling, especially evening sedges and spinner falls, is often in low light at dusk. According to W. B. Willers' *Trout Biology* (1988), "feeding intensity is greatest at lower light intensities typical of early morning and late afternoon. Many fish species feed most actively during these so-called crepuscular (twilight) periods." An amber lens, acting much like an orange or yellow filter in black and white photography, will filter the blue and the grays to give higher contrast and sharper detail. Some polarized lenses, whether amber or gray, may be too dark for these twilight periods. Select the lightest color polarizing lens available. In low light, an amber or pale yellow lens that sharpens detail is preferred. Available, too, are light tan polarizing lens designed specifically for low-light conditions. Some have a silicon coating that repels grease and smudges. Due to this hydrophobic film, water also beads and runs off. To test a lens for polarization, rotate it over a known polarized lens. The test lens will darken and lighten if the other lens is polarized.

2

THE KNOTS

THERE ARE NUMEROUS KNOTS AND CONNECTIONS AVAILABLE to the angler. But an angler needs to know, and know well, only a few. These selected knots have served anglers well. Knots should be formed smoothly and securely. There are two ends to a line: the tag end and the standing part or section. The knot is tied at the tag end. The standing part, the main or longer section, connects to the source and is opposite the tag end. Closing friction on dry monofilament can heat and weaken the line. When tightening or closing a knot, always use a lubricant, such as water. Some anglers use a small, push-up container of lubricant; however, some lubricants may float the knot or cause it to slip. Be especially careful when using ultrafine tippet material. To increase the knot strength to hooks, insert the tippet twice through the hook eye. This distributes the strain better than a single wrap. Some knot closures, however, may not allow twice through the eye.

THE DUNCAN LOOP

The popular Duncan Loop or Uni-knot attaches the tippet to the fly.

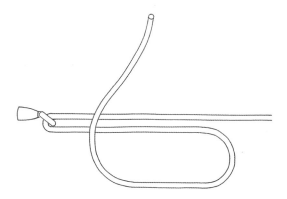

1. Pass the tippet through the eye of the hook. Then, make a bend in the tippet and fold the tag end back to create a loop.

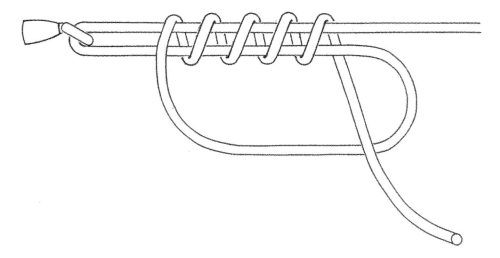

2. At the fly side, pass the tag end four or five times through the loop and around both strands. To begin the knot closure, lubricate the line before pulling the tag end to moderately close the loop. Do not tighten the loop firmly before sliding the knot down to the fly. This may create crinkled and weakened line. After sliding the knot down, firmly tighten the knot at the hook eye and trim excess.

To create an open loop, tighten the knot down about 2″ to 3″ from the fly. An open loop will allow a pattern, such as a surface popper, greater movement and absorb the strike shock. Additionally, an open loop allows the pattern to dart and dance erratically during the retrieve. In this case, the water lubricates the closing loop during a strike. The strike also closes the loop.

The Duncan Loop is also used for connecting backing to the reel arbor. Wrap the backing twice or thrice around the arbor. The tag end (and the location of the Duncan Loop Knot) should pass over (not under) and around the arbor to connect to the backing. When recovering backing, this reverses the knot line around the arbor to lock down the backing.

THE BLOOD KNOT: TIPPET TO LEADER OR BUILT-LEADER SECTIONS

The Blood Knot or Barrel Knot, originally a gut knot, is symmetrical and strong. The multi-wraps absorb some strike shock. Although four to five wraps are standard, fine diameter lines may require six or more wraps. The blood name apparently derives from the somewhat similar double overhand knob knots (with similar reversed loops and turns around the line) used on a cat-of-nine-tails. This would account for the novel name. The Blood Knot, often used for leader making, requires comparable diameter lines. The Blood Knot is neat but not as readily tied as the Water Knot, which appears later. There are two ways to tie the Blood Knot: with matching wraps or opposing wraps. Matching wraps (same direction wraps) create a crossover crotch that locks down the tag ends. Although close trimming of the tag ends is often recommended, flush trimming and extreme pressure might diminish the line diameter and produce knot failure. A strong Blood Knot is a fully bedded knot with 2 mm to 3 mm length tags. Most Blood Knot failures arise from closely cropped tags and dissimilar diameter lines.

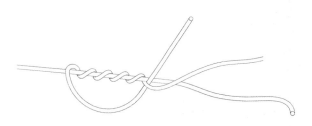

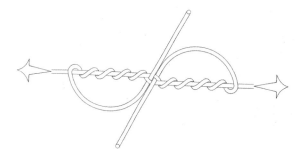

1. Overlap the parallel ends (the tags). Wrap one line over the other four times or more and place its tag end in the crotch created.

2. Then wrap the other line four or more times and place its tag end in the opposite direction through the crotch created. Tag ends must be in opposition. Lubricate and tighten the knot. Firmly pull both main lines and tag ends to maintain parallel wraps.

THE PERFECTION LOOP: LEADER LOOP

The Perfection Loop, or angler's loop, is, "unquestionably the most satisfactory leader loop" (*The Ashley Book of Knots* [1944], Clifford W. Ashley). This is an important knot for fly fisherman; the Perfection Loop aligns the leader with the fly line for efficient energy transfer. Although the knot appears difficult, once learned it is simple and fast. The Perfection Loop is not recommended for ultrafine monofilament. Make the counterclockwise loops in this order:

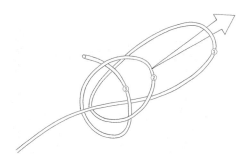

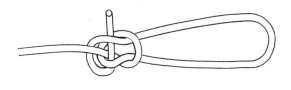

1. Form the first loop behind the standing line. Hold the formed loop between the left thumb and forefinger.
2. Make a second loop in front of the standing line.
3. Now add a third loop between the two previous loops.
4. Finally, pass the second loop over the third loop and under the first loop to form the Perfection leader loop.

Completed Perfection Loop

Lay several inches of the leader butt along the fly-line tip. Fold the leader back toward the line tip and wrap six times over the line, leader, and tube. Use your thumb and index finger to hold the wraps. The drawing depicts open wraps to show placement. When wrapping, however, make tight touching wraps. After wrapping, insert the leader butt into and through the tube with enough length to extend beyond the wraps. Remove the tube and carefully form a tight knot. It is often best to form the knot 3″ or 4″ from the end of the fly line. Then slide the knot down near the end before tightening the knot by pulling both the tag end and the standing end (the section extending from the knot) of the leader. Trim excess leader tag and any short extended line tip.

THE TUBE KNOT: LEADER TO FLY LINE

According to Lefty Kreh (*Practical Fishing Knots II* [1991], Mark Sosin and Lefty Kreh), this traditional knot, done with a horseshoe nail, originated in Argentina and was brought to the United States in the 1950s by noted angler Joe Brooks. A horseshoe nail is illustrated in Joe Brooks' *Fly Fishing* (1958). Although I favor a small brass tube, there are various commercial nail-knot tools available. A small-diameter tube, however, improves forming the traditional Nail Knot. Merely substitute a 4″ or 5″ hollow brass or steel tube for the nail. Select a rigid, hollow tube with an inside diameter slightly larger than the leader butt. A close fit promotes flawless knot forming.

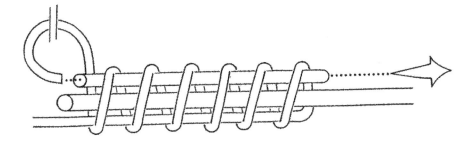

It should be noted that large powerful fish can strip the Nail Knot and the line coating off a fly line. Other connections, such as loop-to-loop, should be used for heavy, aggressive freshwater game and saltwater fish. The Tube Knot forms the same relatively smooth, in-line connection as the Nail Knot. However, like the Nail Knot, the Tube Knot is permanent, must be retied for leader replacement, and can catch on the rod guides. To permit smooth passage through the guides, some anglers coat the knot with a flexible waterproof glue, such as Softex glue, Dave's Flexament, or Clear Cure Goo. Other anglers attach a short length of heavy monofilament to the end of the fly line with the Tube Knot. They then connect their working leader with a loop or Blood Knot. This accommodates some quick leader changes.

THE SEAGUAR KNOT: TIPPET TO LEADER

The Seaguar Knot, with nearly 100 percent breaking strength, is fast, simple, and strong. One hundred percent breaking strength indicates that the knot strength equals the unknotted line strength. It can still break if the strain exceeds the line strength. This bulky, asymmetrical knot, however, can catch on guides and can result in excessive tippet or leader waste. Unlike the Blood Knot, the Seaguar Knot creates a slightly skewed connection. The factory representatives of Seaguar, the largest manufacturer of fluorocarbon line, promulgated this knot, designed especially for connecting fluorocarbon leaders and tippets. The knot may also connect dissimilar monofilament sections. The Seaguar is one of the simplest knots available to the angler. Compare the Seaguar knot with Dr. Mark Lamos' hemostat knot in Lefty Kreh's *Fishing Knots* (2007).

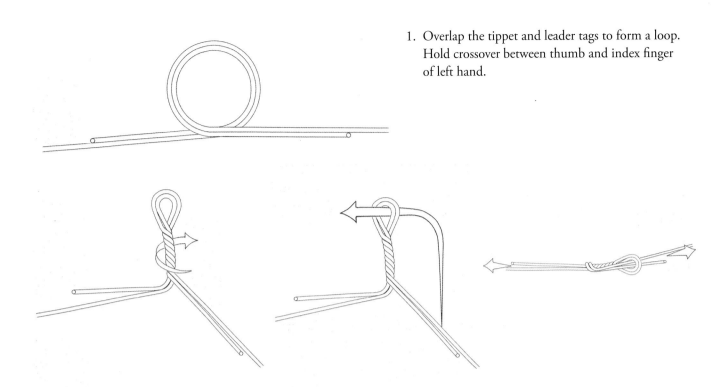

1. Overlap the tippet and leader tags to form a loop. Hold crossover between thumb and index finger of left hand.

2. Place right index finger in loop and rotate three full times.

3. Then reach through the loop and pull the tippet and leader tag ends (the loose ends of the line) through the loop.

Lubricate the knot before closing. Carefully tighten the knot by pulling evenly on the double lines on each side of the knot.

A short line overlap and loop decreases monofilament waste. The overlap, however, must offer sufficient grip for closing the knot. One method to minimize monofilament waste is to use a Loop Turner, a stiff wire with a terminal hook, to twist the loop and pull the leader tag and tippet through. This can be done with 4″ or less line overlap. Despite its unattractive asymmetrical bulk, the Seaguar Knot is remarkably strong and quick.

THE SPINNING KNOT: FLY TO TIPPET

The Spinning or Twirl Knot can be tied in ten seconds or fewer and—once the tippet passes through the hook eye—in total darkness. Unlike some knots, the smaller the fly pattern, the easier it is to tie. This knot, akin to a reversed or inverted Duncan Loop, is spun in the loom of the hand. For increased strength, the tippet may be looped twice through the hook eye before tying. Although the directions may first appear complex and awkward, brief practice results in a swift and secure connection. For decades, this has been my trout knot for fly to tippet; it is well worth learning. The Spinning Knot, like all knots, should be tied with smooth, continuous movement.

1. After passing the tippet through the hook eye, hold the tippet end (the tag) between the thumb and index finger of the left hand. With the right thumb and index finger, slide the fly down the tippet.

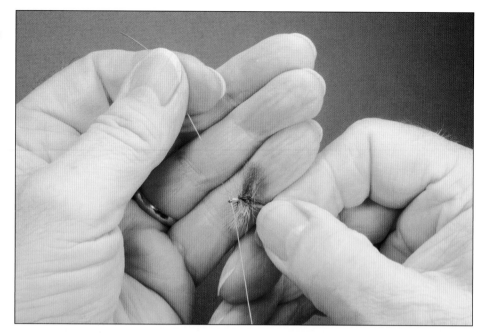

2. Pass the fly over the left palm, around the little finger, and behind the back of the left hand. Then draw the fly (with the fly riding on a created tippet loop) between the index and middle finger of the left hand.

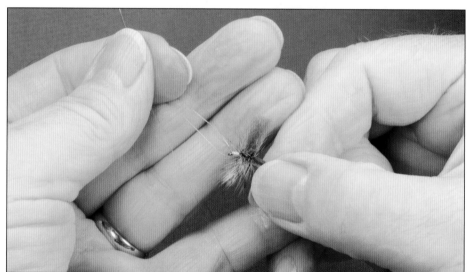

3. Spin or twirl, in either direction, the looped fly five or more times around the tippet section held taut in the left palm. Arc the fingers in the left hand to create spinning space and a taut tippet.

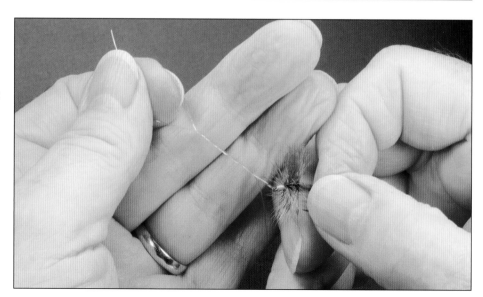

4. With the fly still in the right hand and while still holding the tag end of the tippet between the thumb and index finger of the left hand, relax and remove the left hand loop fingers from the loop. Continue to hold the tippet tag or end as the left fingers rotate to grasp the wraps made around the tippet.

5. Now, with the right hand, slowly pull the fly away from the knot. Pulling the fly away from the knot minimizes excess tippet waste. Once the knot has been loosely drawn closed, lubricate the closing space in front of the fly. Now continue to pull the fly, sliding the knot against the hook eye. If the knot tightens before it stops against the eye, a crinkle may occur in the extended tippet. The knot must remain loosely formed until it is drawn against the hook eye. Finally, firmly tighten the knot against the hook eye and trim excess.

THE BACKING LOOP

The backing line connects the fly line to the fly reel. Although a powerful fish may pull an entire fly line from the reel, the attached backing line still keeps the fish connected to the reel and angler. A large backing loop, formed from the backing itself, allows fast fly-line changes. Changing or replacing a fly line is now simple. Once the backing loop enters through the rear fly-line loop, it then passes over and around the reel or line spool (when the reel is mounted on the rod) to complete the loop-to-loop connection. Fly lines can now be quickly changed to match different angling conditions. A fly-line loop, now common on quality fly lines, and a backing loop make a convenient, knotless connection.

The loop is formed by inserting and porpoising the backing in and out to create a smooth, strong loop void of knots. To prevent possible slippage, the backing must be inserted through the core for an adequate length. For changing fly lines, the final backing loops should be about 16" to 18" in circumference to readily accept a fly reel or fly-line spool. This is the preferred method for creating a back loop that connects with the fly line.

Spliced loops require a braided or woven backing line with a hollow center or core. Based on the Chinese finger trap, the stronger the pull, the greater the grip. The backing must have a hollow core and enough diameter for the fine-wire tool. Friction holds the backing loop securely under tension. Furthermore, this knotless connection—adequate for all but heavy big-game fishing—slides smoothly through the rod tip and guides. The key to its strength is the length of backing buried within the backing center.

The term tag end refers to the free end of the backing line. Use a long, dull needle or a folded music wire, such as a stainless-steel guitar wire— .015" (.38mm) or finer—to pull the tag end through the center of backing. Cortland's Micron backing line, 30 pounds (13.6 kilograms), works well. This thin braided line lies flat for increased reel capacity. Select a bright, vibrant color that instantly announces when the fish is into the backing. When a powerful fish bolts, ultrafine backing can cut the fingers. Two methods are presented: the needle method and the folded-wire method.

The Needle Method

First, extend approximately 3' of woven backing to make the backing loop and the center buried line. Attach the tag end (the free end) to a dull needle and enter the backing center about 3' up from the tag end.

Continue to work the needle and tag end through the center of the backing for about 10". Then push the needle out through the backing wall. The needle and tag end are now outside the backing.

Next, pull the slack backing through the center to create and retain a 6" diameter terminal loop. Re-enter the needle approximately ¾" farther along the backing. Again, work the needle another 10″ through the center of the backing and exit. This inserting and porpoising stitches intermittent lengths of backing within the backing center.

Now advance the tag end by re-entering the backing wall, working the needle and tag end through the center for another 10″, then exit. Again, re-enter the needle approximately ¾″ farther along the backing.

Continue to enter and exit until approximately 20″ or more of the tag end is buried within the backing center. Make the final buried spacing longer than the tag end so that the tag end becomes trapped within the backing center.

The Folded-Wire Method (illustrated)

Unlike the needle method, the preferred folded-wire method produces long lengths of buried line through the backing center. The backing must have a hollow core with adequate diameter for the fine-wire tool. A tightly folded, fine stainless steel wire—such as a steel guitar string—forms the tool. Tightly compress the fold in the middle to create a sharp point. Create opposing micro-bends in the wire approximately one inch from the end. This opens a diamond hoop once the wire point passes out through the backing. It is now easy to capture more backing to pull through. The wire tool should be about 6″ to 8″ long when folded. Use tape to protect the sharp wire ends.

In the following photographs, the backing-loop length, the tag-end length, and the center-travel distances are radically reduced. Please note the dimensions presented in the text.

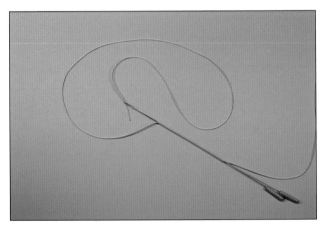

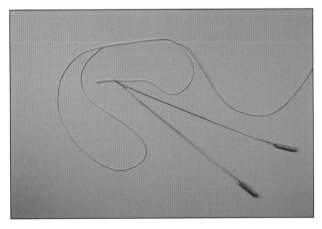

1. The folded tip, which threads the backing line through the center, must point toward the tag end (the free end) and enter the backing wall approximately 4 feet from its tag end. Push the wire, pointing toward the tag end, through the backing wall and into the hollow center. Then carefully work the wire approximately 10″ through the backing center toward the tag end. Now, exit the wire tip through the backing wall and insert the tip of the tag end in the crotch of the tool as illustrated.

2. Next, pull the tag end and excess backing completely through and out of the backing until a 6″ diameter backing loop forms. The loop, when folded, should be about 9″ long. Do not decrease the loop size as you pull more backing through the backing core.

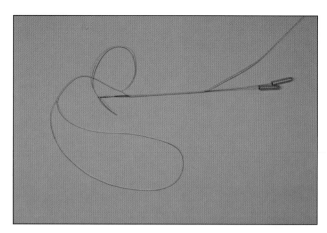
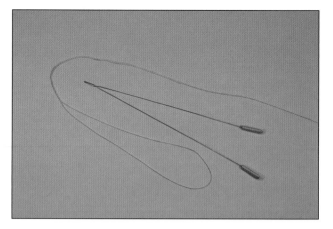

3. Then remove the tag end from the wire and re-enter the wire, pointing toward the loop, approximately 10″ above (away from the loop) where the tag end exits. Work the wire tip down and through the backing wall to within ¾″ of where the tag end exits. Now, capture the tag end again with the wire tool. Leave a short length of backing, approximately ¾″, outside the holes. This short exit-entry section facilitates locking the line down. Again, enter backing about 10″ from the last hole and capture the tag end.

4. Now pull the tag end back through the center again. Exit the backing and remove the tag end from the folded wire. This porpoising stitch buries intermittent lengths of backing within the backing center. Continue to enter and exit the backing until approximately 20″ or more of the tag end is buried within the backing center. For adequate loop strength, pull a minimum of 20″ of backing inside the backing center. Several entries and exits serve to lock-in the loop. Make the final entry-exit spacing longer than the free tag end so that the tag end becomes trapped within the backing core, then remove the wire tool. Finally, trap tag end within the backing core.

This strong knotless connection slides smoothly through the guides.

THE PITZENKNOTS: FLY TO TIPPET

The late Edgar Pitzenbauer of Bavaria created this small simple, strong knot that indicates when it is properly tied. You will actually feel the knot set as it reverses or overturns at the hook eye. Pitzenbauer, a celebrated and creative angler, developed this knot for the large selective grayling and trout of Slovenia.

1. Pass the tippet through the hook eye and slide the fly about 8″ down the tippet out of the way.
2. Fold the tippet back and allow the fly to dangle. This keeps the fly away from your hands while tying the knot.
3. Wrap the tippet three times only back toward the fly.
4. Pass the tippet tail through the loop as illustrated.
5. Pull the standing part away from the fly so that the knot slides and snugs against the hook eye. Then, pull again until you feel the knot set, a turnover of the knot against the eye. If you fail to feel the knot click, retie the knot.

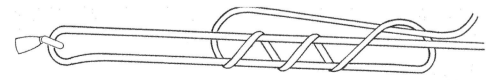

THE DOUBLE PITZENKNOT

The Double Pitzenknot, a clinch knot variation, may be improved with three or four wraps before lubricating and closing. The original double-wrap knot is illustrated here. The singular disadvantage of the Double Pitzenknot is that an ultrafine and supple tippet material may make it difficult to form. Otherwise, it is a strong, simple knot.

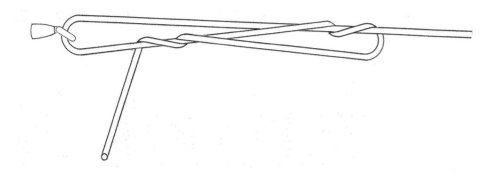

1. Pass the tippet through hook eye.
2. Wrap tag end twice around tippet.
3. Fold tag tip back and pass twice around eye loop
4. Lubricate and firmly pull to close.

THE PITZENBAUER SILVER-RING LEADER SYSTEM

Edgar Pitzenbauer also created a unique (perhaps the best term) leader system. Half of this knot is a small silver ring. Pitzenbauer developed, "some years" before 1997, an effective and inexpensive line to leader and leader to tippet system. The leader is fifteen pound (.015″) Sunset Amnesia memory-free monofilament, available in high visibility red or high visibility chartreuse. He preferred the high visibility red, but I chose the high visibility chartreuse for most angling. In 1997, he playfully wrote to me that the leader dealers will not like this idea; one leader can last all season. And he wrote, "The Amnesia is always straight; the red color easy to see. And my artificial flies do not like this cast: they have no possibility of wrapping around a knot." The angler only changes the size and length of the tippet as needed. A Duncan Loop knot attaches a small silver ring (diameter approximately 2.5 mm) to the end of the leader. The tippet rings, which are sufficiently strong and light enough to float, are available from some specialty fly shops and websites. The silver rings also permit low-light knotting in dusk or dawn. Another Duncan Loop attaches the tippet to the silver ring.

Pitzenbauer Silver Ring Leader System

I use a modest method for attaching the leader to the fly line. I merely link the leader to the fly-line loop with a small Perfection Loop. Tie the Perfection Loop on the leader butt and connect it to the integrated fly-line loop. This small double-loop connection is strong and readily passes through the rod guides. Although moderately bulky, the leader may also be attached with a standard Nail Knot. Pitzenbauer, however, favored a smooth superglue connection. Either connection allows the angler to begin casting with a leader only as long as the rod. *The significant mass of the un-tapered Amnesia leader alone can be cast and the line extended, even for a short 10′ cast.*

There is no need to pull out fly line from the rod tip for an initial cast. This is particularly convenient when you are waist deep in flowing water. Although I favor the small Perfection leader loop to line loop, I offer brief but complete directions for the line-leader superglue connection.

PITZENBAUER LEADER-LINE CONNECTION

The Amnesia leader, an 8′ or 10′ length, inserts into the end of the fly line and secures with superglue (cyanoacrylate cement). First, with a razor blade create an ultrafine taper at one end of the Amnesia section. The fine taper allows the Amnesia to pass through the eye of the needle and to be pulled up through the center core of the fly line. Next, use a needle to initially penetrate the center tip of a fly line. Work the needle through the center core of the fly line for ½″ or more and out the side. This preliminary entry and exit allows the Amnesia to pass more readily into and through the fly line tip. Now pass the Amnesia taper through the eye of the needle and work the Amnesia up through the fly line tip and out the side hole. Pull the Amnesia a few inches beyond the side hole and tapered end. Then, with fine sandpaper chafe a ½″ or more section of Amnesia exiting from the side hole, the section that will be pulled back into the fly line core and locked inside. Now, coat the chafed section with superglue and carefully pull it back down into the fly line tip. Position the chafed and glued section carefully within the tip of the fly line. Finally, trim the tapered Amnesia tag outside the side hole. The Amnesia is now glued within the center tip of the fly line and allows the leader and line to pass smoothly through the guides. This connection should be adequate for most trout fishing.

THE WATER KNOT: TIPPET OR LEADER TO LEADER

The Water Knot is one of the oldest knots in angling. And, as with many anglers, it is my standard connection. The "water knotte" is first mentioned (but not illustrated) in *The Treatyse of Fysshynge Wyth an Angle* (1496). The term has been given to various knots. Most scholars believe that the *Treatyse* knot was later illustrated in *The Complete Angler*. This Water Knot, depicted in a copper-plate cut, appears in the John Hawkins edition of Izaak Walton's *The Complete Angler* (1766) and later in Frederic Halford's *The Dry Fly Man's Handbook* (1913).

The Water Knot, sometimes erroneously called the Surgeon's Knot, is only vaguely similar to the original Surgeon's Knot illustrated in the Peter Owen's *The Book of Outdoor Knots* (1993). Although more awkward to tie, the original Surgeon's knot, with extra wraps, is an effective knot for fine tippets.

Halford noted that the Water Knot "has been adversely criticized by modern authorities," yet he found "no practical disadvantage from its use."

This copper-plate cut of the Water Knot appears in John Hawkins's 1766 second edition of *The Complete Angler* by Izaak Walton and Charles Cotton.

In Halford's day the Water Knot was a gut knot. Although neither as aesthetic nor as symmetrical as the Blood Knot, it is strong and simple. When connecting fine tippet material, five or more wraps may be required. The Double Water Knot—especially appropriate for connecting an ultrafine tippet to a heavier leader—is tied exactly like the standard Water Knot; however, the terminal portion of the fine tippet is first doubled, then treated as a single line section.

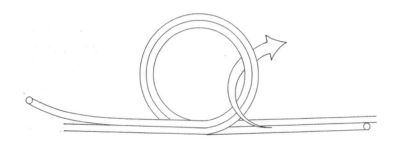

1. With the tag ends pointing in opposite directions, overlap the two sections to be joined about four inches.
2. As illustrated, form a loop in the middle of the doubled sections.

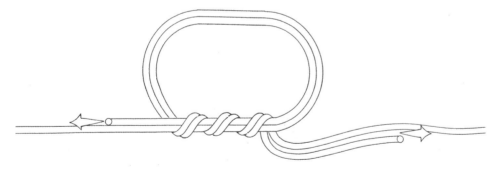

3. Pass both ends of the tail section through the loop.
4. Continue to pass both ends of the tail section through the loop five or more times. Remember that both sections, the tail and the tag end, pass through the loop.
5. Lubricate the knot and close it by pulling all four strands. Finally, trim the tag ends.

FLY CASTING

THE ROLL CAST

The roll cast is often the first cast taught. Not only does it illustrate proper overhead trajectory, but it also extends line in front for the standard overhead cast. The roll cast permits a forward cast with minimal backcast space. In the roll cast, the energy and force of the backcast (which the roll cast lacks) are created by the watered line (the water anchor) and the "draped belly" (the suspended line weight off the rod tip) of the fly line behind the caster. The term roll cast is a misnomer. It is neither a circular nor arcing cast. Furthermore, the fly line rolls out above the water surface, not on the water surface. Like all efficient casts, the forward roll should be rather narrow (i.e. a tight loop), and all forward line energy should be dissipated or expended before the line falls and touches the water. In the forward cast position-1, the roll-cast line forms a D-cast with the rod as the near-vertical stroke and the fly line as the curving belly behind the caster. Each forward roll cast must be done slightly to the left (for right-handed casters) of the watered line. This prevents crossing over your own watered line during a roll cast. Due to the lack of a backcast, it is often used when there are obstructions behind the caster. A roll cast can also aerialize a line (pickup) for an overhead cast. It can also help to aerialize a sunken sink-tip line before making a backcast. When strong winds prevent a backcast, a roll cast with a rear wind can throw a long forward cast. In addition, the roll cast is claimed to assist in releasing a fly caught in water debris when used with a reverse pull of excess line. This is done by stripping off a few feet of excess line and then executing a roll cast above and beyond the snagged fly. The roll cast, however, may just make it more difficult to extract a caught fly; the line pressure alone often buries the hook deeper.

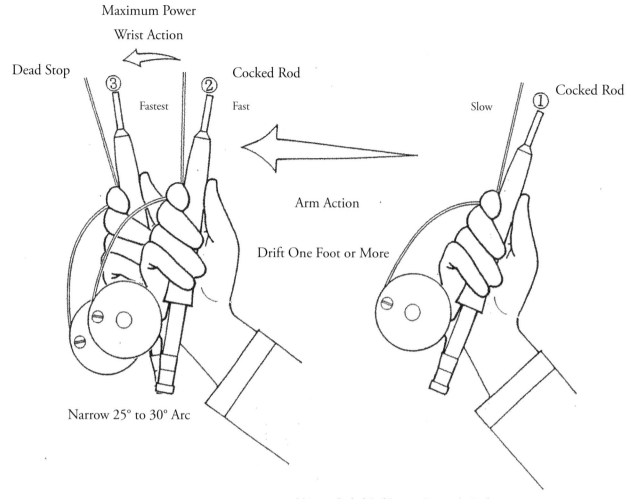

Maintain Cocked-Rod Position During the Drift.

The Roll-Cast Paradigm

Each roll cast places the line to the left of the watered line. Once the line is too far left on the water, a roll cast can be made to the right. This is done by keeping the rod and the casting stroke on the right side (for a right-handed caster), while placing the rod tip over the left shoulder. Remember that the roll cast is made with straight rod-tip trajectory, *the same stroke used in the overhead cast*. Anchor the fly line under the trigger finger or several fingers. The line must not move up through the guides during power application; a fly line must be attached to the rod to receive power. The line should roll out above the water surface approximately chest high in a tight loop. *The roll cast should be done with smooth, authoritative acceleration until the dead stop at position-3*. Although there are three distinct rod positions described here, the actual roll cast has smooth, continuous acceleration. Nevertheless, for class instruction, a full stop at position-2 with acquired line tension (watered line and full drape) can demonstrate the roll-cast components.

Only the shallow spring lever from rod position-2 to rod position-3 throws the line. Consult "The Rod Grip and Line Hold" starting on page 59 for the standard hold and line lock.

Roll-Cast Mechanics

Begin the roll cast with about three rod lengths of extended fly line on the water. An adequately watered or anchored line is required for the roll cast. Swing or drift the rod tip moderately low and horizontal to maintain maximum water and line contact while reaching up in back to create the drape before assuming forward cast position. Drag as much line on the water as possible. Avoid lifting the line up and off the water (a common error) while pulling the line back and forming the rear belly drape: *this removes all line tension and rod load.*

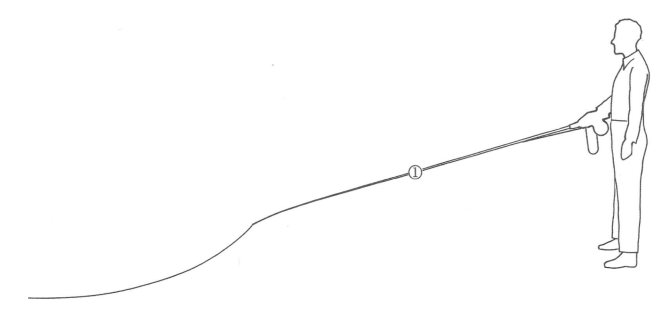

The Start Position with Watered Line and Low Rod Tip

To create maximum belly or drape, extend or raise the rod tip high in the back before assuming the lower, more comfortable position-3, *which now becomes position-1 for the forward cast.*

Drape the line off the rod tip behind you. Remember that in the forward-stroke position-1 (a cocked rod position), the rod tip slants slightly rearward and away from your body line. The watered line should be relatively straight with minimal slack. The more watered line, the more rod load.

Rod position-3 is now forward cast position-1; apply the standard overhead casting stroke. The stroke travels from position-1, through position-2, into position-3 and stops dead. This is the standard very slow to very fast casting stroke. And like the overhead cast, the rod tip travels a straight horizontal line.

The Preliminary Setup and
Drift, Rod Positions-1, 2 and 3

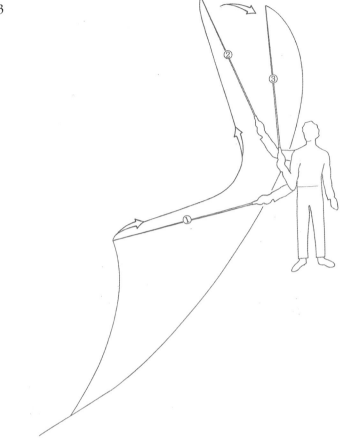

The Forward Casting Stroke

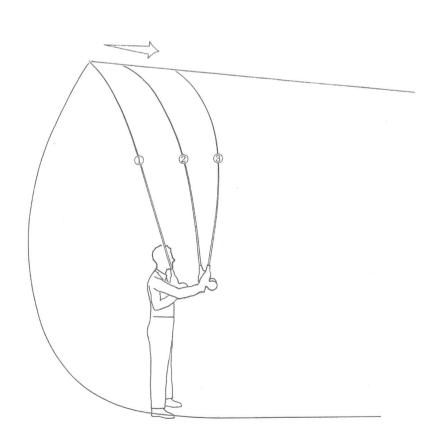

If you can make an efficient overhead cast, you can make an efficient roll cast; if you can make an efficient roll cast, you can make an efficient overhead cast. Remember that the roll cast is not made with an arcing or circular rod-tip motion. The force from position-1 to position-3 must bend the rod. To a significant extent, it is the rod bend that throws the fly line, not the caster. The traveling position-2 is a cocked rod without a stop before the wrist snap at position-3. Avoid arcing position-3 down toward the water.

The line should extend straight out above the water. After the line extends forward and begins to drop, the rod tip follows the line down. The keyword is follows. The rod tip should not pull the line down in front. *During the casting stroke the rod directs the line; after the casting stroke, the line directs the rod.* Finally, all forward fly-line energy should be expended before the line touches the water surface.

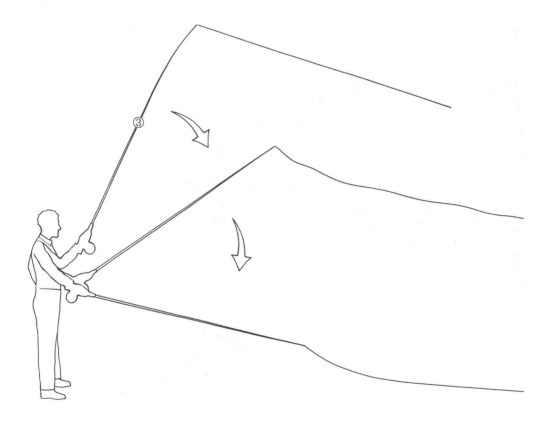

The Forward Line Extension and Fall to Water Surface

THE ROLL-CAST LINE SHOOT

With the new heavier weight-forward lines, it is quite possible to shoot extra line forward on the roll cast. To shoot line and increase casting distance, first strip off some shooting line from the reel. Then, instead of simply draping the fly line behind you, use the rod tip to forcibly drive or kick a large power-belly behind you immediately prior to the forward stroke. The larger the back belly, the longer the shoot.

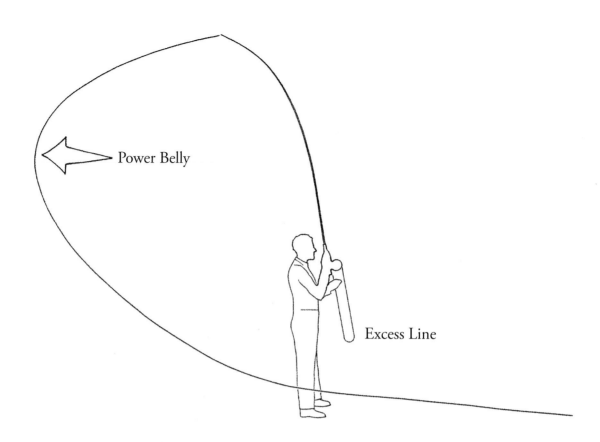

Power Belly

Excess Line

Haul and Shoot on the Forward
Roll-Cast Stroke

To increase line speed and distance, execute a forceful haul (pulling line down and back through the stripping guide) during the forward roll-cast stroke. The haul may be brief or protracted, depending upon the particular weight-forward fly line. The roll-cast shoot may require a heavier than normal weight-forward line, a slender shooting-line section, and a commanding back belly drive. Perhaps the most dramatic shoots occur with heavy weight-forward fly lines, such as The Royal Wulff triangle taper Ambush lines. Contrary to the static drawing, the haul positions A to B occur during the forward stroke. (Consult the section on the double haul for details on hauling.) Release the shooting line instantly after the forward stroke. The power belly also may be done with an authoritative roll cast without a line shoot.

THE OVERHEAD CAST

The overhead cast is the standard for presenting the fly to the fish. A fly rod is a long lever designed to bend. *Casting is rod bending.* Although each rod position is described separately here, the actual overhead cast has a smooth, continuous acceleration (passing through each position) that bends the rod. *Essentially, fly casting is merely drawing straight rod-tip lines in the air with enough energy to allow the fly line to continue drawing that imaginary straight line.* This is the simple secret of proficient fly casting. The fly line travels an imaginary line (drawn by the rod tip) as it extends and unrolls. Proficient casters preserve the straight lines. There is a satisfying sensation in a rod loading and unloading fly line; enjoy your rod time. While casting, periodically check for wind knots by sliding your fingers over the leader and tippet. Also, secure the rod sections prior to casting, and never cast with a loose rod section.

The Rod Grip and Line Hold

First of all, consider the rod and line hold. There are different ways to hold a fly rod. Right-handed anglers commonly configure the reel for left-handed retrieve. This allows the rod to remain in the right hand while fishing, thus eliminating the need to change hands when retrieving (spooling in) the fly line or when landing a fish.

For maximum power and comfort, grip the rod handle with the thumb directly on top of the handle. This standard hold places the thumb in line with the target. The lower four fingers and the hand heel will apply most of the power, especially when lifting the line off the water and into the backcast. In the forward cast, the thumb generates the final thrust to the rod. This grip is sturdy and secure but may encourage rod and reel twist during the casting stroke. Supposedly, a twisting rod reduces the efficacy and accuracy during the cast. The twisting rod, however, may have little effect on the cast and may be deliberately done to avoid catching a shooting line on the reel handle. Care must be taken to prevent the standard hold from arcing the rod too far back.

The Standard Rod-Grip Position

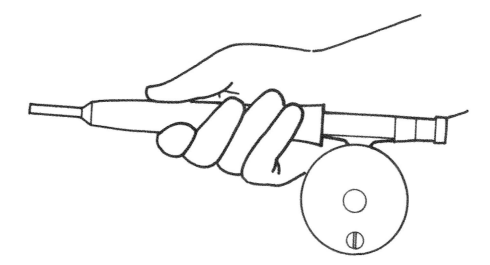

The alternate continental grip, generally used for light-line rods, extends the index finger along the top of the handle. Although some claim that the continental grip produces accurate casts by pointing, the lack of wrapped fingers probably produces a weak, less secure grip. The index on top hold usually lacks power for rods heavier than a 6-weight.

Another hold is the V or tournament grip. The V of the thumb and index finger is positioned on top of the rod handle with the thumb along the side. This free-wrist hold, sometimes called the split grip, provides a powerful wrist-snap. The V-grip, advocated by John and Richard Knight in *The Complete Book of Fly Casting* (1963), places the lower joint of the index finger (where it meets the palm) on top of the rod handle. Those who place the V to the side of the rod and the base of the index finger (the first knuckle) directly on top of the handle along with the back of the hand generate an uncomfortable and unnatural grip. However, with the reel seat under the forearm, this grip has inordinate lifting powers.

The standard thumb-on-top hold is recommended and illustrated here. In any hold, the grip should be relaxed and comfortable, applying pressure only when required. To lock the line to the fly rod, capture the line beneath the trigger finger (the index finger); this allows maximum rod energy to pass directly to the fly line during the casting stroke. To set the hook when a fish strikes, the line should be locked beneath the trigger finger. An angler can control a fleeing fish with slight trigger-finger pressure, releasing and stopping line as required.

An angler can also retrieve line or fish by stripping line down from behind the index finger. A fighting fish may pull line from beneath the index finger, but pressure from the finger can usually control most fish.

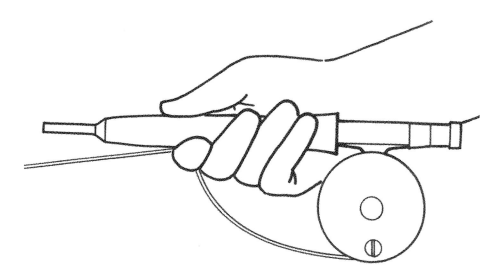

The line draped from the trigger finger can be stripped in to recover the line. For increased control, strong fish should be put on the reel as soon as possible. To do this, the excess line is returned to the reel. This is done by trapping the fly line under the little finger and reeling in under tension. This maintains pressure on the line for smooth, firm reel wraps.

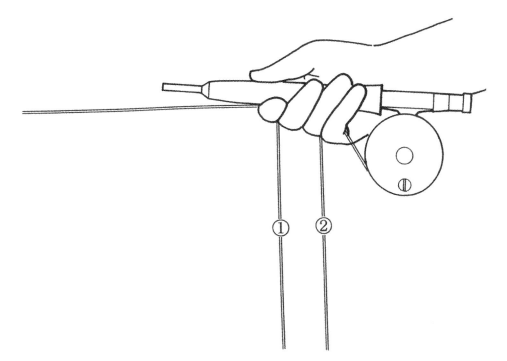

The Rod Grip and Line-Recovery Position

The Casting Stroke

It is the casting stroke that creates the cast. Straight rod-tip trajectory controls accuracy and line placement. For the overhead cast, the straight trajectory is slightly up in back and slightly down in front, about chest high above the water. Begin the casting stroke with smooth tension; avoid jerking the rod into the stroke. If adequate force is used in the backcast, the fly line will pull the rod tip back, creating a spring that will help launch the line forward during the forward cast. In the backcast, there should be sufficient energy to bend the fly rod and straighten the fly line. Avoid soft, limp casts. After the forward cast, the rod tip should stop dead just beyond vertical on the trajectory line. A basic fault is advancing the rod tip beyond vertical before the final wrist snap. In other words, if the rod is beyond vertical at position-2, the wrist snap merely throws the line down into the water. The caster has erroneously drawn a hook at the end of the straight rod-tip trajectory. If the caster arcs down a few inches off the straight rod-tip trajectory track, the fly line will arc down several feet off that trajectory. In brief, the cocked attitude of position-1 (in both the forward and rearward cast) is maintained as it accelerates into position-2.

In a manner of speaking, the rod butt should lead the casting stroke from position-1 to position-2. In fact, a rod may go far back as long as the rod bends deeply and the rod tip draws a straight line on the forward stroke. Once the rod stops, the fly line continues to travel along the track as it unrolls. To help draw that straight rod-tip line, *the fly rod must bend to become shorter in position-2.* This is the simple secret of proficient casting.

The rod travels from slow to fast to fastest in an accelerating casting stroke. Proficient casters often have a very slow one to two and an extremely fast two to three. I often instruct beginners to slow down their slow and speed up their fast. Both the backcast and the forward cast consist of three positions. Position-1 is forward in the backcast and rearward in the forward cast. Position-1 to position-2 is essentially accelerated arm action. Position-2 to position-3 is a commanding, shallow wrist snap. As previously mentioned, the wrist snap (making a narrow arc of 25° to 35°) from position-2 to position-3 bends the rod then stops dead. The accelerating rod tip throws the line. At position-3, the rod stops and slants forward (forward cast) or rearward (backcast) approximately 15° to 20°. In the forward cast, the rod should follow the line down only after the fly line has fully extended forward, having eradicated all forward energy and begun the drop toward the water. *During the casting stroke, the rod commands the line; after the casting stroke, the line commands the rod.*

The Complete Overhead Cast

The overhead cast begins with a fairly straight fly line extended on the water (the watered line) in front and the rod tip near the surface. Some students may wish to extend line with a rod rattle. Pull out about four long line strips from the reel. Point the rod tip down toward the water and, while gently guiding the stripped line with the line hand, briskly shake the rod tip on its axis to drive the line down and through the rod tip and onto the water. The rod butt is static; only the rod tip forcefully wags horizontally as it dispels fly line. When sufficient line is on the water, reach back and up into the roll cast start position. This should straighten most of the watered line. Now, execute one or two smooth roll casts to extend and straighten the required length of fly line on the water. Line can also be extended with aerial hauls and shoots until line is suitably lengthened.

Start with about 2½ to 3 rod lengths of straight watered line. If necessary, strip in some line to straighten the watered line. During the smooth slow-fast pickup, the water tension will load and bend the rod. To prevent the aerialized line or fly from catching the caster, slant the rod 5° to 10° away from the body line. Elevating the rod during the casting stroke quickly fatigues the arm. Long rods allow a natural and comfortable casting stroke. The following directions describe in detail the line pickup, the backcast, the forward cast, and the line laydown. Finally, it should be noted that the casting strokes and body movements (such as weight shift and line management) are more flowing and more comfortable than depicted in these static ink drawings.

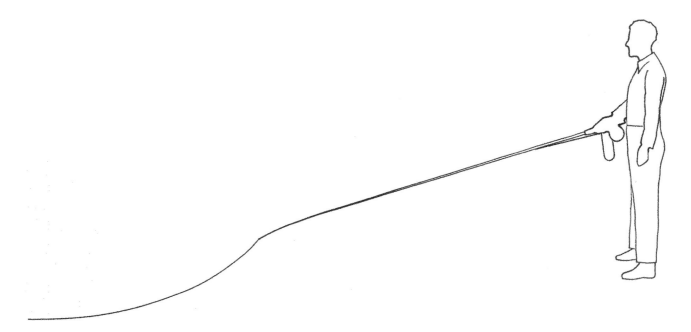

The Start Position with Watered Line and Low Rod Tip

The Line Pickup

Begin by locking the line on the rod handle with the trigger finger. Never start the cast with a high rod-tip position and slack line; this stroke lacks loading distance and must travel too far back. Instead, with the rod tip close to the water, lift about half of the watered line off the surface before accelerating to position-1. The rod should slant forward about 15° to 20°. The backcast begins with position-1 in the front. *Lift the line more up than back.* Do not disturb the water appreciably during the continuous slow-fast pickup. Avoid ripping back and furrowing the water during the pickup.

Facetiously, I often note that these water ditches can trap trout until they drown. Avoid making ditches. Now, do not stop at position-1. After loading the rod well, continue the casting stroke into the backcast.

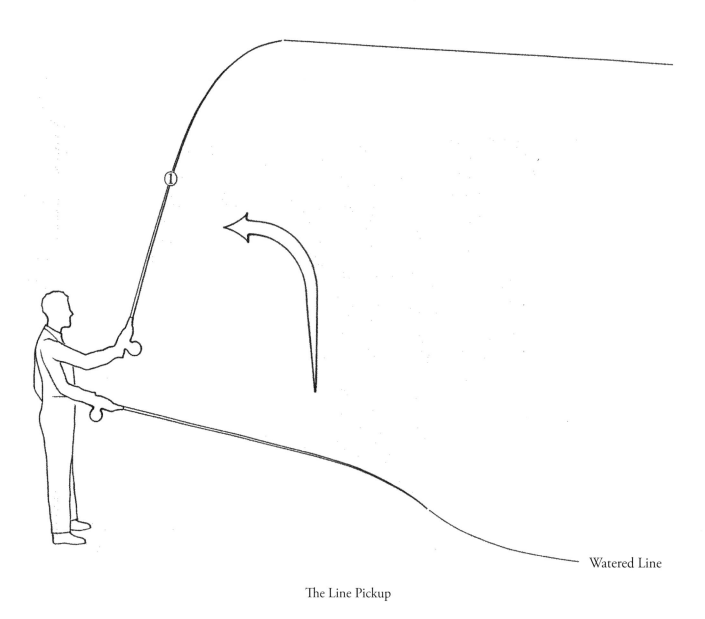

Watered Line

The Line Pickup

The Backcast Stroke

Begin casting instruction relaxed and, if possible, with a qualified casting instructor. Fly casting is a pleasure (and a sensual pleasure) as the muscular rod loads, accelerates through the stroke, and stops dead to throw a long, soft fly line. When done properly, casting is strangely simple. Each casting stroke—whether a backcast or forward cast—begins with position-1 and travels through to position-3. Accordingly, the backcast and forward cast start at opposing positions and move in different directions. The following casting paradigms illustrate this number reversal.

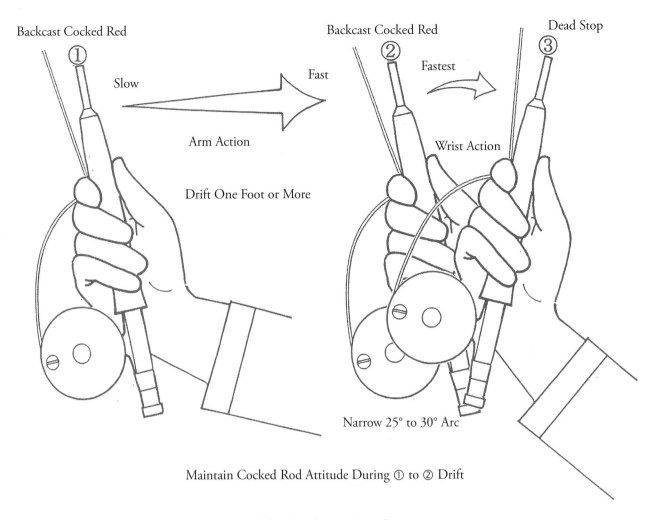

Backcast Cocked Red ①

Slow

Fast

Arm Action

Drift One Foot or More

Backcast Cocked Red ②

Fastest

Wrist Action

Dead Stop ③

Narrow 25° to 30° Arc

Maintain Cocked Rod Attitude During ① to ② Drift

The Backcast Paradigm

The rod travels from slow (position-1) to fast (position-2) to fastest (position-3) in an accelerating casting stroke. Position-1 to position-2 is arm action; position-2 to position-3 is wrist snap. The wrist snap is the last lever that bends the rod farther and launches the fly line. At position-3, the rod stops, but the line continues. During the stroke, the rod travels back with the same forward cocked attitude to position-2. *An excellent soft forward cast grows from a powered backcast.* Match the rod energy to the cast distance. If there is 30′ of line out in the forward cast, there will be 30′ out in the backcast plus the distance (approximately 5′) that the rod tip travels. Thus 30′ of line results in about 65′ of fly travel—the front 30′ plus the 5′ of rod drift plus the 30′ extending back. This travel takes time. Consequently, the caster must wait for the line to travel. Do not rush the stroke. A casting axiom claims that if your backcast is proper then the forward cast is usually proper. However, if the backcast is improper, then the forward cast is always improper. In terms of proficiency, *the backcast is the most important cast done*. While learning timing and control, turn your head and watch your back cast. Watching will reveal the quality of your backcast. You will learn to place the fly line high in back and learn how long it takes for a given line length to travel back.

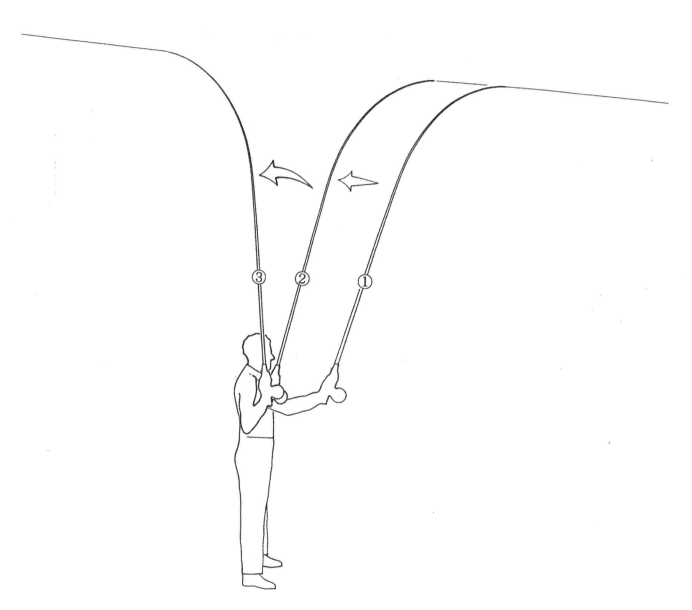

The Backcast

To draw a straight rod-tip line, *the fly rod must bend to become shorter* during the casting stroke. The casting stroke, without curving or slicing, is commonly a foot or more (and may be several feet) before the wrist snap, that final authoritative thrust from position-2 to position-3. Generally, the longer the straight stroke, the greater the rod stress and the longer the cast. I often share an absurd but perceptible tale with my students: 90 percent of the cost of a rod is for the lever alone, also known as the flex or bend of the fly rod. Make certain that you use the bend.

Then, with the arm, smoothly accelerate through position-2 with straight rod-tip trajectory. At position-2, the wrist snaps the rod back (the final spring or lever) into position-3 and stops dead. The backcast should extend rearward, slightly above the horizontal. This shallow, speedy wrist snap, from position-2 to position-3 stops the rod approximately 15° to 20° slanting back. Even a rearward stop at true vertical can create a notably efficient forward cast. Remember Norman Maclean's pronouncement, in *A River Runs Through It*, that "man . . . will always take a fly rod too far back."

The line now extends in the backcast. The backcast, which should smoothly load and bend the rod, is essential for a good forward cast. The stored power in the bent rod during the backcast will be released and used in the forward cast. Consequently, use adequate power in the backcast. The rod becomes a vertical spring or lever that throws the line. *Cast the fly line, not the fly rod.* A fly rod does not have to travel far to throw a long line far.

Backcast Line Extension

When you stop dead at position-3, the line continues to unroll, extending the backcast line slightly up and back. Again, the longer the line extends, the longer the pause. Wait until most of the line extends, then slowly begin the forward cast (thus straightening the line) before increasing the forward acceleration. Do not allow the rod tip to go back again before going forward, the so-called Inverness twitch of a two-handed salmon rod. In summary, *once you initiate the forward cast, continue the forward cast.* There is nothing obscene about watching the backcast unfold behind you. It should be reasonably straight and extended before the forward cast.

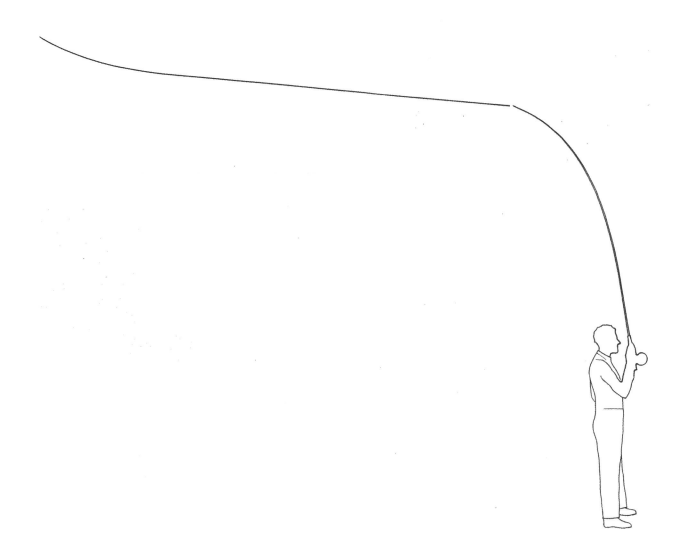

The Backcast Line Extension

The Forward Cast

As noted, coming out of the backcast, the forward cast begins slowly to create a straight fly line. The degree of straightness in the backcast extension is more critical than commonly supposed. If the forward cast starts at extension-1, then the line terminus swings over and down beneath the straight forward trajectory as the fly line advances, tempting wind knots or erratic flight. If the cast starts at extension-2, then the initial slow-fast stroke totally straightens the line and prepares it for increased acceleration. If the fly line is totally straight at extension-3 before starting forward, then the forward timing is critical, almost too late. The line may actually sag while advancing.

Once the rear line is nearly straight during the back stroke, apply maximum power to the line when the rod hand is in front of the ear. Only modest energy from the angler is then required for the forward cast. Some of

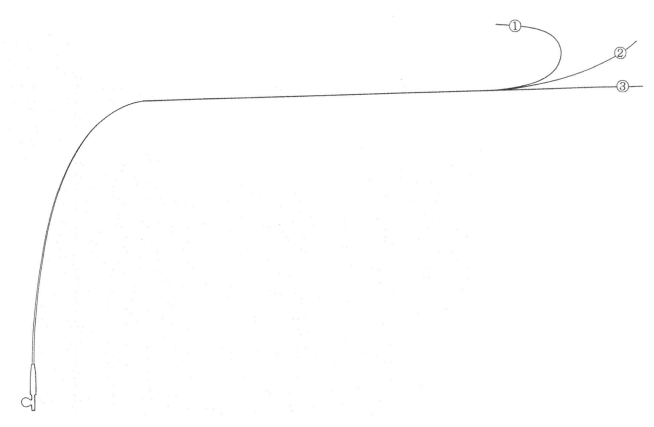

The Backcast Line Extensions

the energy used in the forward cast comes from the bent rod (the backcast) rather than from the caster. The caster merely amplifies the forward energy.

Now the numbers reverse for the forward cast. The backcast position-3 now becomes the forward cast position-1. In the forward cast described here, position-1 begins in the rear with a cocked or angled rod. In the cocked position, the rod should slant back approximately 15° to 20°. Do not, however, slant the rod so far back that the rod tip cannot trace straight rod-tip trajectory. As noted, the bent rod assists in describing straight line trajectory. The rod, maintaining the same slanted or cocked attitude, accelerates forward to position-2. Position-2 has the same cocked hand as position-1. This is a slow-fast movement. Position-2 continues to advance. At position-2, the wrist applies the final power, the wrist snap lever that launches the line forward.

The rod tip must not advance to vertical during the forward casting stroke; the rod should remain cocked (i.e. if a vertical line were drawn down from the rod tip, it would align behind the rod hand). The rod butt, in a manner of speaking, should lead the casting stroke into position-2. Now, as the rod passes position-2, maximize the rod speed with a powerful wrist snap (about a 30° arc or less) into a shallow position-3 and stop dead. Bend the rod to create a spring that throws the fly line forward.

Although conventionally described as such, a fly rod does not rotate like the hands of a clock. This common clock image, a classic icon of casting instruction, only creates poor casters. *The rod butt should not simply rotate on a given point.* A sweeping arcing down rod tip only produces a sweeping arcing down fly line. Unlike the hands of a clock, the rod should follow a horizontal, cocked drift from position-1 to position-2. Furthermore, unlike the clock simile, the vertical fly rod is pushed and pulled horizontally. There is, however, a slight, shallow tip arc from position-2 to position-3 that throws a straight, compressed rod tip forward. Essentially, *the fly rod is a vertical spring that travels horizontally.*

Various metaphors often occur when describing the final short and decisive throw of the forward cast: a hammer hitting a nail or flipping a mud dab off the end of a stick. This action is short, swift, and forceful. Remember, too, that the rod tip travels a relatively straight line, slightly up in back for the backcast and slightly down in front for the forward cast. The fly line should extend forward about chest high above the water then float gently down to the water. *Do not cast into the water.*

Summary

The following forward cast paradigm details the rod positions. Positions-1 and position-2 are cocked rods (*i.e.*, the rod tip angles to the rear). Accelerating from position-1 to position-2, the rod must maintain the same cocked attitude. Once again, if the rod arrives at a slanted forward position-2, then the final power snap drives position-3 down in front. Thus the fly line fails to follow straight rod-tip trajectory. Hooking the rod tip down on the forward cast is a fundamental error. Keep the flowing position-2 fairly vertical to allow enough hand rotation for the final power snap.

Maximum Power

Wrist Action

Dead Stop   Cocked Rod   Cocked Rod

③ Fastest   ② Fast   Slow   ①

Arm Action

Drift One Foot or More

Narrow 25° to 30° Arc

Maintain Cocked-Rod Position During the Drift.

The Forward Cast Paradigm

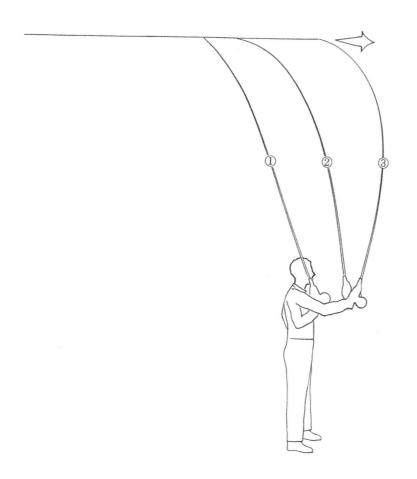

① ② ③

The Forward Cast

Furthermore, reverse this illustration to describe the backcast. Position-3 in the forward cast becomes position-1 for a backcast. The new position-2 now becomes the tight power snap that throws the fly line behind you into a new rear position-3 (the original forward cast position-1).

As an instructor, I use white batons or sticks (approximately 20″ long) to teach the proper rod angles for the backcast and forward cast. This illustrates the angles of a cocked rod at position-2 during the casting stroke. As previously noted, a fundamental fault is a vertical rod at position-2; this error often causes a downward arc past position-3, throwing the line down. Once the students gain some rod angle muscle memory, casting becomes simple and effective.

Forward Line Drop and Rod Follow

The rod stops dead at position-3. All the forward line energy should be spent or depleted before the fly line falls and touches the water surface. As the line extends and falls, the rod tip must follow the line down in front. *The rod tip does not pull the line down.* The fly line now commands and controls the fly rod as the line falls. The final position (with watered line and rod tip near the water surface) is the starting position for the next overhead cast.

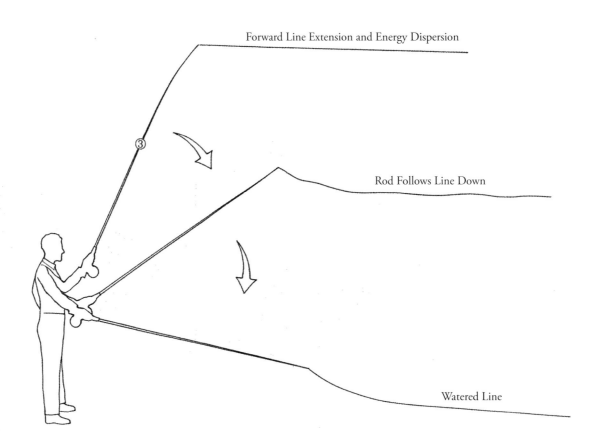

The Relaxed Line Drop and Rod-Tip Follow

The Tailing Loop

Casting requires control and care. Improper trajectory and power can promote casting problems, especially the so-called tailing loop. The tailing loop encourages the fly to snag the line or to create wind knots. Wind knots—which are the result of improper casting rather than wind—tie overhand knots in the tippet, leader, or, at times, even in the line. Wind knots profoundly weaken a leader or tippet (by as much as 50 percent or more depending upon the diameter) or impede the fly line. To avoid a tailing loop, which is an erratic displacement of line and fly, follow these four key points of a proficient forward cast:

1. Allow the line time to nearly straighten in the backcast before initiating the forward cast.
2. When initiating the forward cast, drag the line slowly forward before applying power. This straightens the fly line and loads the rod prior to maximum power application. In short, come out of the backcast slowly before acceleration.
3. Do not give maximum power, the so-called wrist snap or power snap to the fly line until the rod hand has passed in front of the ear.
4. Finally, apply straight rod-tip trajectory by drawing a straight line in the air with the rod tip.

Avoid excessive or weak line extensions on the backcast and maintain constant rod-loading pressure (rod stress) throughout the forward casting stroke. Avoid looping or dipping the rod tip down and up during the forward casting stroke. Casting is pushing and pulling a flexible vertical beam horizontally through the air. When the rod tip draws a straight line in the air (slightly up in back and down in front), the fly line continues in that efficient, straight trajectory as it extends forward. To demonstrate what creates tailing loops, I produce them for my classes by dipping and then abruptly raising the rod tip during the forward casting trajectory, thus throwing the line into itself. These demonstrations frequently produce wind knots, flying tangles, and tailing loops.

STRESS AND STRAIN

Rod action may also be explained by elastic deformation. A fly rod works by elastic deformation, a type of strain. Stress (moving the rod) creates strain (bending or loading the rod). Strain is accompanied by change in size or shape. In fly casting, it is the rod shape that changes; the rod bends. In elastic strain, the applied energy is absorbed and stored in the rod as the rod undergoes deformation. Once the applied force (the stress) is released, the rod returns to its original shape as the energy is released in a usable form: energy that throws the fly line. Elastic strain is the capacity of the rod to store and release energy. If the elastic limit of a rod is surpassed, then it will either respond by plastic strain (a permanent bend) or brittle strain (a break). Modern fly rods are designed to bend and are remarkably efficient in storing and releasing energy.

I have described the overhead casting stroke with three positions. However, in practice, the rod hand may actually rotate slowly forward into the shallow running wrist snap at the end. *Important Note: The descriptions and drawings of the casting stroke have notable limitations.* Even with limitations, these descriptions and drawings have produced excellent and informed casters. During a forceful casting stroke, the rod handle may actually achieve a slight forward slant or inclination before it arrives at the forward position-2. Nevertheless, the forward position must always allow distance on the trajectory line for the shallow wrist snap. Due to a moving and bent rod, the rod tip (in a trailing cocked position) will be above and behind the rod hand. This explication of the fluid motion of a fly cast reveals an essential truth: casting is dynamic. I often tell my students to visualize the rod butt leading the casting stroke until the wrist snap, that narrow arc at the end of the cast. There is some truth in this tale. The forward hand rotation or pivot may actually briefly glide down the forward casting stroke before the wrist snap. Rarely do rod hand position-2 and rod hand position-3 occupy a single point in space. They can, however, share a single point in space when demonstrating a slow, methodical roll cast that stops at each hand position. In the roll cast, a complete forward stop and wrist snap can lay out a long line.

THE DYNAMIC CAST

Perhaps it is best to visualize that only the rod handle actually assumes the three rod positions rather than the complete fly rod. When the forward cast begins in the rear, the rod tip bends back and down under the stress while advancing. Then, during the stroke, the handle position slowly rotates to near-vertical (even though the rod tip is bent back) as the rod tip advances. Finally, a decisive wrist snap sends the handle forward into position-3 as the rod tip bends, throwing the line forward before rebounding back.

THE MUSIC OF THE ROD

A fly rod sings. Rod sound—the sound made during the casting stroke—defines the casting stroke. Listen to what your fly rod tells you. If the casting-stroke sound is *a low, long swooooosh*, then too much of the whole rod passes through the air; the rod was neither fast enough nor bent enough. The full length of the rod is pushing air. Conversely, if the sound is *short and high-pitched*, then the tip section has traveled faster than the middle and butt sections and, consequently, launched the line properly. Only the narrow, fast top section pushes air. *A proficient cast is a succinct soprano.* In other words, cast the loaded rod tip, not the rod. Do not sweep the whole rod through the air. Listen to the music of the rod. A precisely matched line and rod may only whisper; nevertheless, listen carefully to the song of the stroke, to what your rod tells you.

THE DOUBLE HAUL AND FORWARD LINE SHOOT

The overhead double haul and forward line shoot is often considered the most efficient and the most challenging cast. A forward line shoot creates maximum line speed and distance, especially with a weight-forward fly line. A double haul (a haul during the line pickup, a backcast, and another haul during the forward cast) may be dramatic or surprisingly subtle. It can be just a tense whisper. Even a nearly imperceptible soft and short double haul offers remarkable line tension and control. It can penetrate a wind or hurl a long line. The key to the double haul is the coordination between the rod and line hand. For additional information, refer to the double-haul mechanics explicated in the *Ground Method Double Haul. Note: Rod positions are designated with numbers, hand position with alphabetic letters.* All directions are for right-handed casters.

Begin with two or three rod lengths of fly line on the water. To prepare for a line shoot in the forward cast, strip four or five feet of excess line from the reel. Later, when released, this extra line shoots forward for a longer cast. Note that adequately watered line (the line on the water) is required to flex the rod to extend line back and to pull line in the backcast. Some instructors use an overloaded rod to accelerate learning. With standard-weight fly lines, overload the rod (e.g. an 8-weight line on a 6-weight rod or a 6-weight line on a 4-weight rod). An exaggerated line communicates more rod-line information to the caster.

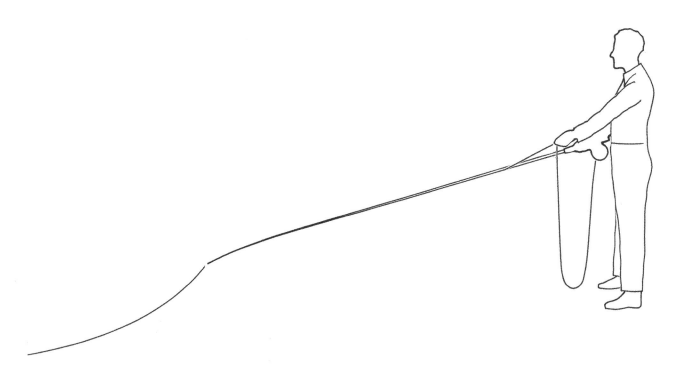

The Start Position

The watered line should lie fairly straight and the rod tip should be near the water. To begin the backcast pickup, reach forward and grasp the fly line immediately below the stripping guide. During the line pickup for the backcast, pull the line down (a smooth, swift accelerating haul) through the stripping guide toward your side during the rod lift. In the beginning, use smoothly accelerating short hauls, approximately 8″ to 15″. Longer hauls can come later.

The Pickup

Begin by securing the fly line in the left hand. Then start the pickup slowly while lifting the line up off the water. The rod lift and the countering line haul accelerate the fly line. This overcomes water resistance and creates immense line energy into the backcast. It is important to apply the three basic rod positions (1—2—3) during each double haul. Consult the cast paradigms in *The Overhead Cast* for rod numbers if required. During the backcast stroke, continuous rod tension must be kept on the fly line. Continue the rod lift and first haul into rod position-1. Then smoothly power into position-2, and finally snap back to position-3. Extending or shooting line in the backcast requires a straight rod-tip trajectory from position-1 to position-3. Never allow the fly line to creep through the stripping guide toward the rod tip during the backcast stroke. Line creep—fly line slipping through the stripping guide toward the rod tip during the casting stroke—dissolves line energy.

Shooting Line in the Backcast

Now, as the fly line extends straight back and pulls in the backcast (the line extension in the rear), allow the line weight to pull or draw the line hand (from hand-A to hand-B) up toward the stripping guide. This extends line in the backcast (akin to a controlled rear shoot) and prepares or cocks the line hand aft for the haul in the forward cast.

At nearly maximum rear-line extension, the line hand prepares for the forward cast. This backcast rod position-3 now becomes the forward cast rod position-1. The rod and line hand (near the stripping guide) are then ready for the forward haul (the second haul). Begin each haul slowly before maximum acceleration. The second haul (a smooth, strong accelerating pull) draws the line down through the stripping guide as the rod travels forward through position-1 and position-2. At the dead stop position-3, the fly line will be released and shot forward. Double-haul casters often pump and shoot the fly line through the rod guides with several casting strokes to maximize line speed for greater distance.

Now, begin the forward haul—hand position-A to hand position-B—immediately after the rod bends into the forward cast. With tension on the fly line, a haul may be moderately short for increased line speed. Both the cast and the haul should smoothly accelerate. The haul distance—hand position-A to hand position-B—must be either maintained or increased during the forward casting stroke. The hand and line must not move or creep toward the stripping guide during the forward power application. The rod can only give power to the fly line when the line does not move or when a haul is made. When the line moves toward the stripping guide, all line energy is lost. If the haul distance increases during the forward casting stroke (making the forward haul), then line energy increases, creating an efficient cast. Never decrease the distance between the stripping guide and the hand once the haul is made. *Keep the distance.* Once the haul is made and the line extends forward, the excess line held at hand position-B may be released and sent forward (shooting line on the forward cast).

The Forward Haul

The Forward Line Shoot

At dead stop rod position-3, the fly line travels forward, completing its trajectory and extension. This forward line momentum can now draw any extra fly line forward. Timing of the line release is critical. Thus, the forward moving line weight pulls extra line (the now-released slack line) through the rod guides. This is the forward shoot. If a long line is stripped off the reel before the double haul, then a long line may be shot forward. To prevent the stripped loose line (the extra line available for the shoot) from catching on the reel, reel handle, or rod butt, it may be beneficial to loosely direct (without impeding) the line with the line hand during the forward shoot: consider the open line hand as the first rod guide. The shooting line should slide freely through the line hand. During the forward stroke and shoot, some casters rotate the rod and reel on its axis 45° counterclockwise (turning the rod thumb left for right-handed casters) at rod position-3. This points the reel handle down and tucks the rod butt away from the traveling slack line, making the rod or reel less likely to snag a loose shooting line. In any case, longer shoots are possible when the hand guides the shooting line through the stripping guide.

Double hauls may be made without line shoots. Several fore and aft line shoots can create immense line energy and speed for a long forward shoot. Subtle shoots can control line in windy conditions. A double haul may be just a delicate tension that controls line movement.

The Fly-Line Coil

Use the fly-line coil to increase the length of the shooting line in a double haul. This method of managing excess shooting line while wading is to coil it in the left hand (for right-handed casters). If the coils are the same length, they may tangle. To avert such tangles, capture diminishing line lengths under the left thumb as illustrated. Form three loops with the second loop ¾ the length of the first loop and the third loop ¾ the length of the second loop. Note that the line travels from the reel three times around the hand and then to the stripping guide. Held in this manner, the fly line is readily released for a long line shoot immediately after the forward casting stroke. To release or shoot the line, merely relax the line fingers into a cone. The length of the first long loop is based on the wading depth and the particular angling conditions. This standard method reduces tangles and water drag on the fly line.

The Fly-Line Coil

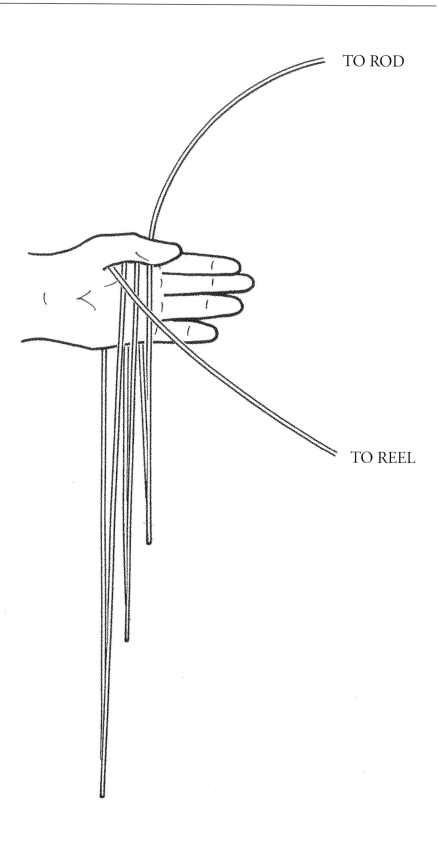

TO ROD

TO REEL

As the line shoots forward, gently control the loops as they feed forward. For long powerful casts, shift the body weight back for the backcast and forward for the forward cast. Additionally, the upper body (the turned torso and the shoulder muscles) adds power to the cast. The forward haul distance may be short and smooth or long and authoritative. Once the double haul mechanics are understood, longer hauls that draw the line hand to the hip—from hand position-A to hand position-B—or beyond can be made.

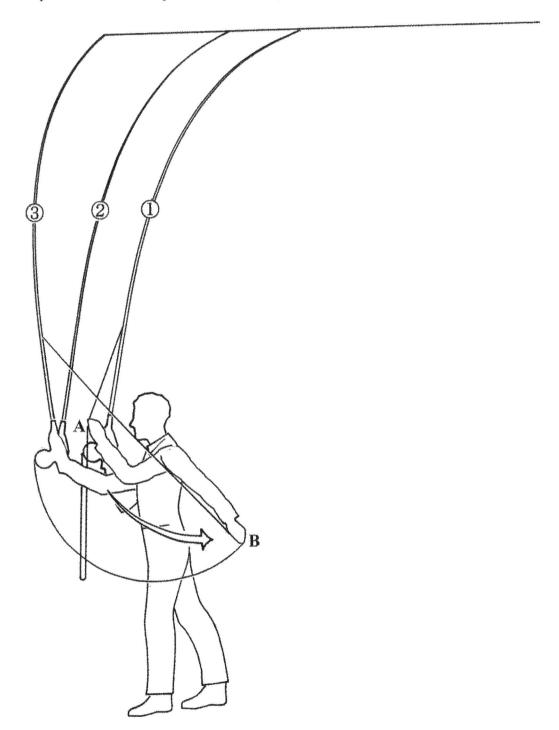

The Extended Forward Haul

The haul distance, essentially, must be either maintained or increased during the forward cast. If the A to B distance increases during the forward stroke, then the line energy increases. The line must never creep toward the stripping guide during the forward stroke. If the line moves up through the stripping guide during the stroke, then the accumulated line energy and rod strain dissipate. To illustrate the detrimental effect of line creep, make a forward cast while drifting the line up through the stripping guide. Or more dramatically, make a forward cast without holding the fly line stationary as the rod travels forward. The result is a limp line that, at best, only stumbles forward. There are three ways that a rod can command and accelerate the line: (1) if the line is trapped by the fingers against the rod handle, (2) if the line-hand to stripping guide distance remains the same, and (3) if the line-hand to stripping guide distance increases, thereby amplifying the rod action. The double haul uses distance increase, or a haul. In brief, never decrease the hand-to-stripping guide distance during a casting stroke. Feeding line toward the stripping guide of a bent rod quickly kills the cast; *keep the distance*. Finally, note that shooting line both fore and aft requires a straight rod-tip trajectory. Arcing or hooking the casting stroke prevents line shoots and extensions. The proficient double haul is hand, rod, and line in an angler's ballet.

THE GROUND METHOD: LEARNING THE DOUBLE HAUL

Lefty Kreh, the celebrated doyen of American fly fishing, promulgated an exceptional method for learning the double haul quickly. Consult his *Ultimate Guide to Fly Fishing* (2003). This method teaches the mechanics of the double haul by casting with a low rod tip about two or three feet above a grassy surface. During each forward and rearward horizontal cast, it may be beneficial to slightly lift or lower the rod tip to prevent line hits on it. Moreover, if the casting arc is too wide, the arcing line will fail to shoot. A line that will not haul is a line that will not shoot. Each casting stroke should be short, low, and horizontal with the rod tip tracing an effective straight line. As illustrated, the ground method is done in front of the caster to allow a complete view of the double-haul movements. The caster should fully focus on each haul and each shoot. On this horizontal trajectory, the forward cast (for right-handers) is to the left, and the backcast is to the right. Once the caster has put muscle memory into the ground double haul, the rod is then slowly aerialized to a front overhead haul and a rear overhead shoot. Then hauls and shoots may be made both forward and rearward.

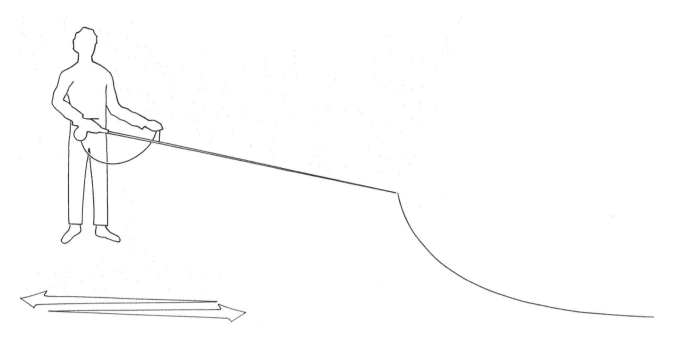

The Horizontal Start Position

First, begin by extending about 20′ to 25′ of fly line on the grass to your left. The rod tip should point slightly to the left. Next, reach up and grip the fly line near the stripping guide.

The Left Start Position with Grounded Fly Line

Then execute a low horizontal cast to the right while hauling on the fly line. Before the cast, eradicate any slack line. Begin the stroke by tensioning the line while on the ground before executing the cast and applying maximum power. This tensioning is important when applying power to the static start of any cast. This aids in creating a short, powerful stroke. It is imperative that the casting stroke bends the rod and that the rod tip travels a narrow arc.

The Haul to the Right

The line now shoots to the right, as the line hand follows the line toward the stripping guide. The line hand should stop near the stripping guide. Remember that the haul and shoot need not be long, only a few inches or more. If necessary, refer to the double-haul casting instruction in the text. *Note that in a single casting stroke there is a haul and a shoot.* The line hand works harder than the rod hand.

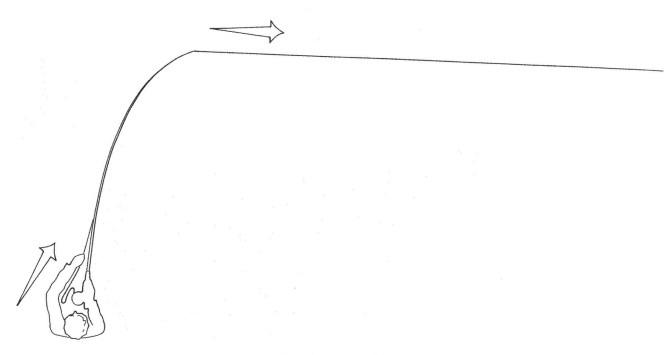

The Shoot to the Right

Again, when the line falls on the ground, wait. Think about what your hands have done and what must be done next to execute a haul and shoot to the left. Do not rush the haul and shoot; wait and think.

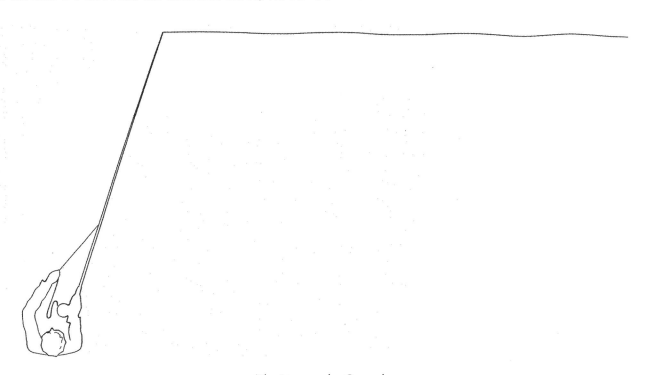

The Line on the Ground

Visualize what must now be done. When ready, make a haul, one casting stroke, and a shoot to the left. During each haul shoot, keep the hands reasonably close together.

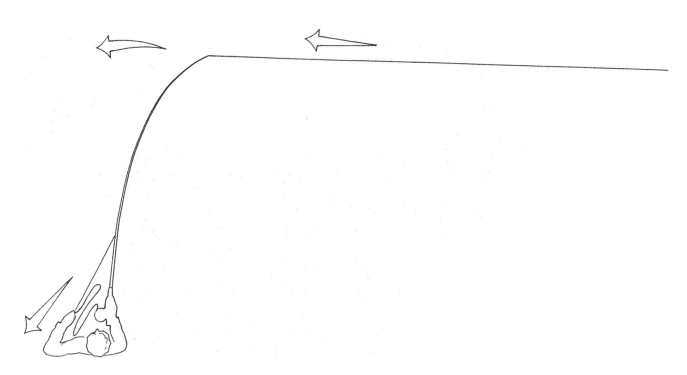

The Haul to the Left

The fly line now shoots (extends) to the left, as the line hand rides the line toward the stripping guide. The line hand then stops near the stripping guide. Remember that the haul and shoot need not be long, only a few inches at first. Longer hauls and shoots can come later. Allow the line to fall on the grass. This returns the rod and grounded line to the left start position illustrated above.

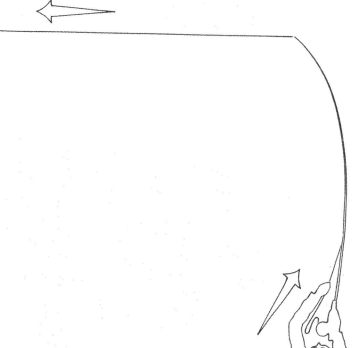

The Shoot to the Left

THE OVERHEAD DOUBLE HAUL

Continue to make double hauls and shoots on the grass in front of you. Pause after each haul and shoot to visualize what must be done for the opposing haul and shoot. Then execute the opposing cast. This creates the muscle memory for smooth haul shoot strokes. When the mind and hands remember the haul shoots on the ground, slowly aerialize the haul shoots fore and aft into a standard overhead double haul. Do not rush the double hauls; give the rod and hand time to haul and shoot the line. This method, especially with an overloaded rod, often teaches the double haul in one brief session.

Note: *I often include this addition for my casting students.* If the rod is over-loaded with a fly line heavier than normal by skipping one line weight—such as an 8-weight line on a 6-weight rod or a 7-weight line on a 5-weight rod—then the effect is amplified and learning is faster still. For teaching the ground and overhead double haul, an excellent rod-line combination is a fast 6-weight rod and a Royal Ambush Triangle Taper (TTAM6F, 235 grains) floating line. This line has a short, heavy 20' head and an ultrathin running line. This combination exaggerates the haul and the shoot, thus offering the fastest possible means for learning the double haul. Other over-weight lines (such as those ½ weight heavier than normal lines) may also work. The caster can feel the drag weight of the haul and the pulling tug of the shoot. Once the mechanics (especially the hand movements and timing) of the double haul are achieved, the caster can then return to the standard rod-line combination.

THE SINGLE-HANDED SNAP-T CAST

The Snap-T cast, attributed to Günter Feuerstein of Austria in the late 1980s, uses the same traditional C-snap that recovers a fly or tippet for change or inspection. Briefly, the C-snap is done with watered line extended in front. The angler then lifts the rod to about 40° and executes a swift, short stroke immediately beneath and inline with the draped fly line. This action sends the forward line back toward the caster. Some experienced cast-ers then catch the leader or line as it returns. This, however, also sends the fly hook back toward the caster. The safer and preferred method is to direct the stroke angle to the side so that the line comes back and catches on an extended horizontal rod. This keeps the returning fly away from the angler. Although the purpose and execution differ, the Snap-T is akin to the C-cast.

The Snap-T is a change-of-direction cast, taking an extended downstream line and placing it upstream in preparation for a roll cast. The Snap-T forms the letter T when the fly line crosses the rod on the upstream throw. There are similar casts, but the basic Snap-T is simple and popular for trout work with a floating line. An effective Snap-T can replace the standard single-handed

Spey cast. Although often considered a double-handed cast, the following Snap-T directions are for a right-handed caster with a single-handed rod.

Practice the Snap-T without an attached fly or hook. Now, once the fly and line is downstream and extended on the dangle, angle the rod downstream while eliminating any slack. For efficiency, begin with a taut and tensioned fly line. This allows the fly line to receive instant energy from the fly rod. Moreover, it permits a shorter stroke and a straighter trajectory.

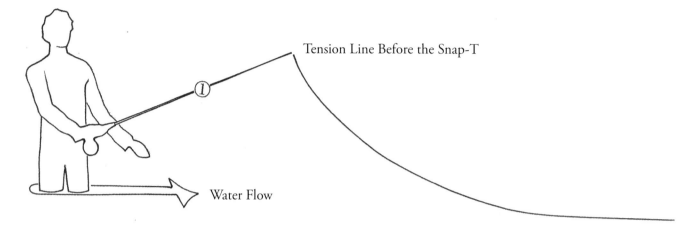

Tension Line Before the Snap-T

Water Flow

The Line on the Dangle

Remember that the rod-tip trajectory determines the line path. Rather than a single stroke that sends the line upstream, make a double stroke that sends the line upstream. To do this, make a short lift and draw with the rod tip and then a powerful snap under and inline (positions 1 to 2) with the downstream draped fly line. Make the power snap as short as possible. As the rod tip drives downstream, the line and fly hurl upstream over the rod. "To every action," Sir Isaac Newton reminds us, "there is always opposed an equal reaction."

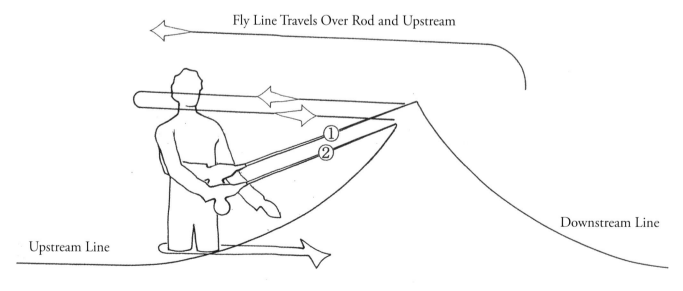

Fly Line Travels Over Rod and Upstream

Downstream Line

Upstream Line

The Line Snapped Upstream

Once the line touches upstream, swing the rod to the side, driving rearward a full belly drape in a cocked rod position. The fly and line then drifts downstream to align for a roll cast. Once the fly attains the proper position, immediately execute a quarter-upstream roll cast. The fly and line must be on the upstream side of the roll-cast stroke. In addition, *never perform a roll cast with fly or watered line directly in front.* This forces the fly back toward and perhaps into the caster. Casters have found the single-handed Snap-T both simple and effective.

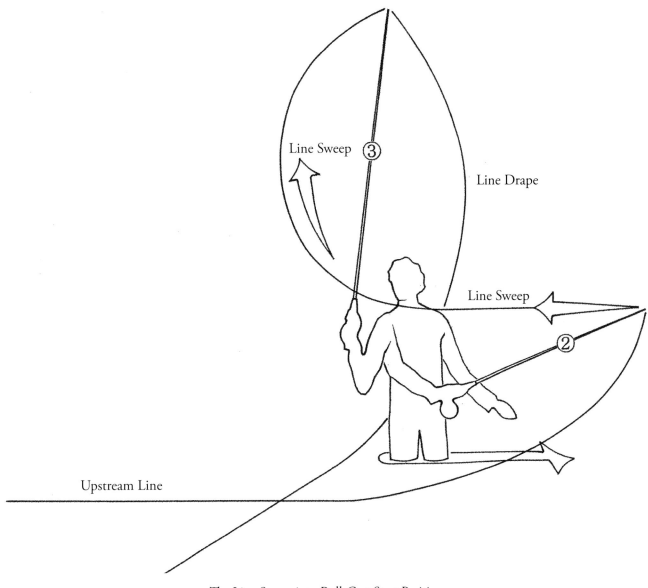

The Line Sweep into Roll-Cast Start Position

THE CENTER CURVE CASTS

This cast within a cast—a single spiral cast within a forward horizontal cast—allows the angler to throw curves within the line around boulders and rocks or upstream into fast currents. Additionally, an up-current curve can land a fly beyond a fast current tongue into slack water, allowing time for the fly to be seen and taken before drag captures it. Otherwise the fly would immediately zip across the water when a straight fly line touches the fast current.

Presentational casting—casting a mended line—is remarkably efficient. Instead of mending line on the water, the angler casts a shaped or mended line. The value of casting a mended line is significant; it can minimize fly drag, counteract currents, travel around obstacles, conquer fast flows, and properly address a rise. A line mended on the water can cause water disturbance, but a midair mend falls already formed with the proper line configuration. There is, obviously, a limit to how far the curve can travel down a falling line. This technique is best for close casts on small, boulder-strewn streams or on small streams with swift current tongues.

A stiff rod and weight-forward line can deliver a line curve about 35′. A double-taper or a long-belly weight-forward line may increase that distance. Usually, curves are sent shorter distances. Although other line tapers are more efficient, the ubiquitous weight-forward fly line can throw curves. But unlike a double-taper or a long-belly line, a steep, overpowered weight-forward line can actually straighten the running curve before the line touches the water. Yet with practice and proficiency, there is no need to change lines just to throw curves. Above all, avoid the two basic errors caused by overpowering the curve cast: (1) excessive energy in the overhead cast can straighten the running curve, and (2) excessive energy in the wrist roll can recoil the fly line back toward the caster.

The Left Curve

Note that on the forward stroke, the rod should stop slightly beyond the perpendicular, beyond the cocked position. This rod stop allows sufficient forward rod drift for a sharp recast that will push the spiral down the line. Immediately after the forward cast and while the line extends, complete a forward wrist roll (a near-circle rotation) that rotates the rod axis counterclockwise. *For the wrist roll, draw the rod sharply and briefly back (the recast), and then swiftly spiral forward.* This rotation forces the rod tip out of alignment, creating a forward spiral that drives a running curve along the fly line. This rotational cast is the cast within a cast. *Apply enough power to displace or orbit the rod tip away from its axis.* The circling line becomes a horizontal left curve when it falls on the water. The left spiral loops fly line around rocks or throws slack line upstream into quick currents.

Adjust the timing and power of the stroke for the final curve placement. An early wrist roll puts the curve near the leader, a late wrist roll near the rod. Remember that *the rod should rotate on its axis while the spiraling tip pushes a curve forward down the line.* When done properly, *the line near the rod lands straight, then curves, and then finally runs straight again.*

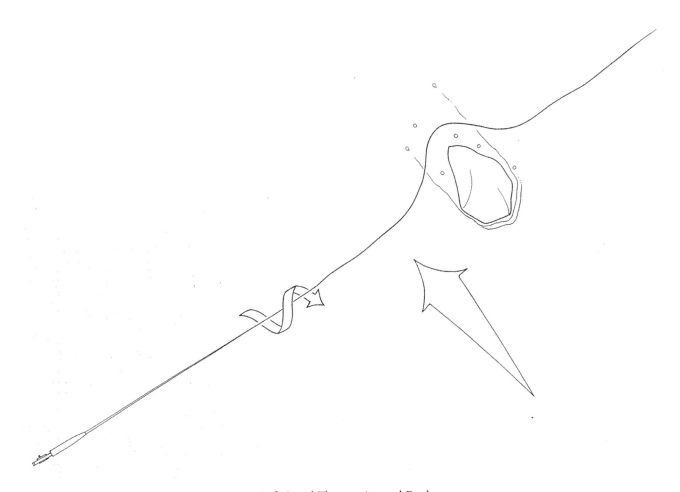

Left Spiral Thrown Around Rock

The Right Curve

The right curve cast is similar to the left curve cast except the wrist roll is clockwise. Again, the power of the single forward spiral should push the rod tip out of axis. The right curve, like the left curve, can be thrown upstream into fast water or tossed around rocks. *Note: There is an alternate method for creating a right-hand curve.* For right-handed casters, the horizontal curve cast method may be more efficient. Like the spiraled cast, it is a cast within a cast. After the overhead cast is made and while it is being realized, a second cast drives a right horizontal running curve down the line. On the initial cast, make certain that the rod does not float too far forward. To create the second cast, merely draw the rod back and then briefly and abruptly forward again into a horizontal cast. When done slightly to the left of the aerialized line, this horizontal cast will drive a horizontal right curve down the extending line. The forward energy of the initial cast should dissipate before the running curve reaches the proper position. Excessive energy in the initial cast can straighten or recoil the second cast.

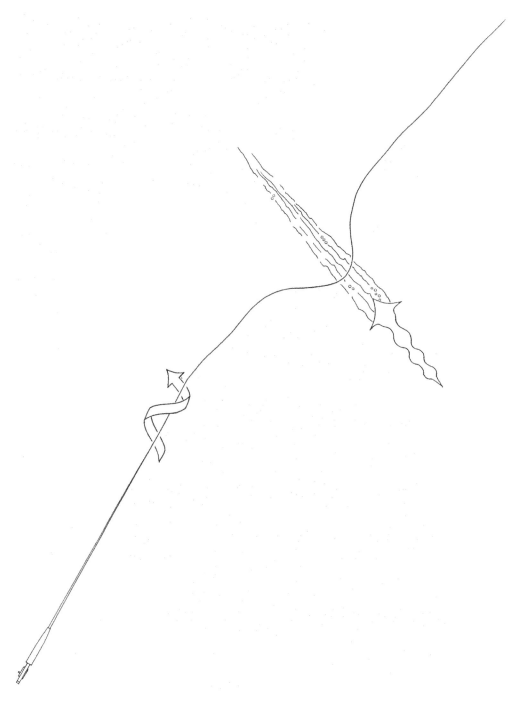

Right Spiral Thrown Up-Current

A fast or stiff rod facilitates casting a running loop. A softer rod has a greater time differential between the caster and the cast and between the cast within the cast. The enemies of casting, such as wind and gravity, are overcome by timing and energy. Casting is a slow-fast action in the backcast and forward cast. This allows the rod to load (to flex and bend) before it accelerates and offers energy to the fly line. If the rod accelerates before it possesses maximum load, its energy is merely absorbed by the rod and not passed on to the line.

Practice throwing right and left curves on the lawn. Place an object on the lawn and execute curved casts on each side of the object. Then do it at different distances. The line should land pointing at the object, curving around the object, and then continuing the initial straight line. Brief practice adds the muscle memory required for the right and left curve casts. A stiff or fast rod facilitates casting running curves. A softer or slower rod produces greater time differential between the caster and cast and between the initial cast and the rotational cast. Only proper timing and energy will determine the curve location when the line lands. With practice, even a fast rod can cast a smooth, soft, curving fly line.

THE LINE DRILLS

Efficient fly-line trajectory requires minimal physical effort to propel a long line. It does, however, require a suitable technique and understanding of trajectory. Here are some teaching tools that demonstrate and assess proper fly-line trajectory. These diagnostic rope methods, best done on a level lawn, require a leader without an attached fly pattern.

The Single-Rope Drills

The single-rope method grew from the double-rope method. The double-rope method (for loop control and accuracy) appears in *1001 Fly Fishing Tips* (Headwater Books, edited by Jay Nichols, 2008). This method requires horizontal casts that land the fly line between two parallel ropes, first placed at 4′ to 6′ apart then, for tighter fly-line loops, at 1′ to 2′ apart. The caster, standing outside the ropes at the middle, casts and lands the fly line between the ropes both fore and aft. This is an effective teaching practice.

The single-rope method, a mild variation of the double-rope method, may offer further insight to trajectory; a single straight rope line guides the rod tip, creating tight loops and straight trajectory. The double-rope method provides a space to cast into; the single-rope method narrows your concentration and offers your rod tip a guide to follow. This may disclose erratic trajectory, especially slicing or hooking a cast.

The Single-Rope Horizontal Cast Drill

1. First, place a straight 40′ to 50′ rope on the ground. A bright yellow poly-propylene rope works well. Position yourself at the middle and to one side of the rope. With the rod horizontal, the rope should lie directly beneath the rod tip. *Begin by extending about 25′ of fly line over the rope on the ground in front of you.* Lock the extended fly-line length beneath the trigger finger to cast a given line length. Stand so that the rod tip is horizontal, approximately waist level above the ground and directly over the rope line. All casts are horizontal and sidearm.

Now that the rope is grounded, visualize an imaginary straight line rising from the rope. Each horizontal casting stroke will trace this projected imaginary straight line above the rope line. Good casting is merely drawing straight lines with the rod tip—straight lines that the fly line continues. This does require a commanding cast that bends (i.e. shortens) the rod in the middle of the casting stroke to trace straight lines. If the rod does not bend, the rod tip will arc or curve, tossing the fly line away from straight trajectory. The rod tip, held above the rope line, should not deviate from that imaginary straight trajectory.

2. Next, above the rope line, execute a horizontal sidearm backcast. During the cast, keep the rod tip above and inline with the rope line for straight rod-tip trajectory. For full line extension, it may be necessary to raise or lower the horizontal rod slightly above or below waist level to avoid passing line hits. Moreover, restrict the length of the casting stroke. With a 9′ rod, the rod tip will travel about 9′ or fewer along the imaginary casting track. A longer stroke may curve or hook the fly-line trajectory just as it would for a standard overhead cast. To fully extend the given fly-line length both front and back, the casting stroke must powerfully bend the rod. After the back-cast, let the extended line land on the ground. Do not immediately recast; take time to analyze each completed cast. The fully extended fly-line length should ideally land fewer than 10″ from the rope. *Try to place the fly line directly on the rope line.* Avoid weak casts that fail to completely extend and straighten the fly line. Only thoughtful practice will consistently and accurately land a fully extended fly line near the rope line. This is demanding; do not be discouraged. For a standard cast, position the reel horizontally during each stroke.

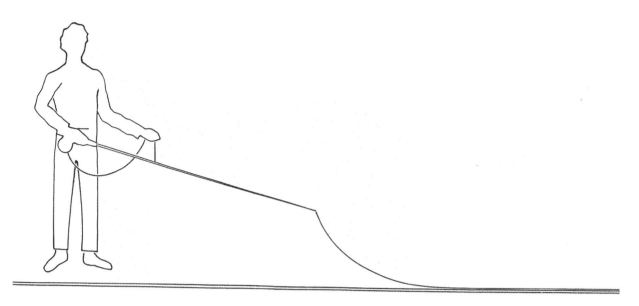

The Start Position for Horizontal Drills

3. Now execute a forward sidearm cast along the imagined trajectory. The backcast and forward cast are completed in the same manner above and inline with the rope trajectory. The fly line should again land within 10″ of the forward rope line. Remember that only proper power and trajectory will fully extend the fly line on or near the rope line. Cast a straight line, voiding all trajectory curves or hooks. The single-rope method, like the double-rope method, encourages efficient, tight line loops. Finally, continue to make back and forward casts along the rope line. Stop and evaluate each cast. Determine the casting fault if the fly line does not land relatively straight and near the rope line.

Finally, after several respectable fly-line laydowns near the rope line, slowly raise the rod to vertical overhead casts continuing to match the power and the trajectory of the rope casts. With a modicum of rope practice, the caster should be able to create straight, smooth casts.

The Forward Horizontal Cast Drill

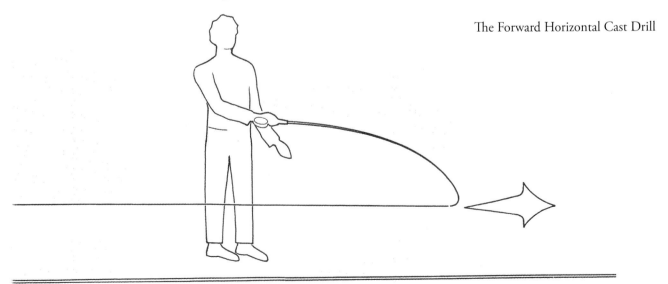

For a concluding challenge, try tracing the rope line with fluid horizontal double hauls and short shoots, landing the extended fly line on the rope after each shoot. This demanding and exacting single-rope method can improve your trajectory and tighten your loops.

The Single-Rope Overhead Cast Drill

This stroke determines the accuracy of overhead rod-tip trajectory. Again, ineffectual curving, slicing, or hooking trajectory is revealed if the line lay out of the casting stroke. Note that the overhead cast is several feet from the ground rope; consequently, placing the fly line near the rope on the ground is more challenging.

1. For forward cast trajectory, stand at the middle of the extended rope. The grounded rope should extend forward and rearward directly beneath the casting arm. Position the extended grounded fly line in front and along the rope.

2. Now, make a smooth overhead forward cast that places the line directly above the extended rope. Allow the fly line to extend and fall directly upon the rope line. The fly line should land close to the rope line.

3. For backcast trajectory, stand at the middle of the extended rope. The rope line should extend forward and rearward beneath your casting arm. Make several overhead casts, both fore and aft in line with the extended ground rope. Then, while observing the backcast, allow it to drop. Again, the extended fly line should fall close to the rope line. Finally, execute blind backcasts without watching the rear cast. Even for a moderately accurate rear laydown, the rear trajectory must extend straight out of the forward trajectory. For a challenge, stand with the rope angled at 45° to your body. Then execute forward and backcasts laydowns over the ground rope. For most casters, the backcast laydown is the most challenging.

The Tippet and Trout Drill

This tutorial teaches proper rod, reel, and line management when fighting and landing fish. It is usually difficult for a beginner to recognize the proper tension and line work required when handling a struggling or fleeing fish. Small fish may be landed and released quickly and carefully. Large fish, however, may require appropriate give and take before they are under control. This drill is based on those fish that require give and take. Continuous tension should be maintained whether the fish is struggling, retreating, or advancing. Raising and lowering the rod tip, stripping in line, reeling in line, and allowing line slippage all aid in line control. This drill demonstrates the elements required in the proper management of struggling fish.

The instructor first selects a rod and line with a standard leader and 6X tippet. A wind knot (a simple overhand knot) is tied in the middle of the tippet. This knot allows tippet breakage if proper tension and care are not taken by the angler. The instructor or selected student (the fish) holds the end of the tippet by the thumb and index finger and imparts a gentle strike, then retreats and advances like a struggling fish. Long sweeping scurries imitate a powerful fish run. During these struggles, the student angler changes rod angle, adjusts reel drag, and manipulates the line to maintain continuous and appropriate line tension no matter what the fish does. Whenever the angler allows slack line, the fish releases the line; the fish has escaped. Whenever the angler stresses the line excessively, the fish releases the line; the fish has broken the tippet. Excessive stress will also break the tippet at the wind knot. If the angler begins with extended slack line (approximately 5' to 6' between the reel and trigger finger) and several wind knots, then the challenge increases. The extended slack line requires the angler to rapidly recover the slack line on the reel all while controlling the fish. After landing a few fish, the angler and fish change places. Students often find that the trout and tippet drill significantly improves their line-handling proficiency.

4

THE PRESENTATION

In 1913, Frederic M. Halford defined fly drag as "any deviation from the natural course governed by the flow of the stream, and any acceleration or diminution of the pace of the living insect on the part of the artificial fly, is designated drag." The cause of drag is simple: the pattern is connected to a tippet. Halford elaborates, "The line is on the water, and the varying speed of the current acting on the different parts of it will tend to retard or accelerate the pace of the artificial fly, or even pull it out of the normal course." Drag, the total unnatural drift of an imitation, not only pulls the dry pattern askew of the natural drift line, it may also pull the pattern under. A fly pattern with drag is often a trout-rejected fly pattern. Drag is usually identified by the resulting wake; however, even an insect dragged along by a breeze can produce a wake. Perhaps the difference is the degree of drag or the appearance of the drag. Regardless, drag, though never entirely eliminated, is diminished by several factors.

DIMINISHING LINE DRAG

1. *By selecting the most appropriate drift line.* Choose the line of approach with the least change in current speed. This is usually directly above or directly below the rise. Lateral presentations normally extend over several varied water speeds. Use forethought in anticipation of drag.

2. *By line manipulation as drag occurs.* An angler can throw slack or a reach cast to readjust the drift as currents create drag. In heavy, fast water, line manipulation may begin as soon as the line lands and may continue throughout the drift.

3. *By short-line casting.* Less line on the water means less drag and more accurate casts. The traditional upstream presentation from the tail (the blind side) of the trout usually allows the nearest approach. If a longer float means more drag, then the pattern should alight above and outside the trout's window. This position may be calculated as about one foot upstream (technically 13.5″) for each foot of trout depth. This will place the pattern outside the trout's window. The extreme difficulty, of course, lies in an accurate estimate of trout distance and depth.

4. *By using supple lines and leaders.* Despite the current rage for stiff fly lines that rifle through the guides, a soft, supple line and leader may, at times, be advantageous. Such lines and leaders have current response; they reply quickly to the complex currents and go with the flow. Hybrid lines with a short head and ultrafine running line may offer some supple properties and a forward thrust. A long-belly line, whether a double taper or weight forward, offers better line control and mending. Additionally, a long-belly fine-diameter 3-weight line follows the flow better than a 6-weight line. Matched to a long rod, it will roll cast efficiently and drape with less water contact. Supple lines, leaders, and tippets tend to conform to the current, thereby decreasing drag and fostering more natural floats.

5. *By reading the currents.* Spring creeks and other slow waters present complex currents—undulating weed beds produce micro-currents that push and pull the pattern in a distorted dance on the surface, a dance often rejected by selective trout. Water is retarded or accelerated by objects and slope. It is deflected by banks and rocks. Weed patches produce twisted skeins of currents that coil and unravel in the flow. Complex currents fold (where a stronger flow dominates a weaker flow) and boil (where plant mass or undulations of the streambed push water patches to the surface). They produce seams (where two drifts zipper together) and rips (where equal currents collide and lift). The shallower the water and the faster the flow, the more the riverbed topography transmits to the surface. Study the surface to determine the proper drifts. Your dry fly should ride these wet wrinkles and flowing furrows naturally.

6. *By presentational casting.* Halford confirms the advice given by dry fly anglers: Never throw a straight taut line. Presentational casts or aerialized mends can land on the surface with the proper configuration for the particular drift, allowing the pattern to approach the rise without excessive drag. Presentational casts include curves, loops, hooks, ripples, and serpentines. Consult line tactics below.

The skill in presenting a dry pattern softly and accurately is fundamental to success.

Other considerations include the casting distance and cast angle to the rise. If possible, take advantage of riparian cover and move slowly. Avoid line flash and shadows cast over the water. Unless an active larger fish is selected, cast to the closest fish first. Water conditions will determine how far from the rise the fly should land. Before casting, determine which presentation angle is best and what currents may compromise the float. A rapid and unnatural skidding fly commonly frightens fish. In spring creeks, thick aquatic weeds often disperse and divert the flow into twisted skeins that catch and drag the fly. Change the cast angle or lengthen the tippet. Over cast the delivery and pull the pattern back to land a long slack tippet. And not all flies should land directly in front of the rise. Often a fly to the side is more effective. A fly to side requires the trout to turn and look. It must turn its body to turn its head. That body turn may initiate a take that may not have been done otherwise. Remember that a deeper trout sees more than a shallow trout.

THE TROUT WINDOW

The concept and diagram of the trout window—based on the optical laws of the angle of incidence and the angle of trout vision refraction—was popularized in Alfred Ronalds' *The Fly Fisher's Entomology*, published in 1844. Later books have continued the research, notably Col. E. W. Harding's *The Flyfisher & the Trout's Point of View* (1931), Vincent Marinaro's *In the Ring of the Rise* (1976), and Brian Clarke and John Goddard's *The Trout and the Fly* (1980). Early writers usually understood the window in this manner: the 160° sight cone of the trout becomes compressed by refraction into a 97° cone through which the trout views the world. Yet the trout does have difficulty seeing beyond the surface mirror. It can see the dimpling of hackle feet in the surface, but color and detail are "through a glass darkly." And the window, that ring of bright water, is backlit so that again little color and detail are evident. Colonel Harding noted that surface-feeding trout watch beyond the window and recognize the insect by the tiny surface dimples created by their feet. Like the hunter, the trout follows the spoor before it sees the prey. Vincent Marinaro was one of the first modern writers to draw attention to the fact that the trout places the fly at the edge of the window for the purpose of observation. Brian Clarke and John Goddard make reference to Snell's circle, the circular boundary between the mirror and window. They argue most convincingly that it is at the ledge of the window that the trout first views the full fly. They also conclude that, when dressing some stillwater nymphs, a reflective strip should be mounted on the back of the pattern to reflect a spot of light against the otherwise dark background of the mirror. Flashback nymphs are now common.

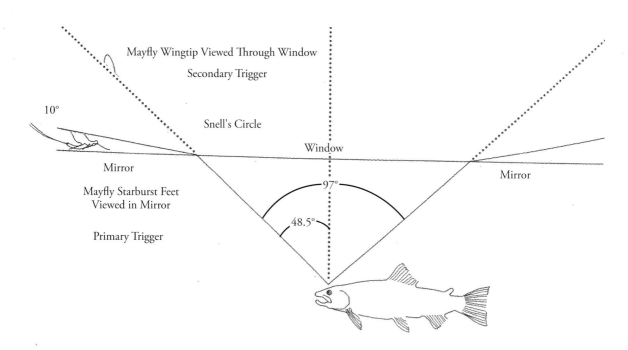

As the mayfly sails into the trout's view, the mirror first reveals the starburst of feet. Shortly thereafter, the wings enter the window.

Although the mirror reflects the world beneath the surface, the starburst of light from the legs and the imprint of the body do appear. Brian Clarke and John Goddard believe that "these star-bursts of light created by the indentation of the feet of the dun floating on the surface . . . are the first triggers to the trout's predatory mechanism" (*The Trout and the Fly*, 1980). The second trip mechanism is the wings of the dun as the insect drifts toward the window.

THE LINE TACTICS

The Figure-Eight Retrieve

The figure-eight or palm retrieve recovers line smoothly and continuously when nymphing. While holding a line loop between the thumb and the index finger, twist the hand to the left while capturing the loop with the lower fingers (the middle finger, the ring finger, and little finger). Next, release only the thumb and the index finger while twisting the hand to the right. Take an advanced grip on the line with the thumb and the index finger, rocking the hand back to pull line into the palm with the last three fingers. While rocking the hand and retrieving line, allow the loop or loops to gather in or fall from the palm. The palm retrieve creates a continuous, steady pattern movement that can vary in speed. It is an excellent method for imitating the movement and emergence of chironomids, caddis, mayflies, and swimming damsel nymphs.

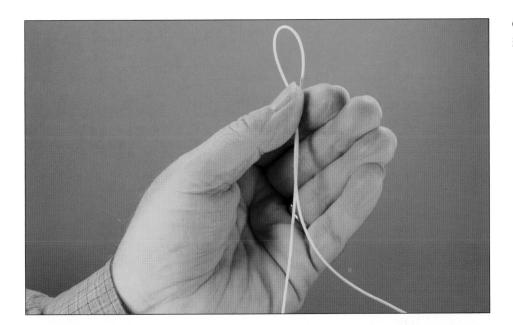

Grip line loop with thumb and index finger.

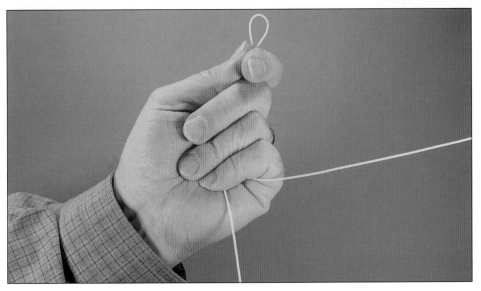

Then close lower fingers over line loop.

Next, twist hand right to recapture more line with thumb and index finger. Remove lower fingers to capture the newly gathered loop within the palm.

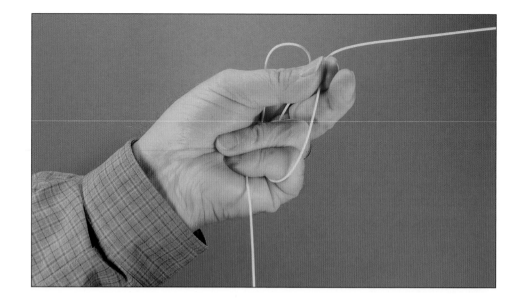

Again, rock hand left to gather new line into the palm with the lower fingers.

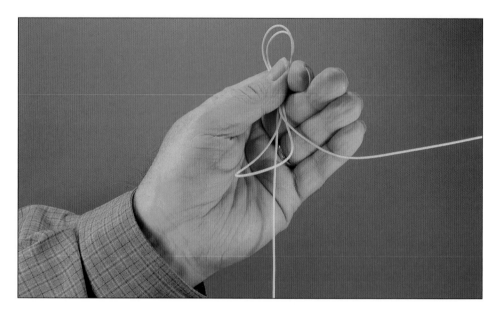

After palming the gathered line, reach forward for another thumb and index finger line grip. Continue the rocking twists to capture, palm, and retrieve more line.

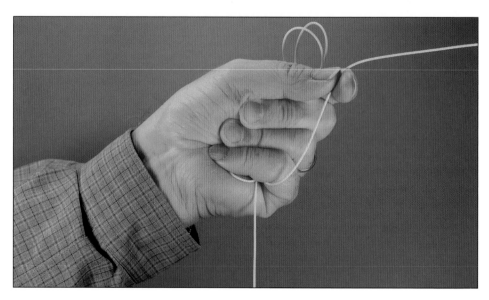

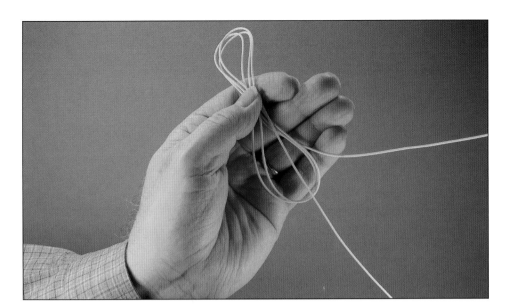

Finally, while holding the line with thumb and index finger, the palmed fly line may be dropped or, for increased line distance, released by the thumb and index finger and shot forward.

The Downstream Drift

The antique anglers knew. In *The Practical Angler* (1857), W. C. Stewart of spider fame enumerates four advantages for fishing upstream. (1) The angler approaches the fish from the blind side—the tail. (2) The angler strikes against the fish, whereas in downstream fishing the fly may be pulled away from the fish. (3) The angler disturbs the water below the trout rather than above. (4) And last, the angler presents the fly more naturally, that is, without drag. Stewart, a borderer, lived when wet-fly downstream was the accepted technique. He bucked the current. Upstream angling is older than Stewart. The first mention of upstream angling, according to John Waller Hills' *A History of Fly Fishing for Trout* (1921), appears in Robert Venables' *The Experienced Angler* (1662).

For the right-handed caster, the usual presentation is from the right bank upstream. A diagonal line presents the fly above the trout while a slack drag-free leader and line drift beyond the fish's view. The trout should only see the fly. The US Environmental Protection Agency defines the banks looking downstream. When facing downstream (the direction of flow), the right bank is on your right side and the left bank is on your left side. In some cases, it may be advantageous to work the waters from both banks upstream and downstream.

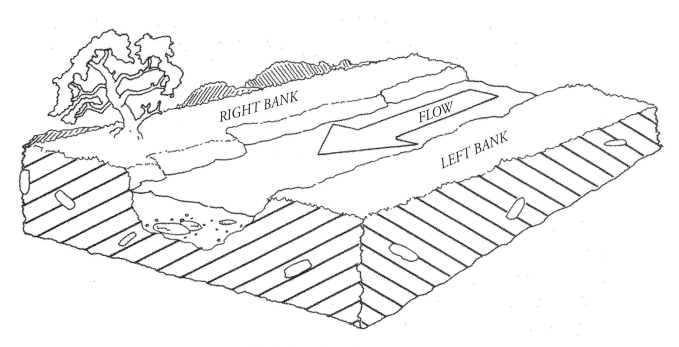

The Traditional Bank Designations

Hills assesses the value of the downstream drift.

Downstream fishing, here and now, in this twentieth century, is better for certain persons and certain occasions. You avoid many difficulties. Wading is easier, and casting less incessant. Your line is taut and you are more likely to hook a fish. Also, as it is always taut, you know where your fly is and know where to look for rises. This is the great difficulty of upstream fishing, especially in quick and broken water.

Although, according to Hills, "there is a certain reticence to-day about downstream fishing," the downstream drift is used to a greater extent than supposed. Although the upstream cast drift has historical precedence, the downstream cast and drift can be valuable.

It is true that a fairly long line must be thrown downstream simply to reach fish before they are disturbed. This is what Hills calls a long-line downstream and a short-line upstream. But if the angler wades slowly with care, then fish may again rise to a hatch within a short time and distance. Because the current straightens the line, downstream fishing is often considered a novice method. Downstream fishing can be, however, an art unto itself. The first mend should be made before the line hits the water. Do not wait until the fly acquires drag. Then it is too late. If a downstream slack drift encounters a rising trout, the chances of a take increase. The slack downstream drift obscures the tippet and eliminates some drag.

Frederic Halford, in *The Dry-Fly Man's Handbook* (1913), states that when wind and occasional places demand a downstream float, "then it is possible to fish downstream or partly across and partly down even with a floating fly." The downstream float, which Halford called drifting, "requires that the angler should let out a length of line far greater than that required to cover the fish rising below him. As the line descends in the forward position of the cast it is checked not only by tightening the grip, but also by bringing the rod-hand back towards the body." This allows the fly to land above the rise with slack line. As the fly floats down, the angler's rod lowers and the fly passes over and beyond the rise. It is recovered slowly either by retrieving line gradually with the line hand or "by returning the fly laterally over the bank below the fish." To Halford, the downstream drift was "a manoeuvre of desperation" that seldom led to a second cast. Nevertheless, where waters are wadeable and fish difficult, the downstream drift may prove productive.

The Pitzenbauer Downstream Drift

The late Edgar Pitzenbauer of Bavaria fished, for more than twenty-five years, the clear exacting waters of Slovenia. His quarry, the grayling, has prominent dorsal fins, a forked tail, and an under-slung mouth. Grayling also have a reputation; they challenge both the angler and the pattern. There is a mid-European legend that grayling, more a gourmet than a gourmand, feed upon gold nuggets. Some of these "nuggets," these small patterns, also work well for selective trout. But unlike most active trout, large shy grayling require small flies, accurate casts, soft presentations, and at times long drifts. Any threat detected by the gregarious grayling often alarms the entire shoal. Pitzenbauer wore olive clothing and waded silently to avoid spooking fish. Unlike trout, who often grab a passing fly, grayling slowly rise and softly suck. Such a take requires accurate strike timing. And grayling often follow the fly extended distances before taking, thus the necessity for a drag-free float. Consequently, selective grayling are often considered far more difficult than selective trout.

Pitzenbauer's presentation was a study in the downstream drift. First, he waded very slowly downstream. Then he faced or quartered downstream and placed the rise either below or to one side. If the delivery is to the side, the fly should not float down the wading turbulence. He then cast a concise length of line relatively high and parallel to the water. He bounced the line back, which allowed the fly to land directly above the rise. Next, he dropped the rod tip. In so doing, the line created a loop approximately 20″ in diameter on the water near him. His rod tip halted high in the cast, dropped, and then slowly extended (a downstream reach cast) during the drift. As the water lengthened the slightly serpentined line, the loop dissolved and the line extended into an 8 meter or longer float. This extended, relatively straight fly line allowed quick hooking. The trout's pointed-mouth profile, however, is not conducive to the downstream take. A slightly off-line drift

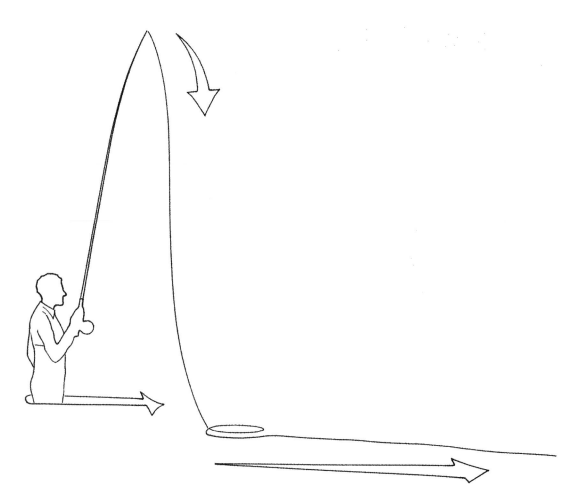

The Pitzenbauer Drift

usually solves such problems. Nevertheless, the Pitzenbauer downstream drift has seduced some sage grayling and trout. Consult *Knots* for the Pitzenbauer Silver-Ring System.

WATER ENTRY AND WADING

Water entry and wading should be done with quiet caution. According to Bill Willers's *Trout Biology*, the territory of a trout depends upon the degree of visual isolation. There may be border zones between territories that are occupied periodically by occupants of each territory. Vegetation, rocks, turbidity, and other components screen trout from one another allowing greater trout density and, consequently, smaller trout territories. When an angler enters a trout territory, the inhabitants flee to another, thereby dislodging trout from their territories up and down the stream. An angler may be completely unaware of this hidden alarm system that disrupts the trout territories and hierarchies for meters around. Trout are attentive to each other; to scare one trout is to scare several. Most salmonid studies support the view that trout, except when spawning, refrain from making extensive movements beyond their territories. Because all members of a hierarchy will defend a particular stream section, any intrusion will cause disruption. An exception to the territorial imperative is the errant trout; a large wayward trout that prefers to cruise and forage rather than establish a territory. In any case, entry and wading should be made with care and, if possible, cover. Placing a plant mat or rocks between you and the rise may allow that rise to continue.

THE FUNDAMENTAL LINE TACTICS

A fly may drift unnoticed. However, pattern movement can provoke a fish, or the pattern can be delivered in a realistic manner. Line tactics, executed by hand and rod, (1) imitate various insect movements (such as the Leisenring lift and the deferred strip) or (2) configure the line for proper presentation (such as the Pitzenbauer drift and the curve cast). As with all imitative insect actions, the speed and frequency should vary. Ask yourself what the pattern imitates and how it moves. Although all insect actions cannot be imitated by rod and line, some can. Insects move in diverse ways: rowing (*corixidae*), curling (*chironomidae*), undulating (*baetidae*), winging (*hymenoptera*), jetting (*anisoptera*), and swimming (*zygoptera*). During insect movement, nonswimming legs are usually folded against the body. Remember that most insect movement is slower and more subtle than the action often imparted to an imitation. Even large dragonfly nymphs, propelled by anal expulsions, attain speeds of only 50 centimeters per second for short bursts.

Rod action and angle are significant in how the movement is transmitted to the pattern. They can diminish drag, mend lines, throw curves, create hooks, toss running loops, and invite strikes. Rod angle also has an important duty. If the rod tip points toward the pattern, use a lengthened tippet to absorb some of the strike shock. Angling the rod to the left or right of the retrieve direction may also offer some yield to a hard take. A soft-tipped rod held high may merely absorb the quick staccato strips so that the pattern runs smoothly rather than expressing the desired pattern pulses. Here are a few essential line tactics, some more proficient and expressive than others.

The Short Strip

The short strip, which imitates scuds and nymphs, is a brisk retrieve of 5″ or 6″ of line through the index finger—the trigger finger—on the rod. Keep the rod low so that the staccato pulses are transferred to the fly. Strip immediately behind the index finger. As the rod is low and inline, the restricted rod flex may snap a tender tippet. Avoid strong rod strikes. Angling the rod tip slightly to one side may reduce snapped tippets.

The Damp Scrape

Heavily hackled patterns are scraped 2′ or 3′ across the water surface. Small sparse patterns may move, to use Leonard Wright's phrase, only "the sudden inch." This disturbance, mimicking the struggling or skating caddis, leaves a seductive dimple or wake that may attract trout. Vary the suddenness imparted to damp patterns. With small patterns, the movement may be accomplished with the rod tip alone. Merely flick or lift the tip to imprint the pattern on the surface. This imprint may draw fish.

The Errant Run

The errant run imitates the movement for erratic swimmers, such as scuds, corixa, and emerging caddis. With a combination of short-strip and rod-tip movement, make the pattern run erratically with twitching, sporadic speed. Use rod movement and palm retrieves to impart the motion.

The Leisenring Lift

The Leisenring Lift, primarily a stream tactic, allows the angler to present a pattern realistically to a visible trout. Cast the pattern above the trout and allow it to sink before addressing the trout. When the pattern drifts within range, lift the rod tip to emerge the pattern directly in front of the trout. This is an excellent tactic for the various bubble emerger patterns. A somewhat similar phenomenon occurs in lake fishing, where a natural, such as a chironomid pupa, emerges from the depths. As the bubble-jacketed insect rises, the bubble expands, increasing buoyancy and acceleration. A deep-retrieve tactic includes increasing the acceleration of the retrieve and applying a sudden stop. Somewhat akin to Wright's "sudden inch" retrieve, the abrupt stop encourages a following or trailing trout to intercept and capture the pattern. Due to a natural feeding response, the trout may take—a take perhaps never committed to originally. Obviously, some trout may turn away without a take. Occasionally, however, these sudden stops can seduce trailing trout.

The Swimming Nymph

Cast with a fairly straight line and use a drop retrieve, a figure-eight retrieve with falling loops, to maintain constant contact with the pattern. This generic retrieve imitates a variety of aquatic insects. Due to the continuous tension, the strike must be quick but gentle. The rod tip may be angled away from the retrieve line to absorb the shock of a take. Some anglers allow the line to slip during the strike, preventing break-offs produced by taut straight lines. The problem here, however, is knowing when to let it slip.

The Deferred Strip

Cruising trout, particularly in shallow sections of spring creeks, may be startled by line movement or a sink-pattern entry. To prevent this, cast softly beyond a cruise lane or across a pool, and allow the pattern to settle. Wait. When a cruising trout nears, gently lift and swim the pattern. Even the gentlest motion may attract attention. On one small spring creek, I cast and tucked myself behind a tree. I waited. When a cruising trout neared, I merely touched the pattern on the bottom. The movement produced a puff of silt that attracted a trout. He came, he saw, he took. This ambush technique may be combined with a variety of retrieves.

The Draw Cast

On tightly rising trout, cast above and beyond the drift line. Draw or scrape the pattern along the surface to align the drift to the rise. To avoid frightening the fish, the draw is done a distance from the rise. The tactic may be used for either upstream or downstream drifts. Once aligned, it may be necessary to toss slack line with a ripple cast into the drift, especially if the fly has a propensity to swing away from the drift.

The Anchor Cast

Eric Taverner, in *Trout Fishing from All Angles,* describes two anchor casts: the cross-weed and the cross-country. Sometimes it is necessary to cast over and on a weed bed or bank. Spring creek wading often places a weed mat between the angler and the trout. The weeds, although screening the angler, present a problem. The mat will immediately arrest or anchor any line or leader that touches down. To produce a natural float beyond the anchoring weeds, over cast and bounce or ripple the line back to produce slack, thus offering extra leader and tippet for the drift. The cross-weed cast anchors on weeds. Taverner concluded, "After many attempts I stumbled upon the solution: to cast a slack line over the weeds a little above the fish, so that the line and the top of the cast [leader] rested on top of the weeds and the remainder pivoted round and went down to the fish at the pace of the current."

The Taverner Cross-Country Cast

This cast also entails a pivot. For a close-lying bank trout, the cross-country cast drops the fly line on the ground and the leader, tippet, and fly on the water. The fly is retrieved by slowly drawing it through the riparian vegetation. A bushy or stiff fly hackle avoids most snags. To prevent rod and line flash, cast horizontally when possible. The most difficult part of any anchor cast is in determining where to place the anchor or pivot point on the weed patch or bank. These line tactics are best for close-rising trout on a near bank.

The Ripple Cast

The ripple cast, a vertical wave cast, throws slack line by driving a subsequent second cast into an extending and descending cast. First, execute an overhead cast and line layout. During the forward stroke, stop the rod hand in a near-vertical position. Immediately after line layout, drive a tight, short stroke down the same rod-tip trajectory. The cast should shoot extra slack line down the previous cast. This cast also permits an angler to add slack to a watered line or completed cast. The ripple cast is a more powerful slack-line cast than the conventional horizontal rod-tip wag used to create a snake on the water. It also allows the angler to toss extra slack into a fast current for improved drift or float. Excessive ripple force may cancel sending slack line; instead, the initial cast may recoil toward the caster. An effective cast will ripple line beyond the rod tip and, consequently, ripple some line back to fall slack on the water. With supple leaders, it has a further advantage of producing more leader slack than line slack. The ripple cast also allows the angler to toss slack into fast flow for an improved drift. This cast, done inside an extending or completed cast, works only for short distances.

The Ripple Cast

The Reach Cast

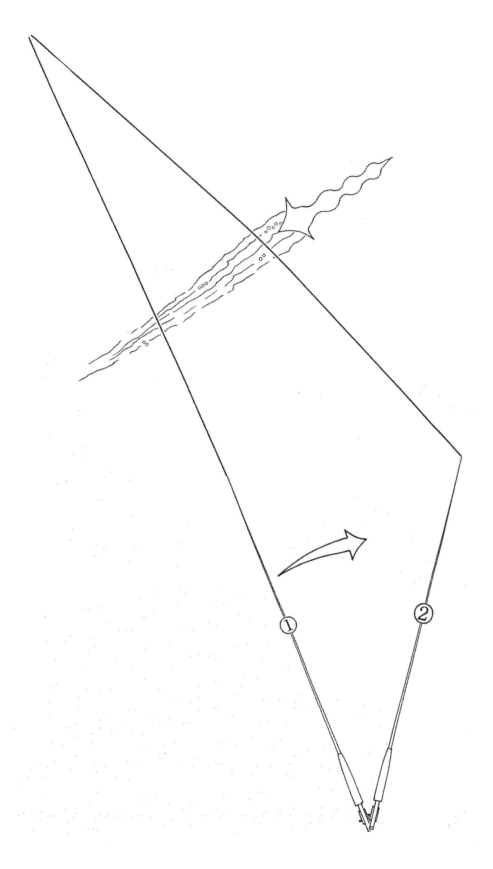

The Reach Cast

The reach cast is simple and effective for close casts. While the forward cast extends, the angler merely fully extends the arm and rod left or right looping the aerialized line upstream. The angled line then falls into a proper angle to address the current. It is a cast-reach motion that mends the line above the water. Long rods increase the length of the mend. The reach cast can introduce slack line across currents for a few more feet of drag-free drift. The pattern flies to the target, but the large line bow or curve falls onto the faster current flow. Thus, a bowed upstream fly line and a long fly rod may grant the fly an extended drift before drag occurs. The reach cast is most effective when the faster flow is relatively close to the angler. Longer drifts may require the up-current curve cast or an S-cast. To execute the reach cast, first cast an aerialized line toward the target. Then fully extend the arm either to the left or right upstream. Once the line falls and touches the current, follow the drifting line with the rod tip.

The S-Cast

While the fly line extends forward, narrow horizontal wiggles create a chain of curves in the line that falls on the water. When done early in the casting stroke, the wiggles land the waves near the fly, when done late, near the rod. This slack line cast can place up-current slack onto fast flow. Only the rod tip should wiggle, creating modest waves; avoid moving the complete rod through the air. The rod tip directs the fly line to describe small wiggles and waggles that will fall upon the water. The rod wiggles should begin as soon as the aerialized fly line unrolls forward. The S-cast is also known as the serpentine cast.

The S-Cast

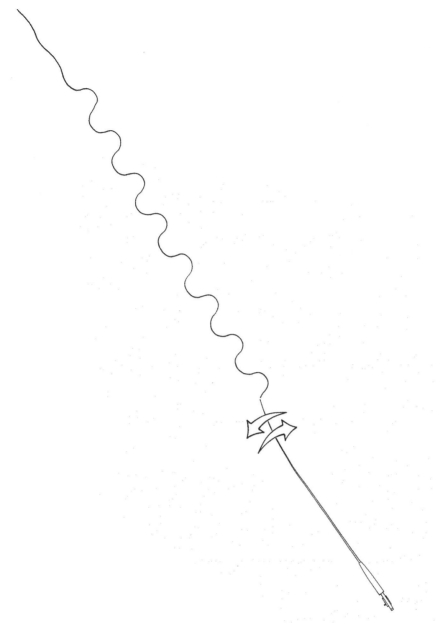

The Circle or Ring Cast

A more powerful variant of the ripple cast is the circle or ring cast. In this cast, the angler throws a vertical circle down an extending or completed cast. This powerful short-stroke cast propels a line circle or ring above and down the fly line. The brief forward stroke, in fact, shoots the circle along the line. A series of such vertical circles can be driven down the fly line to greatly increase line slack. Pushing circles down a static or fixed line length does not lengthen the fly line. Extra slack line must be stripped from the reel and gained by the rod before each circle cast. To do this, the caster must add new slack line by drawing the rod tip abruptly back, slipping more line through the guides to gain more slack. This extra slack (essentially a short-line drape from the rod tip) is then rolled down the fly line.

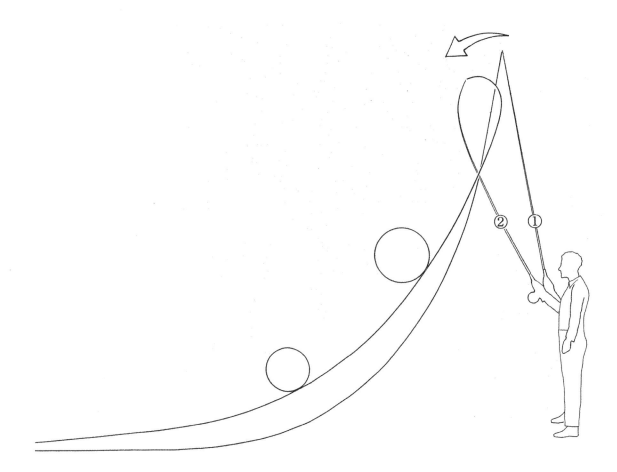

The Circle Cast

THE HOOK CASTS

The terminal hook cast throws a hook or curve to the left (a positive hook) or to the right (a negative hook). This allows an angler to throw a curve around obstructions or address an upstream trout in such a manner as to hide the leader. Taverner labels this the shepherd's crook cast and describes the left-hook cast,

> The simplest way to do this is to cast underhand to a spot a little to the right of the place to which the fly would normally be aimed and to cast a great deal harder than is necessary to propel the fly that distance. The fly thus travels at considerable velocity to the full extension of the gut and having reached that point has still some energy left which it expends in curling around to the left...

A left hook or curl is thrown with a backhand horizontal cast. For a right-handed caster, the right hook is difficult and usually done with an under-powered loop. For a modern caster, Taverner left out a critical part of the hook cast. The mass (the weight) of Taverner's gut leader would help power the sweeping hook. The light modern leader, however, requires greater energy. This is accomplished with a horizontal cast and then a sudden haul near the point of maximum extension. As the fly line nears full extension, the line hand accelerates the leader and rod-tip swing with a single short jerking haul. Only a late haul will work. The haul then sweeps the fly and leader into a terminal left hook. Based upon right-handed casters, John and Richard Alden Knight (see below) call the left hook the positive curve.

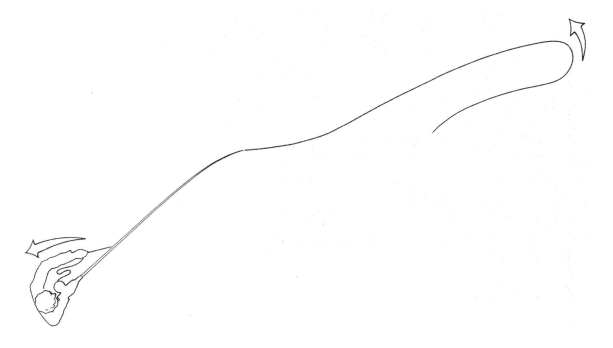

The Left-Hook Cast

The Right-Hook or Curl Cast

This is sometimes thrown with a horizontal backhand cast and haul. Unfortunately, the backhand cast produces only still-born curves rather than hooks or curls. For a right-handed caster, the right hook is problematic and usually done with an underpowered loop to the right. This underpowered loop is then laid on the water. In *The Complete Book of Fly Casting* (1963), John and Richard Alden Knight best describe the right-hook, or as they phrase it, negative-curve cast:

". . . throw the backcast almost in the horizontal plane, following through with the rod tip. In the forward cast, apply power with the middle rod only, leaving the upper rod out of the cast just as you do when throwing a wide bow [*i.e.* loop]. Apply just enough power to start the line forward, but not enough to complete the cast. The result is a half-hearted attempt with a wide bow [curve] which falls to the water before the bow has had a chance to complete itself. Actually, the cast is an incomplete forward cast."

The right hook, unlike the left hook, is a rather close incomplete horizontal forward hook cast. Most right hooks occur within about four rod lengths. The power required for a longer right hook cast usually straightens the fly line. Furthermore, to preserve the terminal curl, it is a soft cast. The rod shifts slightly left to open the hook. It is a soft fetal cast easily led astray by the whims of wind. Nevertheless, with diligent practice, the negative curve can produce a close right curl.

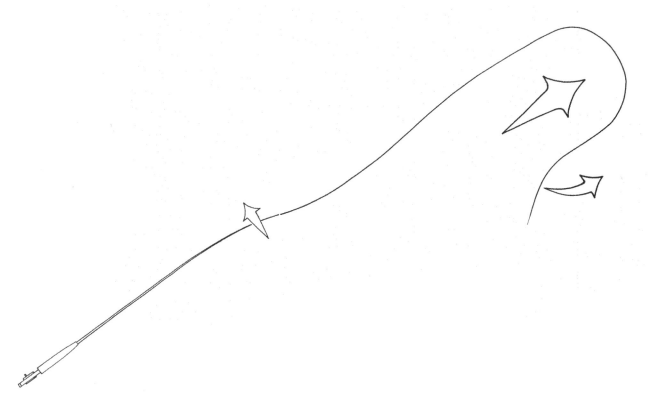

The Right-Hook Cast

THE DROPPER

This is a standard method for fishing two flies, especially a dry fly and a small nymph. The dry fly allows the nymph to drift beneath the surface at a determined depth. Always check angling regulations before using a dropper or more than one fly pattern. A barbless two-fly maximum is often the legal limit in many fly-fishing only waters. Some selective gear rules allow a maximum of three barbless flies. Three flies are typically more difficult to cast and more than likely offer little or no advantage. With the dry and wet pattern combination, a strike may occur on either fly pattern. The dry pattern becomes a strike indicator and locator for the sunken pattern, especially for tiny nymphs, such as size 18 Gold-Ribbed Hare's Ear or Pheasant Tail nymph. Fast-water dry flies should be bushy and buoyant; still-water floaters can be less so. For attaching droppers, some fly-tyers add a short monofilament loop—with 2X or 3X tippet material—beneath the tail of selected dry flies. Such loops should be firmly secured with thread and cyanoacrylate cement, super glue, before tying the pattern on the hook. Dropper patterns then attach to this small butt loop. Otherwise, the dropper fly is usually attached to the bend of the dry fly hook as illustrated. Make certain that the dropper knot is firmly secured, especially when connecting to a barbless hook. A dropper knot can slip off a barbless hook.

The dropper length from dry to nymph is usually about 18″ to 30″. The dropper length, however, should be calculated by the speed and depth of the water. The closer the nymph to the dry, the more control the angler has. In still waters, the dropper length may be restricted only by the angler's skill in preventing casting tangles. The dropper should be about one to two hook sizes smaller than the dry fly, such as a size 16 or size 14 to a size 12 dry fly. In running streams, the dropper length is frequently calculated at 1.5X to 2X the stream depth. Depending upon the flow rate, this generally places the nymph about midstream in moving water. Moreover, streams with bottom structures, such as boulders or trailing aquatic plants, may require shorter droppers. The tippet fly is the fly connected to the tippet, the dropper fly to the tippet fly hook.

This tandem combination of tippet and dropper patterns has several permutations:

1. A dry fly and its matching nymph/emerger/ovipositor pattern, i.e. an adult caddis and a female diving caddis.
2. A swamped emerger and its matching nymph.
3. A tippet dry fly and a swamped, sunken adult terrestrial or spent spinner.
4. A nymph and a nymph, tandem nymphs with an attractor nymph as the tippet pattern.
5. A nymph and a streamer, inline tandem wets, such as a Woolly Bugger and a streamer.
6. A dry and a dry pattern, inline tandem dry flies in different sizes or patterns.
7. A streamer and a streamer, inline tandem wets.
8. A dry fly and a dry fly, an attractor tippet pattern and a micropattern as dropper.

Attach the dropper to the tippet fly with a Duncan Loop (the Uni-knot) or an improved clinch knot. A double wrap around the hook bend (the hook heel) may secure the connection on a barbless hook. Double wraps distribute the stress better than a single wrap. No matter which knot is used, it must be firmly tightened against the hook. To thwart tangles, use a moderately open stroke when tossing tandems. I use several nymph patterns previously attached to extended dropper lines. At streamside, they are then trimmed to the proper angling length and attached to the tippet fly. Changing a wet or dry dropper is then quick and simple.

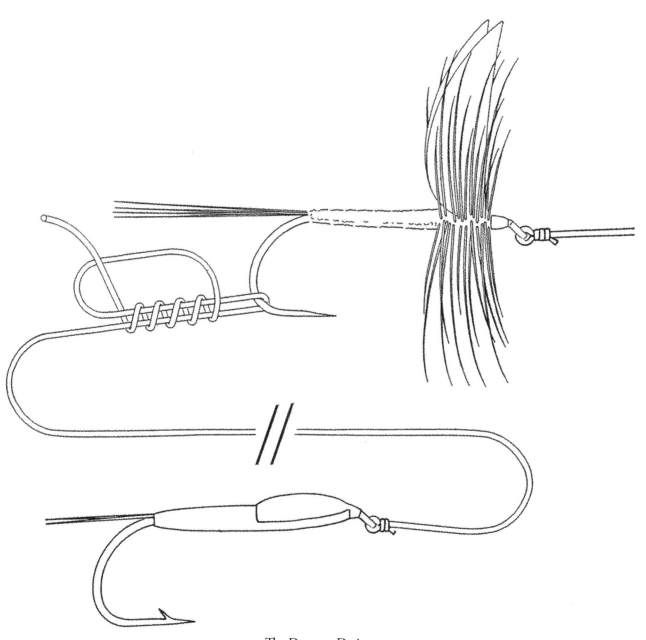

The Dropper Design

5

THE STRIKE AND CAPTURE

IF FLY FISHING IS VALUABLE, THEN FISH deserve our respect. Trout should be landed promptly rather than played. Playing a trout suggests indulgence rather than quickly capturing and releasing an animal. At times, landing a trout has more to do with the angler and the tackle than the trout. Some soft rods are not designed to quickly control and land trout. Stiff, quick-tipped rods that control trout quickly may also snap fine tippets. Clearly, the tackle and methods that protect and preserve the trout are best. Here are some considerations when battling and landing trout.

Several factors make landing trout a problem: small hook gaps, tender tippets, and strike time. Moderate and steady pressure solves most problems. Small hooks and fine tippets usually hold well if sudden trout tugs are absorbed by the rod, leader, and elastic tippet. For this reason, keep the tip elevated and apply lateral pressure only to a moving fish. Furthermore, a hook can be ingested deeply; consequently, greater responsibility lies with the angler to make the strike on time. Only quick but minor pressure is really necessary to home a hook. The strike should be swift but soft. This is not a contradiction.

Be quick but gentle to minimize stress and shock to the fish. Small fish may be landed hastily with a wet hand. Consider breaking a fish off if it cannot be landed quickly. Unduly tiring a trout, especially one that is well-hooked and bound for release, is not necessary. An angler often telegraphs his excitement to the trout, which may only prolong the battle. Trout should be landed with moderate speed and released without breaking water. Experienced anglers can often land and release trout rapidly. For these trout, the battle may have been only a bearable, brief interlude.

Use proper tackle to avoid exhausting the trout. When possible, use a rod and tippet with sufficient strength to hustle in a fish. Remember, too, that a dynamic trout may exert more force than its own weight on a tippet. A static weight increases its weight or force when dynamic and moving. Keep the struggling fish near the top of the water column to avoid weeds and decrease line resistance. A deep trout has increased line drag. Apply lateral line pressure to trout to glide them in. As much as possible, keep the fish's head and body under the water surface. Without water resistance, a trout's struggle is more violent and harmful.

When fighting large trout, rod angle is important. A vertical rod (the antique edict of "point the rod butt at the fish") places undue stress on the mid- and tip section. Conversely, a low rod angle significantly eliminates rod spring that would absorb the frantic struggle. Pointing the rod at the fish (thus putting the fish on the reel) virtually negates rod flex entirely. *For fighting large fish, the appropriate rod angle is 45°.* This angle absorbs the struggle and offers lifting power for controlling large fish.

To decrease line drag (especially in a heavy current), combat trout with as short a line as possible. Long line drag and swift current can release fish. G.P.R. Pulman, in *The Vade-Mecum of Fly-Fishing for Trout* (third edition, 1851), observed that "the resistance of a swift current is alone sufficient to tear a small hook from the firmest hold in the tender mouth of a trout." Keep the fly in the trout's mouth by positioning the rod to create either lateral or downstream tension on the trout. Upstream strain can extract a hook. Never grab a taut line or tippet unless the trout has surrendered, ready for release.

Perhaps the only value of a barbed hook is with aerialized trout on a slack line. Remember to drop the rod tip when a trout jumps to prevent it from falling on and snapping a taut leader or tippet. Keep the rod tip angled to offer the trout as much rod flex as possible. This usually means that the rod should be held at a right angle to the stressed line. Sudden tugs and runs may break fine tippets. To increase rod resistance when mastering large fish, Taff Price, the English angling writer, places the supple section of the rod (the rod tip to midsection) underwater. The reel is still checked and worked above the water. The trout must then labor against the rod flex as well as the water resistance or drag that dampens and cushions the flex. The water viscosity muffles any sudden tugs or runs. By analogy, this is comparable to pounding a nail underwater. This is especially effective during the initial battle, when a large trout has speed and power. Essentially, water viscosity creates a retarding force. The greater the effect, the greater the retarding force. A similar effect is created by placing the hand outside the window of a moving automobile. The greater the speed, the greater the resistance.

Trout that become weeded—by burrowing into the plant mass and hanging up—torment trouters. One method of extracting trout from plant mass is by line thumping or, as Dermot Wilson of England expressed it, by line plucking. When a trout became caught in the plant mass, Wilson placed the rod down and picked up the line between the rod tip and trout. He tightened the line and then plucked it a few times to loosen the trout. Taut-line plucking may encourage a trout to kick free. Once the trout is free, the rod must pick up the slack line to put the trout back on the reel. When possible, all large trout should be contested from the reel. There is an empty feeling if a heavy trout bores into weed and you come away with a weed pennant on the hook. Another method to de-weed trout is to place the rod downstream and work the line through the plant ends. Extract the trout by lowering the rod tip to the water while pulling steadily but moderately. It may even be effective, when the trout is well-hooked, to offer slack line at times. Slack line offers false freedom that may encourage the trout to shift position or move.

Hook selection is also important. Use a single barbless hook for trout that will be released. It is best to file the barb flat on top rather than to pinch the barb down. A pinched barb can leave a hump or, if you're not careful, fracture the hook. The tale is that a few game wardens sometimes test a de-barbed hook by passing it through a cloth patch. If it hangs up, the angler receives a fine. Even if fable, the tale should make anglers sensitive to all regulations. Use bronzed steel hooks rather than nickel, stainless steel, or gold. When stolen by trout, bronze hooks corrode more quickly.

Many anglers are proud that they do not use a net; however, this may be affectation if in the process of landing a fish they must handle it longer and harder than with a net. In fast water or with large fish, proper net work can decrease fight time. But when wading, it may be less stressful to small trout to bring them in by hand and quickly release them. Nets can encourage keeping trout out of water and can cause severe abrasion to the outer mucus "skin" that protects a trout from disease. In some water where there are high banks, stiff currents, and no wading, a net may be necessary to capture the trout. Net movement, though, and perhaps even net color, can cause panicked runs and broken tippets. Additionally, stuffing a large trout into a small net can be frustrating and futile for the trout and the angler.

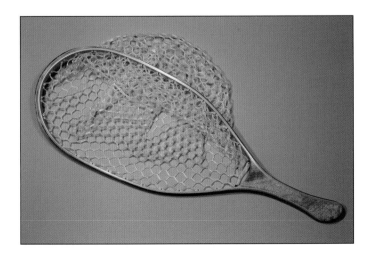

The Ghost Net

Unfortunately, there are rogue nets. Years ago, noted angling author Dave Whitlock trudged toward the beaver ponds on Montana's Big Hole River. A glorious day promised tight tippets. As he clambered through thick brush, Dave's elastic-tethered net snagged on a bush. He did what we all do; he kept walking, waiting for the net to pull free. It did not. He turned around just in time to receive an airborne net between his eyes. After regaining consciousness, he gathered his spiteful net and continued on his way. Few experienced anglers lack a hostile net incident. Even with a benevolent net, there's the connection problem.

Fumbling frustration usually comes when trying to release a net to land a fish or return the net to its connector. Today, the most convenient and expedient connector is the rare-earth magnet. Permanent rare-earth magnets (neodymium permanent magnets) have extraordinary hold, yet they release with a sharp, firm tug. Reattaching the net to the vest is simple; when close, the powerful magnetic field causes the magnets to snap home with a commanding click. Since the 1990s, neodymium magnets have become steadily less expensive. Now, I no longer fuss over obstinate, unruly snaps or clips. Even so, nets can be an annoyance to carry, tangling in brush or disrupting a cast. Nets are best carried hoop up and handle down, at the back center of the vest. Always tether a net to prevent its loss.

It is often illegal to use a knotted cord net basket or bag. Large coarse knots can scuff and scrape a trout. All net baskets should be small meshed with holes perhaps ¾″ or smaller to prevent fins becoming tangled or split. Some catch and release nets have a shallow basket depth and fine weave that reduces trout tangles and speeds trout release. A preferred material is the ghost basket, a clear thermoplastic rubber bag with ¾″ openings. These soft knotless molded rubber baskets avoid abrasion of the trout better than any other material. The ghost basket protects the fish's sensitive slime layer, preventing fin splits and hook tangles. Furthermore, the basket transparency (hence the label "ghost") avoids spooking fish. It also allows for a watery brilliance in fish photography. The singular disadvantage is the increased water drag that the basket produces when placed in fast water. Even a knotless ghost net is neither good nor bad; only the angler makes it so.

Never sweep a net toward a trout. Sink the net, draw the trout over the net, and then swiftly lift to capture. Once the trout is caught, keep the net in the water to cushion any struggle. An extendable net with a rigid bow is popular in Europe. It may be extended to capture a trout beyond the reeds or to probe the weeds to extract a buried trout.

After the take and struggle, lead the fish to moderate water flow for revival. Let it regain its strength by gently holding its head upstream in the current. The gills should work normally, and the trout should gain strength and stability. Never throw a fish back. Gently release trout in moderately shallow water. Usually after the trout regains strength, it will dart away. If it fails to recover when released, recapture and repeat the process. Trout can be exhausted, even "drowned," if kept on a leash when facing or running downstream. There is truth in the adage that only dead fish go with the flow. Trout have a negative rheotropism (flow response); they must face upstream or move through water for oxygen. Exhausted trout should be placed upstream in moderate flow to receive adequate oxygen. Trout also avoid contact with objects, as they have a negative thigmotropism (touch response). One method for reviving a trout is to place it near the surface pointing upstream. The angler then vigorously paddles water in front of the exhausted trout to increase oxygen. The effectiveness of the paddle method, however, is disputed.

Although fish react to touch, fish grip-gloves, such as Spirit River's Grip-n-Mitt, claim to handle fish humanely without undue hand pressure. These net-fabric tailing gloves are readily carried in the fly vest and are especially appropriate for large fish. When lifting a large trout, cradle it horizontally with one hand beneath the body and with the other hand immediately in front of the tail fin on the peduncle (the tail "wrist"). If possible, keep the fish in and under the water. Water cushions the trout's writhing. Avoid touching the eyes or the gill system, and protect it from rocks and other objects. Do not squeeze trout; this damages vital organs, including the swim bladder. Gently spooning the upper throat to determine a fish's diet should be done only when the fish are kept and killed. Fly fishing, especially dry-fly fishing, differs from other field sports. With barbless hooks and a careful release, many fish will fin away to rise again.

In the slender and perceptive book, *A Trout Rose* (1948), R. D. Baird captured the unique relationship between the angler and the trout.

> "It is in this matter of death having to end pleasure, if that pleasure is to be brought to its logical and almost inevitable conclusion, that fishing, and especially dry-fly fishing, differs from all other sports. In fishing, a man can complete his object of outwitting and capturing a fish, and so enjoy his pleasure in the sport to the full. But at the same time he can generally, in the end, return the fish to the river unharmed, none the worse for its adventure, if he desires. In this way, fishing is on a different plane from almost all other forms of sport. The fisherman is a favored mortal, though at the same time it follows that he is in a position of greater responsibility than the man who indulges in other sports, since the power to kill wisely and not wantonly lies in his hands."

R. D. Baird also captured the essence of angling. "A true fisherman does not set out in the morning to catch many fish, rather to spend a pleasant time by the river and enjoy himself in a way that appeals to him. He tests his theories, his methods and his ideas. He would be the last to have unholy joy finding pleasure in the belief, if true, that someone else has not caught fish."

The Release and Return

A note on photography: On occasion, there is a ritual before the release. Anglers catch trout on film as well as on flies. Even in catch-and-release waters, we want memories of a particularly gallant fish. For photography, have the camera ready and try shots with the fish in a natural position in the water. Although this restricts photographs to top and angled views, the best photograph is a watered trout. Better yet, have a companion operate the camera while you secure the fish. For efficiency, explain the camera workings to your companion beforehand. Water calms the fish and expands the fins. A net in the water can cradle a trout for the camera. Do not exhaust the trout in the process of photography. Always minimize the time in a net or out of water for any game fish. If the trout is held out of the water, it is best to have someone help handle equipment and speed the waterless time. To establish size (which is very difficult to determine when there is only trout and water), place a rod or a net near the trout in the water. A digital autofocus camera allows immediate photographic feedback and a speedy process. Those with built-in flashes can quickly capture dawn or dusk trout. A fill-flash (a lighting technique in which the flash provides a lower supplementary light to the main ambient light) provides additional illumination in shadows and darker areas. A fill-flash can make a good image into a great image. A macro lens, such as a 60-mm micro lens (Nikon Nikkor), can create dramatic close-ups of fly and trout as well as function as the standard lens. A circular polarizer (a rotating filter) allows the camera to cut glare and see into the water. Such a filter does require an increase in exposure, which is variable depending on the degree of filter rotation. Automatic cameras correct exposure to make this simple adjustment. A polarizer filter eliminates some surface reflection and haze while increasing contrast and color saturation. The suppression of water reflections are often more successful in the foreground than in the background. Clouds and blue sky become particularly dramatic. Maximum polarization control occurs when the camera is aimed at 90° to a line drawn from the sun to the camera's position. Some field photographers establish this angle by pointing their index finger at the photographic target and by pointing their thumb at the sun, roughly 90°. The camera lens then takes the angle and attitude of the index finger on the target.

6

FLY-TYING TOOLS

Part of the pleasure of fly-tying comes from the beauty, form, and function of the tools. Tool selection is important. It is easier for me to change to a different fly rod than to change to a different tying tool. In short, quality tools can become familiar friends. It is important to note that there are numerous tools and tool models available for the tyer and that only a few are shown here. However, the following tool analyses should offer the beginner knowledge for selecting the appropriate tools.

The range of tying tools available is more comprehensive than essential. Moreover, prices and quality are also comprehensive. Fly-tying does not require many tools, and some tools may even decrease the speed and quality of tying. Seldom will a tool compensate for poor methods and materials. Even so, tying tools are fascinating and pleasurable to own and use. If possible, always purchase quality, and in the beginning, select only those few that are required. Quality keeps its value. The basic tools often include thread, thread bobbin, hackle pliers, scissors, tying vise, hair stacker, wing burner, and whip finisher. Most tyers, however, go beyond the tying essentials.

THE THREAD

Tying thread, though more a material than a tool, is the tension that binds. Thread truly is the sinew and ligament that hug and hold the fragments of a fly. Without thread, most flies could not stand on their tail and barbs. When selecting a tying thread, consider the various features: size, texture, finish, twist, stretch, strength, wax, and color. Certain techniques, such as hair spinning, may require a strong flat thread. Other techniques might require a slick thread, others a textured thread. Most modern tying threads are either nylon or polyester. Silk is still used in traditional salmon and soft-hackle patterns. Dacron is a DuPont trademark for a polyester fiber made from dimethyl terephthalate and ethylene glycol. Dacron strength approaches nylon but, like other polyesters, it differs significantly in elasticity. Nylon stretches up to 30 percent before breaking; Dacron stretches up to about 10 percent. With nylon, when the stretch stops, the thread pops. A fly tied with stretched nylon is under constant pressure. Silk expands about 15 percent of its length before rupture; it silently slides apart. Like silk, polyester doesn't declare its demise.

The modern aught sizing, such as 3/0 and 6/0, is remarkably capricious in the fly-fishing industry. What one manufacturer labels a 5/0 may be an other's 3/0 rating. Some manufactures now specify the denier on their spools. Denier is a manufacturing standard for sizing thread. It is simply the gram weight of 9,000 meters of thread. A 180-denier weighs 180 grams per 9,000 meters. Though the denier designation indicates weight (mass) rather than diameter, diameter is usually relative to weight. Thus, the smaller the denier number, the finer the thread. At present, only a few companies indicate denier on thread spools. Many tyers prefer to select thread according to hook size and tying method. I tie most of my size 12 to 10 hooks with a 3/0 thread. I use a strong flat thread for spinning deer hair, a fine 6/0 thread for tying micropatterns and Trico spinners, and a silk thread for traditional soft-hackle patterns. The following chart lists the denier size and tying comments, courtesy of Wapsi Fly.

Denier 70	Midges and other small patterns, breaking strength approximately 1 lb., recommended for hook sizes 32 to14
Denier 140	For beginners, for the split-thread technique, breaking strength approximately 2 lb., for hook sizes 14 to 6
Denier 210	Streamers, poppers, and most saltwater patterns, breaking strength approximately 3 lb., for hook sizes 8 to 1/0
Denier 280	Heavy hair work, mounting dumbbell eyes, large saltwater patterns, breaking strength approximately 4 lb., recommended for hook sizes 2 to 8/0

The Thread Twist

A smooth thread doesn't push or chase materials around the hook shank. A pushy textured thread, conversely, grips and grabs better. Most nylons are usually slicker than polyesters and may require additional skills in tying. To some degree, thread texture itself can act like wax to hold and bond materials. To increase the texture of a slick nylon, merely twist it. Most modern tying threads have a Z-twist. That is, on a vertical thread, the middle stroke of the Z indicates the direction of the twist. The opposite is the S-twist. Threads may be flattened or untwisted by spinning them the opposite direction of the twist. Most tying threads have a very mild twist. Many waxed tying threads already have a bonding agent that stiffens and consolidates the fibers. A viscous, high-tack wax may be added for greater adhesion when dubbing.

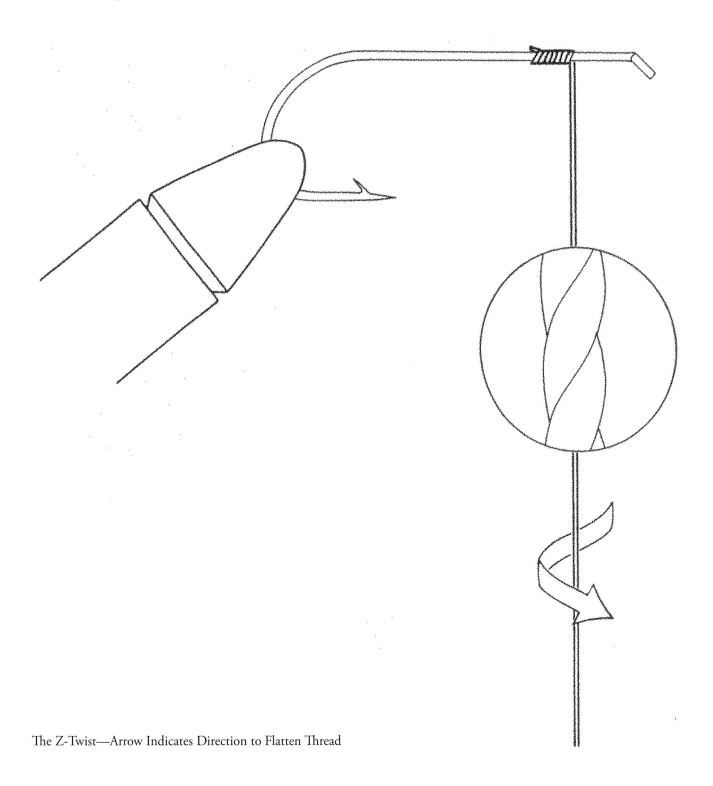

The Z-Twist—Arrow Indicates Direction to Flatten Thread

The S-Twist—Flatten S-Twist
Opposite of Z-Twist

David Foster, in the first edition of *The Scientific Angler* (1882), presented the rationale for untwisting tying thread. "The utility of the untwisting process will be conspicuously apparent in the making of fine-bodied artificials, as the substance of it is reduced by more than one-third." A flat thread, especially a multi-strand flat thread, does not cut into the material, such as quill wings or deer hair, as deeply as a tightly spun thread.

Early tyers often selected thread colors (1) to match the insect body or (2) to meld with dubbing to create the insect body color. Like most tyers, I prefer the subtle polyester colors for trout patterns and the intense nylon colors for saltwater patterns. But the more I tie trout patterns, the more I use just one thread color—white. With permanent markers, I can create colors that are not commercially available. Furthermore, I can change the thread color several times on a single fly. Modern synthetic threads are remarkably durable. Head cement may be more cosmetic than functional and, in fact, may only add unnecessary weight to small dry flies. A tight whip-finish is all that is required. Thread and threadwork constitute the definition of fly-tying.

Wide, Flat Thread Procedures

1. Hair spinning
2. Mounting quill wings
3. Creating smooth bodies
4. Mounting soft tail without flair
5. Forming a smooth head
6. Posting hair wings (wrapping around the base of each wing)

Twisted (Corded) Thread Procedures

1. Beading (wrapping a small twisted knot of thread) to erect wings
2. Creating bulk
3. Applying dubbing
4. Dividing wings
5. Dividing split tails

THE THREAD BOBBIN

In fly-tying the bobbin holds the standard thread spool or the small sewing-machine spool. An adequate bobbin weight eliminates the need for half-hitches during tying. Bobbin features include

1. Rigid spool arms that prevent twisting
2. Adequate weight for thread tension
3. Small-diameter tube for precise thread control
4. Adjustable spool tension and smooth thread flow
5. Smooth tube lips to prevent thread fraying or breaking
6. Alignment of tube and spool to lessen wax removal
7. Comfortable balance and hand conformity
8. Minimal overall length for working beneath the vise head
9. Adequate spool size or spool range

To avoid thread changes, most tyers use different colored threads on different bobbins. Some bobbin arms may be adjusted, allowing fairly straight thread entry; an acute thread-entry angle wipes wax off the thread. Most bobbins will require periodic tube cleaning. A moderately offset tube and spool fits the hand, and a straight thread entry minimizes wax buildup.

There are some simple bobbins, such as the Matarelli, and complex bobbins, such as the MP TT bobbin. On the popular Matarelli bobbin, thread resistance is adjusted by bending the arms that hold the thread spool. The Matarelli Midge Bobbin fits neatly within the hand and accepts sewing-machine spools. The innovative MP TT Bobbin, from Marc Petitjean of Switzerland, has a thread-through system for quick spool changing and threading, an adjustable slider thread tensioner, and a thread hook for axial dubbing-loop spins.

Tying Tools (top to bottom): the Petitjean MP TT Bobbin, the Matarelli Standard Bobbin, and the Matarelli Midge Bobbin

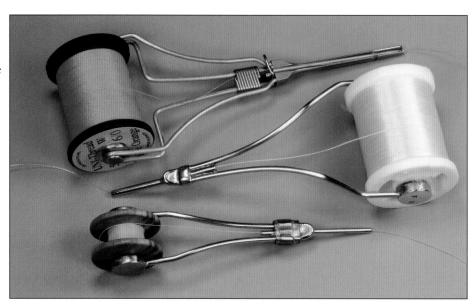

THE HACKLE PLIERS

Hackle pliers are simple and useful tools if designed properly. Poor designs can make wrapping feathers pure torment. The traditional English-style pliers require care in design and construction. Sharp or ill-matched jaws can slip or snip the hackle tip. When hackling, tyers traditionally mount and wrap the feather so that the barbs stand at right angles to the hook shank. Most hackle pliers have a jaw axis at a right angle to the finger hole, encouraging a hackle to twist during wrapping. However, with proper hand control, the jaw angle is not a serious problem. A few hackle pliers have jaws that rotate independently, thereby decreasing hackle twist. They also decrease feather control. Several hackle pliers have springs to cushion a heavy hand. It is best, perhaps, to learn the light touch. More importantly, the weight of hackle pliers should be heavy enough to maintain hackle or thread tension when on the dangle. Here are the features of good hackle pliers:

1. Well-indexed jaws that hold without cutting. Serrations or rubber tips should be avoided.
2. Adequate weight to maintain tension when on the dangle.

3. Adequate point of grip. Pliers should have a large finger hole for rotation.
4. Firm jaw tension with easy opening. Hackle slippage is a cardinal fault. A hackle tip should break before it pulls out.
5. Pliers should be large enough for ease of manipulation, yet compact enough for maneuvering around the hook.

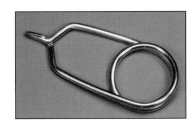

Heavy English Hackle Pliers with Smoothly Indexed Jaws

Small minor tools may have major effects in tying. The Marc Petitjean Magic Tool Clip allows a tyer to clamp together barbs or other materials for insertion in a split thread or dubbing loop. Unlike common bulldog clamps, the transparent Petitjean clip allows a view of the clamped materials. Dubbing needles prick out hairs and furs and dubbing hooks swiftly spin dubbing loops. A fine-nose clamp readily extracts a skewed or cranky barb. And compactors ram spun hairs together.

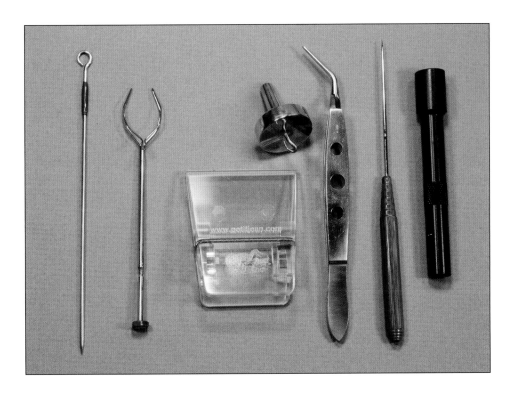

From left to right: Dubbing Hook, Thread Splitter (with a needle tip for dividing the thread and a spreader to keep the split thread open), Petitjean Transparent Clip, Martin Single-Hook Dubbing Whirl, Fine-Nose Clamp, Dubbing Needle, and Hair Compactor.

THE FLY-TYING SCISSORS

Fly-tying scissors may be highly specialized. They should be short for manipulation with finely tapered points for snipping a single barb. Large or adjustable open finger loops, properly termed rings, enhance comfort. Blades touch at only two points: the pivot point and the cut point. The cut point moves along the edges of the shear bars as both blades wrap around each other while closing. Thus a single shear point passes down the edges as the scissors close. Quality scissors are the center of fly-tying: never compromise.

Scissors have two blades: the guillotine (the moving blade) and the anvil (the stationary blade). The guillotine blade connects to the thumb. The other blade is the anvil. To cut, the thumb presses down on the guillotine blade. Most blades are matched to within 1½ points on the Rockwell C hardness scale. A greater differential between blade hardness may cause one blade to attack the other. The blade angles are approximately the same. Some tyers taper the tips for fine cutting. When tapering the tips with a file, do not wipe too much metal off the back of the tips; this lessens the cross-section and decreases the closing pressure.

Blades with microserrations are recommended for cutting resistant materials, such as slick synthetics and deer hair. For optimal efficiency, the serrations should be located on the stationary anvil blade. Serrations on the moving guillotine are less likely to capture material. Smooth blades may push or chase material away rather than cut it. The edge bevel is usually about 25° to 30°, but scissors designed for special materials may be beveled to 40° or more. Both the anvil and guillotine may have the same edge bevel.

Scissors are either right- or left-handed. Right-handed scissors slightly orbit the top finger loop to the left, thereby increasing pressure at the shear point. Right-handed scissors used in the left hand orbit the top finger loop to the right, thereby decreasing the pressure at the shear point. Scissors used in this manner tend to open up, taking the blades apart at the shear point, especially if they have a worn or slack pivot screw.

During tying, scissors may be kept or cradled in the hand. Place the ring finger through the lower loop and nestle the top loop in the palm. The scissors can then be rotated beneath the wrist, where the small finger controls them when not in use. If the index finger lowers the finger loop, then the forefinger is free for tying. When cutting, merely rotate the scissors into the hand and cradle it in the natural fold formed by the forefinger and thumb. The thumb is then placed on or in the top loop for cutting. After cutting, the scissors again rotate beneath the hand while the tying continues. Scissors with large rings may be continuously worn on the thumb and forefinger. Wearing scissors may seem awkward at first, but in time it will become an extension of the hand. Remember also that a single blade edge can closely slice a thread under tension without cutting barbs or other materials. And a fine point can prick out thoracic dubbing.

Usually fine-point, short-blade scissors and long-blade scissors are required for fly-tying. Short-blade scissors are useful for close vise work, and the long straight-blade scissors are good for trimming dubbing loops, chopping dubbing, and pruning deer-hair patterns. No single pair of scissors can do all that is required. Curved blades sculpture spun-hair patterns and heavy shears slice moose mane, thick stems, heavy synthetics, and tinsels.

Features of Fly-Tying Scissors

1. Finely tapered, sharp points (a 15°tapered point is best for fine, close cutting).
2. Large comfortable or adjustable finger loops. Adjustable open finger loops (rings) can be tuned for comfort.
3. Well-meshing blades with a smooth shear action.
4. An adjustable pivot screw. Stamped pivots can seldom be adjusted.
5. Points that register or match when closed.
6. Single- or double-serrated edge for synthetics and hair work.
7. Magnetized tips for selecting small hooks.
8. Uniform angle and width to the cutting bevel.

The double offset scissors, a specialized fly-tying design, have canted blades that allow cutting and trimming not possible with conventional tying scissors. The handles are offset and dropped about 35°for complete cutting visibility; neither the hand nor the scissors obscure the cutting. The hand and the handles avoid the cutting path, so material trapped in a dubbing loop is neither displaced nor dislodged during trimming. The handles are usually adjusted to cross at a comfortable right angle to the finger axis. The offset blades also allow close cropping of fur and hair patches. Moreover, the offset design allows a ready pick-up off the tying table. Another specialized design is the taperizer or thinning scissors. The finely toothed blades of a taperizer allow thinning, blending, and tapering of strand materials, especially synthetic strands on saltwater patterns. Those are just two specialized scissor designs.

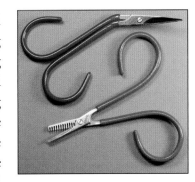

The Original Anvil Double Offset Scissors with adjustable handles and ultrafine points and the toothed Anvil Taperizer Scissors

THE TYING VISE

The tying vise, the tool that holds the hook while fly-tying, differs according to jaw mechanism (draw-cam, push-cam, spring-lever, and screw), mounting systems (C-clamp, table base, screw mount, and handheld), and materials (usually brass, steel, and aluminum). D. H. Thompson is credited with the invention of the simple collet vise, with a single cam lever that closes and opens the jaws. It is generally recommended that tyers mount the hook in a vise with the hook shank horizontal and the point and barb exposed. Mount the hook deep enough to prevent the hook from pinging out and chipping the jaws. However, the jaw should not cover the barb and hook point; jaw pressure alone can cause a furtive fracture in the hook point. Such fractures, unfortunately, may be found only when fishing. Learn to avoid the hook point with fingers and thread. Tying lights, which connect to a standard ⅜″ vise stem, should have cool bulbs and a flexible neck for optimal comfort and positioning.

Not only must a vise securely hold thousands of hooks well, it may also be required to perform special tying functions. A vise should accommodate various attachments and functions with minimal fuss. All adjustments should be simple and secure. Prices vary from the less expensive synthetic castings to precision-milled stainless steel. A quality vise should provide long and faithful service.

Although most fly vises have a draw or push-cam system, recent developments have seen some innovative designs and complex features. There are four fundamental vise systems based upon the manner in which the jaws close:

1. *Draw-Cam Lever*—where the rotating lever, and increasing-radius cam or wiper cam, draws the tapered rear of the jaw bolt into a collet or sleeve, thereby compressing and closing the jaws. Typical examples are the original Thompson A and the modern Standard HMH (Hunter's Multiple Head) Vise.

2. *Push-Cam Lever*—where the cam lever pushes the jaw bolt through the sleeve collet, thereby compressing and closing the jaws. The jaw that must exit a collet is usually smaller in diameter than the typical draw-cam jaw. Dyna-King by Abby is an example of this reverse system. Other cam systems are available, such as the Renzetti Presentation Cam 4000 with a swing-cam lever.

3. *Spring Lever*—the spring lever exerts continuous pressure on the jaws by a powerful wedging or spring action. The jaws, always under tension, require no adjustments other than opening to accept various hook sizes. A typical example of this unique system is the self-adjusting Regal vise often used for commercial fly-tying.

4. *Screw Knob*—in which the rotation of a screw handle draws the jaw bolt against a collet, thereby closing the jaws. This is a variant of the draw system. An example of this system is the older Renzetti Presentation 3000 vise. Although generally slower than a lever system, it is one of the simplest and most reliable closure systems.

Most vises adjust the jaw setting (the distance between the jaw faces) by a threaded sleeve to accommodate various hook diameters. The push-cam system usually has the adjustment sleeve immediately behind the jaws; the draw-cam (or pull-cam) system is immediately in front of the cam lever.

Generally speaking, a tying vise should require little upkeep. A periodic wiping with a silicone cloth, some light oil on working threads, and a lubricant on any bearing surfaces should suffice. A vise should be constructed of rust-resistant metals—if it is not, then a light polish should restore any part to perfection. Care should be taken not to drop a vise. Usually, depending upon the operating system, a vise should not be left with pressure on the jaws. On vises with interchangeable jaws, make certain that the appropriate jaw is used for the particular hook. Do not spring the jaws to accept larger hooks than possible. Do not over-tighten a vise. It should hold securely with minimal pressure. The better vises usually come with a lifetime guarantee that will repair or replace any defective parts as long as there is no evidence of misuse or abuse. Travel vises take the journey best in a soft case, but care must be taken so that parts do not collide.

Vise Features

1. A vise should accept the standard range of hooks with minimal adjustments. Vise jaws with grooves, serrations, or pins for holding and positioning hooks should position hooks securely. Unfortunately, grooves and serrations can fracture a poorly placed hook. Many tyers prefer smooth-jawed vises, especially for the smaller trout hooks. Some vises have interchangeable jaws for patterns both small and large; this allows the added advantage of replacing a jaw that becomes sprung or chipped. Polished stainless steel jaws are preferred over chromed jaws that can, in time, flake and peel. The quality of a vise is determined by the materials, the manufacturing process, and the design. True rotary occurs when the hook shank rotates on its axis.

2. The vise jaw should allow adequate access to the hook shank and exposed bend when tying. Some vises, especially for size 18 hooks and smaller, hold only at the hook heel.

3. All milled threads should be fine, deep, and acutely angled to prevent back-off of adjustments. Lock rings may be added to snug adjustment rings. All knurling should be clean and precise.

4. No matter what the vise-mounting system, it should be stable and secure. Quality vises usually have a pedestal as well as a C-clamp mount.

5. If required, the vise should accept supplementary tools, such as gallows, a material clip, lights, and bobbin cradle. A standard stand rod, usually ⅜″ diameter, should accept future products, even from different manufacturers.

6. All functions—jaw closure, jaw adjustment, jaw rotation, jaw angle—should be effortless and convenient to perform. No extra tools should be required to mount or adjust the vise head.

The following illustrate three different jaw closure systems: the screw knob, the squeeze handle, and the cam lever.

The Screw Knob Renzetti Presentation 3000 Vise with true-rotary for small patterns and detail work.

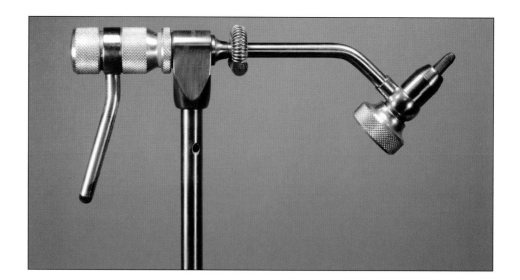

A self-adjusting Regal Vise with squeeze handle. Although occasionally used for small hooks, the substantial jaws may limit detail tying.

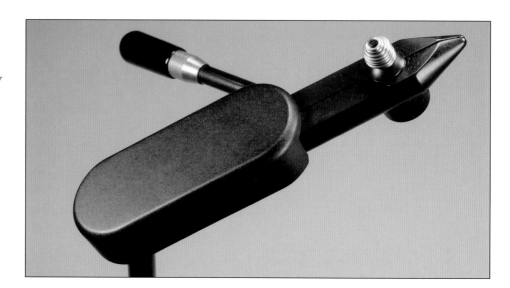

The Limited Edition Premium HMH Fly-tying Vise with Draw-Cam Lever

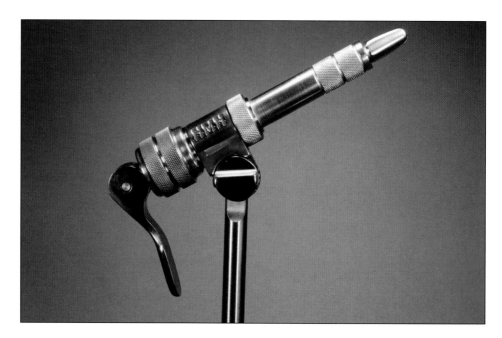

THE HAIR STACKER

The hair stacker is a cylindrical tying tool that aligns, by gentle table tapping, the natural tapered hair or feather barb-tips. There are two basic stacker designs: open and closed. After forceful vertical tamps, several gentle 45° tapping strokes will consolidate and channel the fibers together for removal. This slanted gutter tapping can significantly improve the stacks. Tails, wings, and other bundled fibers are usually stacked. The inside base of some stackers is mildly concaved to produce a natural rounding of the stacked ends, otherwise the fibers may appear too abrupt or unnatural. Depending upon the material stacked, it is best to have stackers of different inside-diameters and lengths. Straight, stiff materials require a small diameter; crinkly strands and those with soft, supple tips require a large diameter. When stacking stiff body hairs, remove all underfur first. For open-end stackers, insert the ends to be aligned (normally the natural tips) into the stacker. Tap the vertical stacker sharply several times on a solid surface, then angle the stacker to bundle the hairs and gently tap several more times. Lift the stacker horizontally before removing the bundled, matched hairs.

Hair-Stacker Features

1. A small-bore chamber (approximately ¼″ to ⅜″ inside diameter) tightly bundles hairs. This is important when few stiff hairs, such as those for tails, are stacked. A wide-bore may allow the hairs to cross rather than pile parallel. Large-bore stackers are useful when stacking crinkled or soft-tipped fibers. Such fibers cling to each other, and their soft tips fold rather than align. These fibers, such as calf-tail hairs, are usually first finger-stacked. Then a large-bore stacker that loosely gathers the hairs gently aligns most of the fibers. Finally, the fingers eliminate the very short and very long fibers, leaving the stack aligned.
2. A positive grip and a wide stable base cushioned for quiet tamping.
3. A smooth, antistatic hair chamber.
4. The male lip of the hair chamber should be thick enough (1/16″ or thicker) so that the hairs are not disturbed when the female section withdraws.
5. A freebore space between the bottom of the stacker and the male lip close enough, approximately ⅜″, to prevent the fibers from moving or falling during removal. An ultrasmall stacker may have only a ⅕″ lip. In other words, the natural fiber tips should be exposed for easy removal, yet not so extended that they fall or touch the female wall during withdrawal from the base.

The Matarelli Open-End Hair Stacker

Standard Closed-End Stackers

THE WING BURNERS

A wing burner is a metal template that holds feathers or fabric so that a flame, usually a butane lighter flame, burns away the surplus, thereby forming a shaped wing for fly-tying. Wing burners come in a variety of wing shapes for adult or nymph, mayfly, caddis, and stonefly wings. The term wing burner is deceptive; burners (perhaps the better term) also make grasshopper legs, emerger wing buds, corixa paddles, and other pattern parts. Wing burners offer several advantages over wing cutters: (1) a wide variety of sizes and shapes, (2) realistic shapes, and (3) no blades to dull. Because the blades bend in wing cutters, the widest part is often near the top, unlike the wings of many insects. Cutters work best on synthetics; burners will fuse the wing edge. For wing burning, select hen feathers that have the barbs at right-angles or nearly so. *Beware: Acutely angled barbs can be burned through at the base, resulting in a truncated or abrupt angle.* Wing burners include the following features:

1. An appropriate wing size and shape
2. A well-matched template edge for clean, sharp wing edges
3. The proper thickness to prevent metal warp or fuzzed wing edges
4. An adequate length for cool handling
5. A secure clamping of the feather
6. A variable feather positioning to accommodate dun, thoracic dun, and spinner wings
7. A template that permits various stem angles.

Carefully calculate stem placement prior to burning. To minimize pattern spin and flutter when cast, position the stem either near the leading wing edge or angled near the wing base. Compare the off-center placement of a bird's flight feather stem or a mast of a sailboat. Both are positioned to effectively penetrate the wind. An advanced or angled stem line reduces casting flutter. Use a center stem placement only for flat nymph wings.

Some commercial wing burners are either the wrong shape or size. Making wing burners is possible. Brass strips—½″ or ¼″ wide and .032″ thick—make excellent wing burners and are available from hobby stores, hardware stores, or catalogs. They are readily shaped with metal shears, files, and grinders. Complete instructions for making wing burners are found in *The Fly Fisher's Craft* (Skyhorse Publishing).

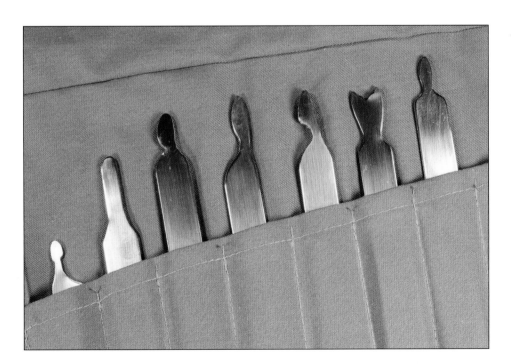

A Medley of Wing Burners

THE WHIP-FINISHER

The whip-finisher wraps one thread several times over another thread so that the under-thread may eventually be tightened to produce a secure knot, such as the final head knot on a fly pattern. Whip-finishers work by a spring-lever side hook, such as the Marc Petitjean, or by a rigid side hook, such as the Matarelli. Some extended whip-finishers can place knots anywhere along the full length of the hook shank. Once mastered, the whip-finisher creates knots with rapidity, control, and pressure during the whip process. According to angling historian Marvin Nolte, an early reference to the knot (though not termed whip finish) appears in *The Fly-Fisher's Guide* (1816) by George C. Bainbridge, "When the fastening off must be effected, by making three or four loose turns of silk at such a distance from the hook, as to admit the end being passed under them. . ." Bainbridge illustrates the knot and adds, "The loose turns must be wrapped closely on the hook, and then the end drawn tight, which will so completely secure the fastening, that if neatly managed, it will be difficult to discover where the fly has been finished. This mode of fastening is called the *invisible knot.*" Consult Chapter 7, *Fly-Tying Tactics,* for detailed instructions on whip-finishing. Although with differing designs, the illustrated whip-finishers all wrap a vertical thread over a horizontal thread to create a secure knot. Each has a rotating handle to facilitate wrapping.

Top to bottom: the Petitjean Whip-Finisher with Spring-Lever Side Hook, the Standard Matarelli Rigid Whip-Finisher, and the Tiemco TMC Quick Finish Whip Finisher

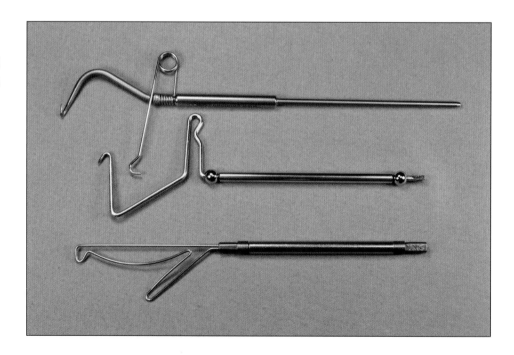

Many tyers collect tools as they collect methods and materials. When possible, purchase quality tools that will acquire time's patina. Although most tying tools require little or no maintenance, a periodic wipe with a silicon cloth or a spot of fine oil ensures their longevity. To protect tools, store them in a cloth or leather case. After more than fifty years of tying, I have some notable historic and original tying tools. They are, one might say, my favorite friends forever.

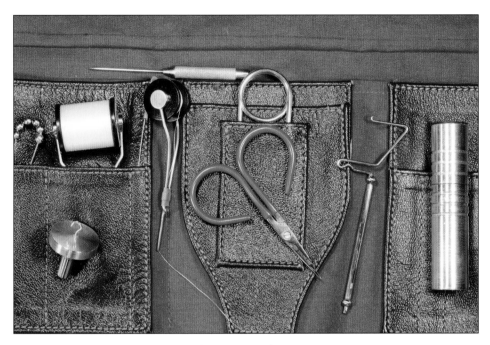

The Tying Tool Case

7

FLY-TYING TACTICS

A FLY-TYER COLLECTS METHODS AS WELL AS MATERIALS. Here are some fundamental tying tactics that apply to numerous fly patterns. Fly-ishing has been described by Scottish novelist John Buchan as "the pursuit of what is elusive but attainable, a perpetual series of occasions for hope." Perhaps this describes fly-tying, as well. Each vise session struggles for that ephemeral perfection.

Fly-tying comes with two heresies: form and material. There is the belief that any variance in the precise proportions reduces a pattern's effectiveness and that only the prescribed materials must be used. Needless to say, this is nonsense. It may be possible to discover better materials and more effective designs. Select form and materials for what they can do for a pattern. Experimenting with form and material often creates astonishingly effective patterns. Note, too, that tying material can exhibit a significant color or character change when wet or when in direct sunlight. The puffy tail of a woolly bugger can become a slender thread. Some tyers wrap for what the pattern will become, rather than what it is. Then again, a trout might have his own take on this. Commercial fly-tyers must maintain a standard; the marketplace demands uniformity. The common tyer, however, can diverge considerably from the standards, especially for innovative purposes. No living art has finality. Many modern patterns are mild variations of previous patterns. Fly-tyers should know the what and the why that has come before them. Only then may they be able to make informed changes.

While experimenting with various methods and patterns, special attention may be given to the twelve basic tying errors:

1. Improperly mounted hook.
2. Poorly proportioned tail, wing, or hackle.

3. Fraying of thread on the hook point.
4. Inappropriate trimming of natural fiber tips.
5. Failure to apply slack or tension when required. This includes too heavy- or light-handed thread management for the particular method or material.
6. Excessive amount of thread wraps, dubbing, or other materials. Tying parsimony requires that each wrap and each fiber do its duty. For delicacy, materials should be mounted sparingly and firmly with the fewest number of wraps.
7. Crowding the wing, hackle, and head toward the hook eye.
8. Uneven stacking or matching of fibers and parts.
9. Improper placement of body parts. Beginners, often unaware of the available shank space, have a tendency to mount body parts slightly forward of their correct position, thus piling wing, hackle, and head together. When mounting the thread, it may be beneficial to leave the head space naked to avoid any intrusion of the wing or hackle. Before tying, pattern part locations may also be marked with thread on the hook shank; if a pattern has a particular mounting point (such as a nymph wing-case at half shank-length), a thread wrap can mark it. An improper start-and-finish point of material—the alpha and omega error—creates awkward patterns. Constantly calculate the space required for the material and the space remaining for additional material. Furthermore, a slight variation in the stance or set of the material may make a significant difference in the function of the fly. The form and function of the pattern should be paramount while tying.
10. Inappropriate materials or colors for the particular pattern.
11. Failure to keep the working thread advanced to the tie-off point.
12. Failure to correct an error before continuing.

THE TRADITIONAL HOOK DESIGNS

There are four basic hook designs: the Limerick, the Perfect, the Sneck, and the Sproat. Each shape has advantages and disadvantages. There are other popular hook bends available, especially the curved-shank hooks, such as Daiichi York bend 1270 and the Tiemco 200 Nymph hook. The York bend, a term introduced by Daiichi Hooks USA, describes a mildly curved shank that makes a continuous and subtle transition into the bend. This flowing meld of shank and bend provides realistic imitations for terrestrials (such as grasshoppers) and nymphs (such as stonefly and damselfly nymphs). Although the curve-shank design is relatively strong, the smaller hook sizes may lack adequate gaps. Other popular hooks include the various round-shank hooks (Daiichi 1130, 1150, and Tiemco 2487, 2457) for emerger, shrimp, and pupa patterns. Select the shape, the size, and the weight of a hook that matches the natural while offering a sufficient gap. The Sproat bend is perhaps the fly fisher's standard hook.

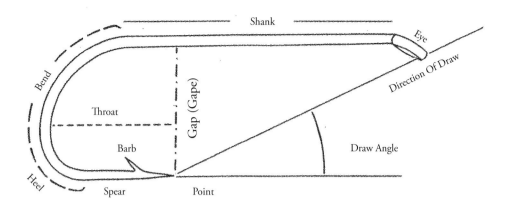

Fly Hook Nomenclature—these standard hook terms appear throughout the tying text.

The Limerick Bend

Advantages:
1. The attractive rakish lines.
2. The hook trails well in heavy water.
3. The set-back point produces a superior penetration angle.

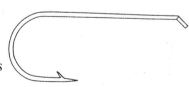

The Limerick Bend

Disadvantages:
1. Limericks with a sharp bottom bend are considered by some to be less strong than those with a rounded heel. The abruptness of the bottom bend varies from manufacturer to manufacturer. It is true that an angular bend gathers more mechanical stress; however, the heavy wire used for salmon and streamer hooks produces a strong bend. Moreover, the point stress may merely push the heel back rather than open the bend.
2. There is a strong extension of steel beyond the body of the fly, which may be a key in the selective rejection of the pattern. However, the trailing feathers and fibers of wets and streamers may cloak the bend.

The Perfect Bend

Advantages:
1. This semicircular bend with the spear parallel to the shank distributes the stress throughout much of the curve.
2. The Perfect opens the distance between the point and the shank, thereby increasing the gap.
3. The Perfect has a medium bite and a moderate heel beyond the fly body.
4. Ernest Schwiebert, in *Trout*, comments that the Perfect bends "offer optimal strength in light-weight hooks designed for high-floating performance."

The Perfect Bend

5. Because of the wide gap, the Perfect bend is appropriate for patterns that bulk the shank, such as the Humpy and the Irresistible.
6. The Perfect bend is a esthetically pleasing to many tyers.
7. The rear shank bend is less angular than the Sneck bend.

Disadvantages:
1. Compared to the Sneck, there is a significant extension of steel beyond the body of the fly pattern.
2. The Perfect spear is curved, perhaps allowing the trout to twist or turn upon it, and the spear length may be short, thereby restricting the depth of penetration.
3. The rear of the shank is more angular (thus weaker) than the Sproat bend.

The Sneck Bend

The Sneck Bend

Advantages:
1. The fundamental advantage of the Sneck bend is that the heel and spear hide directly beneath the fly body. Perhaps the effectiveness of a caddis pattern is due to the overwing and body concealing the heel and spear, which makes them less visible to selective trout.
2. Unlike the Perfect and Sproat, the increase in gap does not increase the steel beyond the fly body. Any shank length may have any gap width.

Disadvantages:
1. The sharp angle where the bend meets the shank gathers the mechanical stress to a single point.
2. The Sneck bend usually requires heavier wire, which violates the lightness requirement on medium and large dry-fly hooks, to compensate for the angular bend. Sneck bends may be made somewhat rounder for increased strength.

The Sproat Bend

The Sproat Bend

Advantages:
1. The gradual curve at the weak point (where the shank meets the bend) makes the Sproat a relatively strong hook design. The Sproat is actually a modified Perfect bend with the upper bend, where the major stress would occur, more gradual and the bottom bend, where the minor stress would occur, more abrupt. It preserves some advantages of both bends—the gentle curve of the Perfect and the wide gap of the Sneck. As a compromise bend, the Sproat moves the spear to the rear for adequate length and a superior acute hooking angle.
2. The Sproat has more bite than a Perfect bend.

3. The Sproat has no abrupt bend, such as the Limerick or Sneck, which may magnify the mechanical stress.
4. The Sproat, a standard fly-tying hook design, has a remarkable range of sizes, weights, and finishes available.

Disadvantages:
1. The Sproat exposes a significant amount of heel beyond the fly body. When used for wet flies, bucktails, and streamers, the extension may be insignificant.
2. The Sproat may not have the gap or the throat of a Perfect bend.

EXTRACTING A BARBED HOOK

Hooks catch anglers as well as fish. This is the medically preferred field method for removing a barbed hook from noncritical flesh. The only tool required is what a fly fisher always carries: the fly line. This method separates the barb from the entry channel made by the point and barb. Carefully follow the three steps. Use this method for any noncritical J-hook penetration. The common J-hook has the spear (the short extension that carries the barb) parallel to the hook shank. *For critical penetration or large-hook penetration, seek medical aid.* Maintaining updated shots, such as tetanus, is beneficial. Wash the wound with soap and water, and watch for reddening or swelling. This is the best argument for barbless hooks that I know.

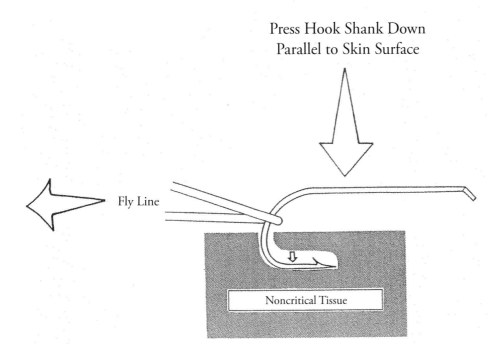

Extracting a Barbed Hook

1. Remove the tippet from the fly hook and loop the fly line around the hook bend as illustrated.
2. Press the hook shank straight down to open the area above the hook barb. Keep the hook shank parallel to the skin surface. Do not merely press the hook eye down.
3. While continuing to press the hook shank straight down and parallel with the skin surface, use a sharp yank or snap of the fly line to extract the hook. Inquire about a tetanus shot or an antibiotic.

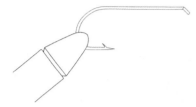

The Mounted Hook

MOUNTING THE HOOK

Begin the pattern by selecting the appropriate hook and tying thread. Then, mount the hook in the tying vise. Adjust the vise carefully to accept the particular hook-wire diameter. The vise jaws should capture the hook heel (bottom of the hook bend and the start of the spear) firmly with an adequate amount of hook anchored to prevent movement during the pressures of tying. A tyer should learn to avoid catching or fraying the thread on the hook point. The point and barb, which are highly tempered, may easily fracture if buried in the jaws. Often such a fracture passes unnoticed. When traditionally mounted, the hook shank should be horizontal.

MOUNTING TYING THREAD

A short length of working thread (1) facilitates avoiding the hook point, (2) promotes tension, and (3) increases accurate thread placement. Usually a 2″ to 3″ working length (from bobbin lip to hook shank) is preferred when wrapping. Depending upon the application, thread may be flattened (untwisted and widened) or corded (twisted and narrowed). It is the thread and the hook that gives form and function to a fly.

Mount the thread with a jam knot. Hold the thread tag in the left hand and the bobbin in the right. With tension, wind the thread several times around the hook shank (clockwise when viewed down the shank from the hook eye). Then continue to wrap back over the foundation wraps, creating a jam knot. Continue to spiral down the shank (toward the bend) with open wraps. The open wraps create a gripping, irregular surface for building a pattern. Some patterns and methods, however, may require a smooth, continuous thread foundation. The placement of the locking foundation knot is usually only beneath the first mounted item, such as the tails or wings. The foundation knot secures the thread so that the various patterns parts (such as the tail, body, wings, and hackle) may be positioned and secured on the hook. Adequate foundation wraps will prevent the thread from pulling loose. Use a bobbin to maintain tension when the thread is on the dangle.

Precise thread handling marks a master tyer. Precise thread work is smooth, sparse, and accurate. Dave Hughes, angling author, once wrote, "If a hook is the backbone of a fly and the materials its flesh, then thread is

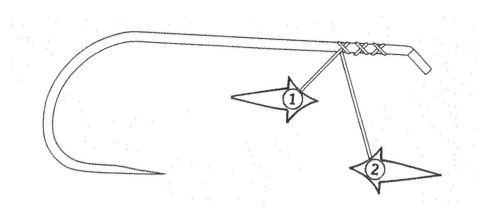

the tendons that hold it together." The pressure and placement of the thread tendons are the most significant skill required in tying. For proper material placement, visualize the start and end point of each pattern component and maintain those dimensions while tying. This avoids compressing pattern parts in the final wraps. Proper thread tactics allow material to be planted, rotated, or even slipped. In other words, material may be held by the thread, moved by the thread, or slipped along the thread. All three skills should be mastered and used when necessary. In the vise of a skilled tyer, even defiant fibers become compliant. Therefore, it is essential to develop accurate thread placement and tension. If thread skills are poor, the pattern suffers. There are several factors that determine thread-work skills.

Thread Tension

Constant thread tension must be maintained by taking advantage of the natural stretch of the thread and by working immediately under the breaking strength of the thread. An interesting thread exercise comes from Dave Hughes: mount the thread, pull the bobbin away, and hold the thread in the tying hand. Now, slowly pull down until the thread breaks. Repeat this several times until the hand knows the breaking point of the particular thread. A tyer should develop a sense of the maximum thread pressure possible and work slightly below it. Establishing and maintaining the correct tying pressure encourages polite, behaved materials. A tyer often has a choice—either he or she will control the material, or the material will work its will.

Minimal Thread Theory

Always use a minimum of thread wraps when tying. Some exceptional patterns, however, do incorporate numerous wraps to form various body parts. Nevertheless, with proper tying tension, seldom are more than three wraps ever required to control material. In most cases, two or three wraps will do. If three wraps will do, do not use five or six. I have watched some tyers actually count the number of wraps for particular patterns. Although I do not advocate tying by the numbers, minimal wraps usually mean that our feathered confections are slender and delicate. The total number of wraps on a pattern does not significantly increase the thread length or pattern weight. However, depending on where the extra wraps are placed, it can produce unnecessary bulk. A typical Light Cahill, tied on a size 14 Mustad 94842 (old designation) with a maximum of three wraps for materials and with a hackle tail, dubbed body, rolled and split wings, dry hackle, and tapered head, consumes 11¾ times the total hook length in thread. By contrast, the same pattern, freely using excess wraps, expends 13¼ the total hook length in thread. The extra wraps use only 1½ times the total hook length more. Thus, there is approximately ten percent more thread consumption with excessive wraps; it is enough to create bulk but little weight. Always practice the minimal wraps. The popular wisdom is that more wraps with a finer thread are stronger than fewer wraps with a heavier thread.

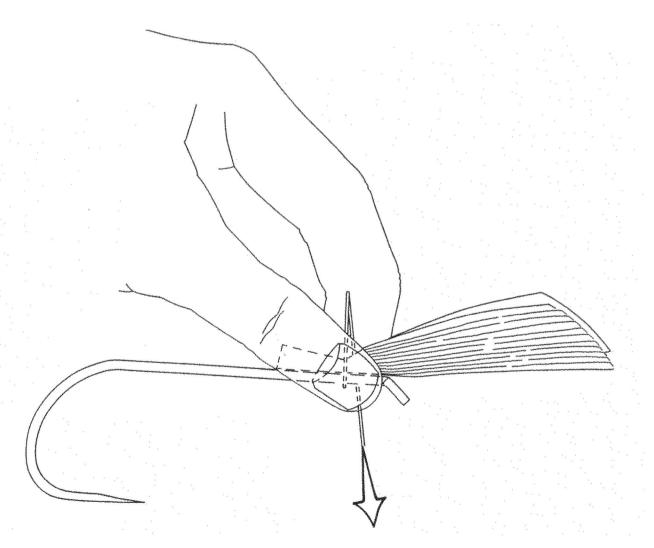

The Soft Loop

THE SOFT LOOP

The soft-loop maneuver, which mounts material at a given point, incorporates the squeeze. With a soft loop, the material is placed directly on top of the hook shank. There are times when controlled relaxed tension, rather than indiscrete or random slack, aids in mounting materials. A proper soft loop may be required to mount materials that are slick and stiff. With lateral pressure on the pinch, the thumb and index finger stack the material in the channel created by the finger tips. The thread then passes between the thumb and the material, loops softly over the material, and then travels down between the material and the index finger. This wrap is usually repeated two or three times. With continuous lateral pressure on the material, the thread firmly snugs down the material. Further wraps are made over or in front of the snug point.

An excellent practice maneuver, especially for beginning tyers, is to spot mount a short 20-pound test section of monofilament directly along the top of the hook shank without foundation wraps. This slick, stiff material resists mounting. The required force and control teaches much about thread work. After brief practice with the monofilament, natural materials may behave. The simple solution is to hold the monofilament at a right angle to the hook shank and overwrap where they intersect. Once secured, mount the monofilament with a series of soft loops along the monofilament on the hook shank. The required force and control teaches much about thread work. Use the soft loop for mounting any materials directly on top of the hook shank with or without foundation wraps.

HACKLING THE DRY FLY

Hackle selection and preparation are essential. Select for barb length and stem length. When mounting a dry hackle, avoid as much webbing as possible by trimming the hackle stem. In this standard method, the hackle stem (with a barbless base about a head-space long or more) is mounted beneath the near wing and parallel to the hook shank. The hackle tip extends left with the dull, concave side facing the tyer. Three or four thread wraps secure the stem. For greater security, wrap the hackle stem both fore and aft of the wing. Next, the hackle is bent vertically with the dull side facing the hook eye. Bend the hackle so that there is some freebore or space before the appearance of barbs on the hackle stem. The barbs should not begin at the thread mount point; to accommodate the twisted stem, allow 2mm or 3mm of stripped stem between the thread wraps and the barbs. Note the alternate method on the next page. This avoids splayed or erratic barbs during the first few hackle wraps. Splayed barbs may sometimes be captured by a rear second wrap before continuing forward. One simple method is to remove the first few underbarbs, those that often go awry, before mounting the hackle. The bottom barbs (which are essential to flotation) are easily trapped by the ensuing hackle wraps. Usually this is corrected by caressing the previous barb wraps back so as not to ensnare the bottom barbs when wrapping forward. Advance the thread before wrapping the hackle forward in tight spirals. Keep the hackle stem at right angles while wrapping. Wrap as many times behind the wings as in front of the wings. The wings should grow from the middle of the hackle. After hackling, capture the hackle tip and trim excess before forming the head. To support a dry pattern, a well-wrapped hackle should stiffly radiate from the hook shank.

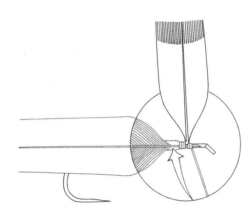

Mounting the Dry Hackle: The concave or dull side of the hackle faces out. This concave side will face the hook eye when wrapped. For improved security, the hackle stem is firmly wrapped both fore and aft of the wing. The stem, however, should not enter the head space. To prevent splayed barbs during the initial hackle wraps, a few under-barbs are removed from the stem side that contacts the body. If possible, wrap the hackle equally on each side of the wing.

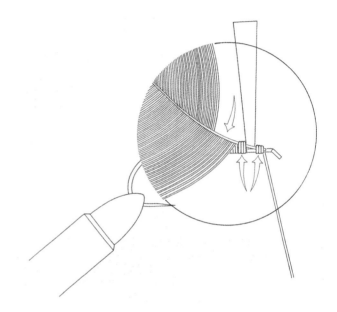

An Alternate Method: The illustrated alternate dry-hackle mount allows the bare stem to wind into position so that the barbs radiate properly.

When wrapping a dry hackle, the first few barbs often flare to the rear. Some tyers use a following wrap to gather them in before advancing the hackle. Wrapping a hackle over a previous wrap, however, may interlace the barbs and secure the stem, but it often creates errant barbs. If the hackle stem is mounted parallel to the hook shank, the stem (which must abruptly bend at a right angle to cock the barbs) twists and splays the initial barbs. As the stem continues around the shank, it eventually aligns itself and properly cocks the barbs. The first few barbs, nevertheless, may strut in defiance. To avoid this problem completely, mount the hackle stem (barbless for about a head space) directly beneath the shank or low on the shank side.

HACKLING THE WET FLY

Although traditional soft hen hackle shields or encapsulates the body, the sparse wraps should reveal the body color. Therefore, the umbrella hackle should mount with limited wraps and dull side toward the hook shank. On a soft-hackle pattern, the hackle is the final component mounted and wrapped. For a delicate wet hackle, remove all the under-barbs (those facing the hook shank when wrapped) before mounting. Wrap the hackle only two or three turns to reveal the body. Consult wet-fly barb length in *Fly Tying Proportions*.

Mounting the Wet Hackle

STRIPPED PEACOCK HERL BODY

Stripped peacock herl, a classic body wrap for well more than a century, is a delicate hard-body imitation. The stripped, bicolored herl (beige with dark tracery) imitates the segmented bodies of many insects. Select the plump, broad herls with stem-color contrast from beneath the eyed tail section. Herl from the eyed section is often too tender and fragile for tying. Removing the fuzzy flue was conventionally done with hot paraffin. The eyed peacock feather was dipped in hot paraffin and then cooled. A fingernail scrapes off the paraffin to reveal a glossy, waxed herl. A simpler and safer method is to remove the flue with a high-tack adhesive dubbing wax. Merely smear the wax on the herls before scraping the flue off with a fingernail. This leaves a glossy, waxed herl ready for mounting. When wrapping a stripped herl body, make certain that the contrasting colors are exposed. Some tyers lacquer or cross-wrap fine wire over a herl body for durability.

HAIR SPINNING

The distributive spin, which creates a slow, controlled rotation of fibers, must be mastered for hair spinning. Various animal body hairs—especially deer, caribou, and reindeer—may be spun with a single thread. The softer hairs, such as reindeer, produce densely spun sections. Select a strong, 3/0 multistrand thread for spinning; it prevents cutting through soft hair.

Stripped-barb spinning is similar to hair spinning. Hackle barbs are stripped and stacked. They are then positioned on the hook shank. A double thread loop lightly traps the barbs so that they rotate around the shank as the thread is drawn taut. The fingers can encourage the distribution of the barbs. More barbs may be added to any vacancy. The distributive spin permits the tyer to use a variety of feathers and fibers, no matter what their length, that may otherwise be discarded.

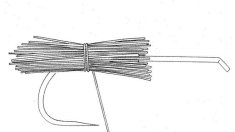 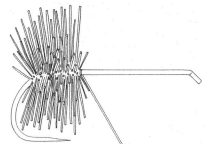 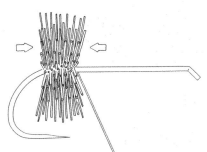

1. Mount the hook securely in the vise, and attach the thread with a small bead wrap (a constricted jam knot) so that all the spinning takes place on a bare shank. This allows each section to spin freely. If a tail is required, attach it with a small secure thread bead. Use a modest amount of hair—about ½ to ¾ the diameter of a pencil. Clear all insulating underfur (the vellus or fine down hair) from the hair, and place one relaxed thread wrap or soft loop around the middle of the bundle and the naked hook shank.

2. Place another thread wrap around the bundle and shank. Slowly snug the thread.

3. Now tighten the thread so the hair flares and encircles the hook shank. While tightening the thread, orbit the hand with the spinning hair.

4. After the rotation has stopped, tighten the thread and pass it between the flared hairs and make a double-shank thread wrap to lock the bundle in place.

5. Prepare and add another bundle as close as possible in the same manner.

6. As each section spins, continue to rotate the thread and hand with the spinning bundle.

7. After two or three bundles have been spun in this manner, use a hair compactor to compress the spun section. Throughout the spinning process, periodically pack the spun bundles. More force may be exerted during compaction if the hook is repositioned lower in the jaws so that the spun sections are forced against the jaw face. *Be careful, however, to avoid the hook point.* Continue adding bundles and packing the sections until the pattern is completed, leaving adequate space for wings and hackle.

8. The spun hair, which is now actually denser than when on the animal, should be trimmed with serrated-blade scissors or razor blades. The fine serrations on scissors grip the fibers.

WINGING PATTERNS

Winging requires special thread tactics. The following standard maneuvers, control and adjust composite (bundled) wings. Adjusting the pliant bundles of wood-duck fibers is not difficult, although a heavy hand may flick the thread through the wing bundle rather than capture and control. However, these wraps are useful, if not necessary, for the stiff and stubborn calf-tail wings as well as for the soft flaring deer- and elk-hair wings. These corrective wraps are used only when required; they are never used to cover poor tying. With minimal wraps, these methods achieve the standard 30° spread between wing bundles and the 90° cock off the shank.

The Figure-Eight Wrap

The figure-eight wrap opens and divides the wings. The thread crosses between the wings and to the opposite shank side. It then passes beneath the shank and comes up the opposite shank side to cross the thread previously placed between the wings. It is easily visualized as a figure-eight wrap with the wings passing through the loops of the eight. To avoid bulk, do not figure-eight beneath the wings.

The Cross Wrap

The cross wrap consolidates, aligns, and erects the wings. The thread, which never drops under the shank, passes between the wings and around the wing bases to cross over the thread laid down between the wings. It then passes around the base of the opposite wing and returns to cross over between the wings. This wrap is best visualized as a figure eight with each wing section passing through a loop of the eight. As the thread is pulled taut, the wing sections align and consolidate.

The Post Wrap

The single-base wrap, often called the post wrap, consolidates and positions a particular wing bundle. A post wrap may also gather the base of both wings together. Similar to the cross wrap is the double-base post wrap, except the thread does not cross between the wings. It consolidates, erects, and aligns the wing bundles together. The thread merely passes around the base of both wing sections. Posting is especially useful for adjusting each individual hair wing. The thread wraps around a single wing base and then anchors the wing. If the thread comes from the outside of the wing to anchor, then the wing bundle draws together. If the thread comes from between the wings and anchors at the opposite shank side, then the wings are divided and pulled back. The particular wing slant determines the direction of correction and anchoring.

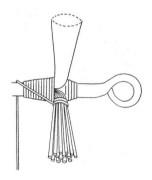

The Post Wrap

THE DUBBING TACTICS

Dubbing is a common method to achieve shape, volume, and color while creating texture and translucency in fly patterns. The term dubbing refers to the material, either natural or synthetic, as well as the method for mounting the material. Early tying descriptions suggest that the body materials, such as wool or silk skeins, were attached at the hook bend and then wound forward rather than attached to the thread and wound forward. Each fiber, natural or synthetic, has specific properties. Fiber size, shape, diameter, surface, and physical structure determine the dubbing characteristics. A tyer cannot threaten his material to make them work as he wants; he or she must select and manipulate the materials properly. *Note*: *All directions are for right-handed tying.*

Dubbing is durable and can imitate a variety of creature colors. It allows light and air to work their wonders. A low twist with high-luster dubbing creates translucent fibers that trap air prisms, which shatter and scatter light much like an emerging insect shrouded in air. In dry patterns, the trapped air increases flotation; in wet patterns, absorbent fibers offer quick water entry and sink. Dubbing is one of the oldest and, with the melding of natural and synthetic fibers, one of the most versatile of modern materials. Before beginning, apply a fine, thin smear of adhesive tying wax to the thread. High-tack waxes make dubbing adhere to the thread. To increase the amount of dubbing, merely increase the number of wraps rather than by increasing the dubbing on the thread. Mastering thread twist masters dubbing.

The Basic Dubbing Method

Mount the thread at the bend of the hook shank. Apply a thin wax smear along 2″ or 3″ of thread. Wipe away any excess wax with your fingertips. Then attach sparse but adequate dubbing along the thread length. Mount the dubbing onto the thread counterclockwise (when viewed down the thread toward the hook shank) by rolling it hard between the thumb and forefingers. For better dubbing adherence, touch the fingertips with wax before rolling on the dubbing. Then, once the dubbing catches, drop the fingers back on the base of the dubbing and thread. *Hold the dubbing along the thread together.* Continue to twist the thread counterclockwise on its own axis until the dubbing tightens around the thread. Once the dubbing is tight, keep a twist on the thread to prevent unwinding. Then, with the hand on the thread and not the bobbin, snugly spiral the dubbing along the hook shank with counterclockwise pressure from the hand. *The counterclockwise pressure comes from slight wrist twists as the hand orbits around the hook shank.* If the hand holds the bobbin, the dubbed strand will unwind. This method applies a given length of dubbing to the hook shank. Early patterns were often sparsely dubbed so that the thread showed through the dubbing. Today there is a distinct tendency to completely cover the thread so that it does not show. Perhaps the modern tyer has lost some of the subtle color play between dubbing and thread.

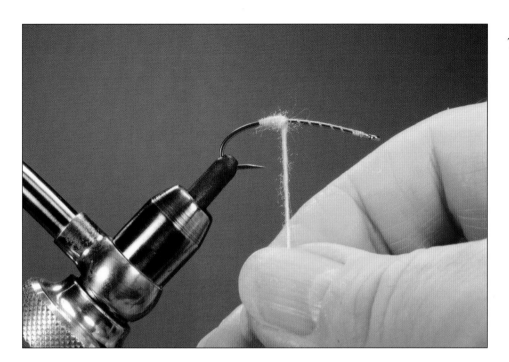

The Basic Dubbing Method

The Palm-Fed Dubbing Method

This method is especially suitable for the soft, long-fibered, crimped synthetic dubbings. Take a loose palm ball of dubbing and mount a small finger-spun strand to the dubbing thread in a counterclockwise direction. Gently hold the dubbing ball in the palm. As you wrap over and away, the dubbing will feed naturally onto the twisting thread. With practice, it is possible to control the amount of the dubbing applied and the degree of twist. If the dubbing is fed quickly, the result is a fast-tapered, segmented body; if fed slowly, the result is a smooth body with a mild taper. I saw this first done, and done with commercial quickness, by Dave Whitlock.

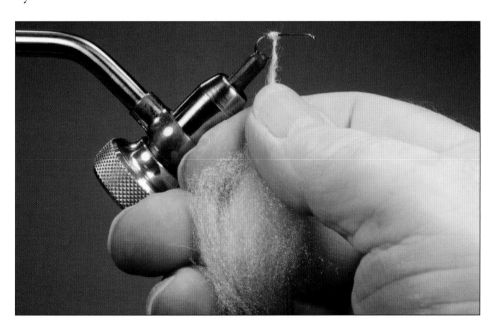

The Palm Fed Method—The last few dubbing wraps may show an increased cording effect.

The long, soft palm-fed fibers swirl around the thread during dubbing. As the twisting and wrapping continues, there is an increase in the twist so that the final wraps display a distinct cording or rope effect. This twisting and wrapping drags other crinkly, long fibers onto the thread. Furthermore, as the dubbing is wrapped on the hook shank, more and more fibers are captured in the twist so that a natural expanding taper results. The cord and taper are more appropriate for some patterns, such as the segmented bodies of adult grasshoppers or stonefly nymphs, than for others. This cord and taper may be modified or eliminated by different hand skills or dubbing fibers. The cling and cord effect is augmented by several factors:

1. The fiber length (long fibers increase cling)
2. The fiber softness (soft fibers increase cling)
3. The fiber crinkle or wave (crinkled or curvy fibers increase cling)
4. The fiber texture (some fibers, especially natural fibers, have scales or structures that increase cling)
5. The fiber diameter (finer fibers increase cling)

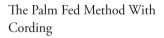

The Palm Fed Method With Cording

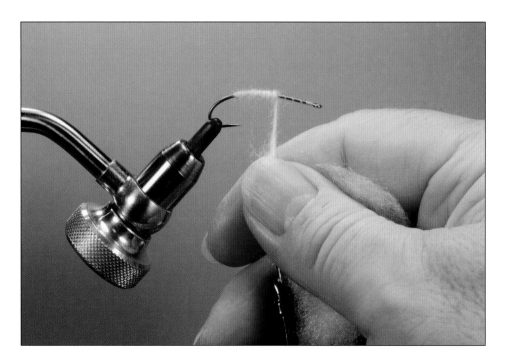

The Dubbing-Dust Method

By contrast, the dubbing-dust method creates a gauzy halo on the hook shank. First, select dubbing—natural or synthetic—that is extremely fine-fibered. Stack the fibers parallel into a dubbing skein. Next, with sharp scissors dice the dubbing fibers into short, 2mm (or shorter) lengths. Then apply a whisper of adhesive wax to the thread. Now, quickly twirl the thread back and forth between your left thumb and forefinger while you daub the thread with the dubbing. Dust the spinning thread until it is suitably hazed.

For a fleecy, translucent haze, merely wrap the dubbing as body. For fine, dense dubbing, twirl and compress the dubbed thread between thumb and forefinger prior to wrapping.

Dubbing-Dust Method

The Dubbing Loop

A thread loop can be loaded with dubbing or various strands and spun to imitate body, hackle, or legs of many patterns. First, form a thread loop. Wrap once around the loop base to consolidate threads at a single spin point. Hang hackle pliers or dubbing whirl on the loop.

The Stripped CDC Hackle

Cul de canard (CDC) barbs may be stripped from the stem, inserted in the dubbing loop, and spun to create a shaggy bubble-snatching hackle. If the barbs are stripped from the stem by hand, then a small foot or hook appears (actually a curlicue of stem) at the base of the barb. The most efficient method for gathering barbs is to stack two or more CDC feathers and pull off, from tip to base, their barbs. Then, keeping the barb bundle together, turn the feather over, and match the stripped barbs with the opposite stemmed barbs. Firmly hold all barbs and strip the opposite barbs, allowing them to bundle with the first cluster. Crop the hooks (the curlicues of stem) and match the ends. Otherwise, the feet or curls would produce a knobby, coarse dubbing. Distribute the CDC barbs evenly within the dubbing loop. Finally, firmly spin the CDC loop to create a buoyant faux

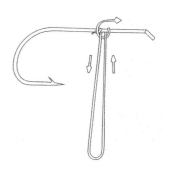

The Dubbing Loop Lock

hackle. CDC feathers may also be stacked and clamped in a bulldog clip or a Marc Petitjean's transparent clip. Once clamped in the clip, the stems can be trimmed and the barb base inserted within a dubbing loop.

CDC barbs also make excellent shoulder and palmer hackles. For a palmer hackle, mount the thread and form a loop at least seven times longer than the hook shank. Insert stripped barbs into the loop. Continue to strip and insert until the loop holds an adequate amount of CDC barbs. For long tendrils, insert the barbs at the base. Trim the barb base that extends beyond the doubled threads. Spin the loop to lock in the barbs and then, while stroking the barbs rearward to prevent overwrapping, spiral the CDC palmer forward on the hook shank. The CDC becomes the hackle and the twisted thread, the hackle stem. This produces a body with extreme floatation due to the numerous trailing tendrils. There is perhaps no better dry hackle than spun CDC barbs. The shoulder hackle is merely a short palmer hackle.

The Single Split Thread

This is my favorite method for a CDC hackle. With a needle, evenly divide a multistrand thread draped over a fingernail. The fingernail flattens the strand for separation. Another method for flattening thread for separation is to press it against the hook shank while rubbing it back and forth. A needle then divides the flattened thread near the hook shank. Keep the split open and separated with a dubbing hook or thread splitter. Insert CDC barbs, held in a clip, into the divided thread, then spin firmly. Wrap the trapped barbs as a hackle. Body dubbing may also be inserted and spun in this manner. This method is appropriate for small and standard patterns, especially emergers and duns.

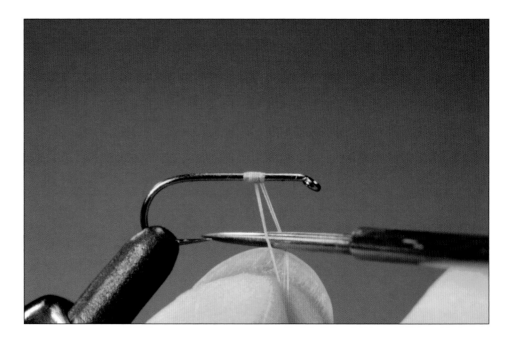

Thread Splitting

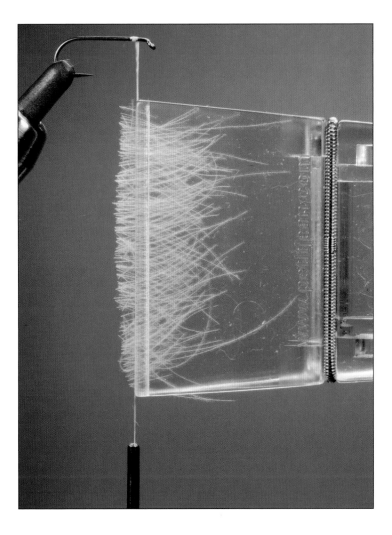

Split Thread Traps Inserted CDC Barbs

WHIP-FINISHING THE HEAD

Traditionally, a fly pattern begins with a locking foundation wrap and ends with a whip-finish at the head. Although the direction of the under-wraps makes little difference, a right-handed tyer should finish the head (the final wraps) by wrapping from left to right toward the hook eye, the direction of reading. This produces a smooth knot with parallel wraps. The head slope should not be so severe that the thread laps cascade toward the hook eye. When pulled taut, the whip-knot butts against the natural taper of the head. Finishing from right to left creates an exposed and unattractive diagonal thread crossing over the final wraps, allowing slack in the diagonal strand. Notice that in the right to left knot illustrated, the thread travels away from where the thread tucks beneath the overwraps. In brief, the final whip-knot should be in the reading direction from left to right. Traditionally, tying thread is exposed only at the head. Other thread wraps are often concealed by material or dubbing.

    To trim excess tying thread, merely pull the thread taut and touch with a sharp blade. Only the taut thread cuts, preserving the hackle barbs. Some

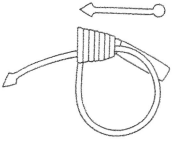

When the final wraps travel from right to left, an exposed cross-thread appears over the wraps. Note that the thread tucks beneath the head opposite to where the thread wraps finish.

tyers sharpen the whip-finisher's extended bottom bar for slicing thread. Consult Chapter 6, *Fly-Tying Tools*, for a complete commentary.

The Matarelli Whip-Finisher

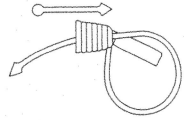

This is the proper direction for the finishing whips. When the final thread wraps travel from left to right, the thread tucks beneath the head. As the tag-end draws left, the resulting knot butts against the head taper.

Although the shape of whip-finishers vary, most work in the same manner—by crossing one thread several times over another thread and pulling the under-thread tight to form the knot. The popular Matarelli whip-finisher, used either with the left or right hand, wraps any size fly. During the whipping process, it is possible to extend the thread for further wraps. Furthermore, the Matarelli whip-finisher is held away from the wrapping point so that accurate thread placement is possible. With practice, tight figure eights may be placed between bead eyes and divided wings. The right-handed sequence is illustrated. The extended-reach whip-finishers are used for body whips on extended patterns with long wings or large hackles.

Some tools can actually hinder or slow the tying process; the whip finisher, however, is simple and fast, creating a tight, precise knot. Few hand methods can match the speed and simplicity of a mechanical whip-finisher once the procedure is learned. All mechanical whip-finishers accomplish the same operation: they wrap one thread over another so that the under-thread may eventually be tightened to produce a knot. The following right-handed whip finish sequence is standard.

Prevent the whip-finisher from turning by placing the fingers over the base of the rotating hook. Loop the thread around the notch (or crotch) as illustrated.

Connect the tip hook near the thread origin and then bring the thread up to form a tight thread angle.

While maintaining thread tension, allow the whip-finisher to rotate as illustrated. The tool will position itself correctly when the handle is held parallel to the hook shank. Note that prior to the wrapping process, the thread will form a reversed number 4 when held above the hook shank.

With the fingers on the sleeve handle, orbit the tool (clockwise when viewed down the shank at the hook eye) around the head space until the appropriate number of wraps is achieved. The perpendicular thread section will overwrap the horizontal thread with each revolution.

To feed out more thread when required, position the whip-finisher as illustrated, and gently rock it while pulling away from the head. To avoid slippage, the tip hook and the thread notch should be approximately the same distance from the whip knot.

To remove the tool after the knot is formed, disengage the thread from the notch while maintaining slight tension on the tip hook. With thread still engaged in the tip hook, pull excess thread away from the knot with the left hand (bobbin hand) until the tip hook stops at the whip wraps. Finally, disengage the tip hook and pull the thread taut. The pressure placed upon the whip-finisher during the whipping process determines the tightness of the whip. Trim excess thread.

Completed Whip-Finish Knot

8

FLY-TYING PROPORTIONS

The traditional fly-tying proportions included here offer an historic standard for fly-tying. Proportion is, though, primarily functional. It determines the swim or surface stance of a pattern. Additionally, proportion often imitates the form of the insect. Fly-tying proportions began early. When *Viator*, in Walton and Cotton's *The Complete Angler* (1766), noted that in London they "make the bodies of our flies both much larger and longer, so long as even almost to the very beard [barb] of the hook," *Piscator* replies that he was given such a fly and "hung it in his parlor window to laugh at." Tying proportions will always be debated, and tyers will always challenge and modify tradition. No matter what proportion is preferred, the tyer should control the materials to create the proportions desired. If proportions are not established and maintained, the fly pattern may lack that stance and symmetry so admired by tyer and trout. However, variations often occur. And some proportions—especially those of the pupa, larva, shrimp, and streamer—offer greater tying freedom. Tying proportions may be ignored for particular reasons but not through negligence or carelessness. Tying should be thoughtful as well as experimental. For special pattern designs or theories, proportion modification can be fascinating.

Although most proportion precepts emphasize material length, proportions may also include such elements as material quantity, shank location, mounting stance, and hook selection. Often the hook itself determines the proportions. Furthermore, some proportions may not be based on the fly performance or on the natural insect. J. Edson Leonard attempted to provide practical functionality to pattern design when he popularized "the ideal float line" in *Flies* (1960). He depicted the dry fly floating on its tail and hackle tips with the hook barely brushing the surface. Theoretically, the hook pendulum cocks the wings up and the hook point down, but the tail

The Theoretical Float Line

The dry fly's tail and hackles provide buoyancy along the float line.

and hackle proportions prevent the hook from touching the water surface. In actual practice, of course, a dry fly quickly penetrates the surface with portions of the hook, body, tail, and hackle. So that the wings appear to emerge from the middle of the hackle, dry flies may have an equal number of hackle wraps both fore and aft of the wings.

The following proportions are based on traditional concepts. Fly-tying proportions, moreover, may further vary according to the individual tyer and region. As Ralph Waldo Emerson once declared, "A foolish consistency is the hobgoblin of little minds." The hook shank begins directly behind the hook eye and travels to a point directly above the rear of the barb. The hook bend usually begins at the rear of the shank and terminates at the beginning of the hook spear. Not all tyers include the head space in the shank length.

Often tail length is shank length. A slightly longer tail (such as one based on the total hook length rather than the shank length) may increase the delicacy of design. Hook length is the distance between the total limits of hook bend and eye. Hook gap (or gape) is the distance between the hook point and shank. The number of ribbing wraps depends on ribbing width and hook length. It is usually five wraps on standard length hooks.

"There is a set convention amongst Scotch fly-tyers that all ribbing on the bodies of trout and salmon flies be composed of *five* turns—no more, no less. Most of the English and some of the American tyers adhere to the rule of five; however, it does not seem to apply in tying the bodies of bucktail and streamer flies." (William B. Sturgis, *Fly Tying*, 1940)

Insects have ten abdominal segments, twice the number of ribbing wraps, with the number reduced in some insect groups.

Many American tyers wrap the dry hackle dull or concave side forward toward the hook eye, and wet-fly hackles dull or concave side toward the body and bend. In the dry fly, this spreads the barbs forward for better support. In the wet fly, the barbs encapsulate the body with an umbrella, perhaps mimicking the transparent case of nymphs and larvae. To prevent trapping the front hackle barbs of a dry fly, William B. Sturgis and Eric Taverner, in *New Lines for Fly-Fishers* (1946), recommend wrapping the hackle with the outside (the shiny or convex side) toward the eye. Wrapped in this manner, the barbs bend back, away from the subsequent turns. "Be sure, when the hackle is raised away from the hook preparatory to winding that the shiny side is facing toward the eye of the hook. Unless this is done it is hard to prevent a few fibres from being folded in." Modern genetic hackles, especially the smaller sizes, often lack the distinct barb curvature. Some hackles may be mounted and wrapped with either side forward.

The following illustrations indicate conventional and alternative proportions. In hook orientation, the front of the shank is at the eye and the rear is at the shank bend. Although this section extends beyond basic needs, it includes all proportions for completeness and references.

THE TRADITIONAL DRY FLY

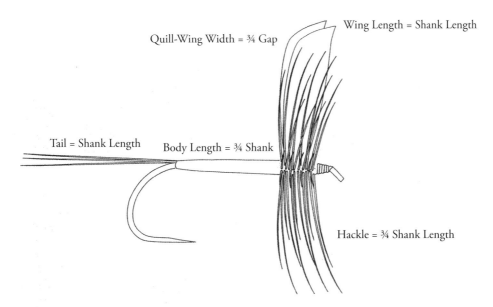

Quill-Wing Width = ¾ Gap

Wing Length = Shank Length

Tail = Shank Length

Body Length = ¾ Shank

Hackle = ¾ Shank Length

The Traditional Quill-Wing Dry Fly

Tail: Hackle-barb tails equal hook shank length or a 2½ hook gap. William B. Sturgis recommends that five or six hackle barbs are usually sufficient. However, much depends on the water flow. Some tyers select tail length slightly proud of the shank length. Dun tails may equal 1¼ shank length, and the longer spinner tails may equal 1¾ shank length. The tail is usually mounted on the shank directly above the rear of the barb. The initial body wraps conceal the tail binding.

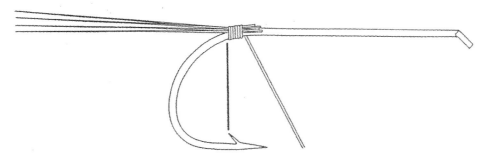

Standard Tail Mount Point

The tail mount point may have derived from tying salmon-fly patterns. James O'Gorman, when tying salmon patterns, began the tag directly above the barb. "Then opposite the beard [the barb] of the hook, put on the tail" (*The Practice of Angling*, 1845).

Body: The traditionally tapered body begins on the shank directly above the rear of the barb and ends behind the wings or hackle. Body length equals ¾ shank length (Eric Leiser, *The Book of Patterns*, 1987).

Wing: The traditional quill-wing length equals hook shank or 2 times hook gap. Maximum wing length equals total hook length. Quill-wing width may equal ¾ hook gap. Wing set begins in the front ⅕ or ¼ of the hook shank. Barb and hackle wing equals hook shank.

Hackle: Hackle equals ¾ hook shank length or 1½ to 2 times hook gap. Some tyers wrap as many turns in back of the wings as in front of the wings; hence, the wings emerge from the center of the hackle cluster. "The standard, average fibre-length suited for any given size of trout hook to be used for a dry fly is one and a half times the gape of the hook, *i.e.*, one and a half times the distance measured directly across from the point to the shank of the hook. Hackles selected for wet flies are a little longer in the fibre" (William B. Sturgis and Eric Taverner, *New Lines for Fly Fishers*, 1946).

THE CATSKILL DRY FLY

The Catskill Dry Fly

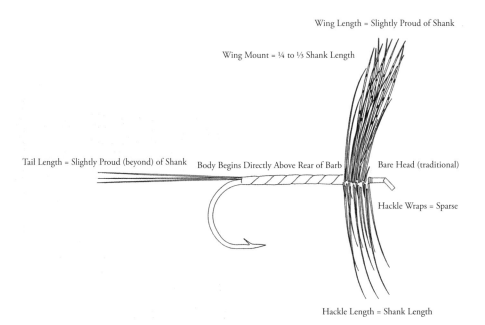

Tail: Sparse tail slightly longer than hook shank.

Body: Body begins on hook shank somewhere above rear of barb and hook point.

Wing: Slightly longer than shank length and sometimes moderately canted forward, mounted ¼ to ⅓ shank length behind the eye. *Note: Catskill patterns may be tied in traditional dry-fly proportions.*

Hackle: A few sparse wraps of stiff cock hackle, often blue dun or ginger.

Neck: A distinct bare neck about one eye-length (or less) from the hook eye. Minimal thread wraps form a modest head. The bare neck may not appear on modern commercial patterns. Originally, the bare neck allowed space for the gut jam knot. The head is traditionally sparsely wrapped. Elsie Darbee once said that anything beyond two head wraps is superfluous. Exactly what the distinctive features of this graceful American style were and who created them is still debated. According to Harry Darbee, Roy Steenrod was perhaps the tyer most accountable for passing on the distinctive features of the Catskill style. Darbee inventories those various features:

1. A generous hook, typically a size 12, perfect bend.
2. A particularly slender and sparse body, usually spun fur or stripped peacock herl.
3. A divided wing often made from the mottled barbs of a wood duck flank feather.
4. A few sparse turns of an extremely stiff, glassy cock hackle, mostly blue dun or ginger.
5. The wings and hackle set back from the eye of the hook leaving "a clean neck at the expense of a slightly shorted body." The hackle moves closer to the balance point of the pattern so that "the fly rides over broken, turbulent waters like a coast guard lifeboat, so nearly balanced that often the tail of hackle whisks (originally a little curlicue of several wood duck barbules [*sic*]) doesn't touch the water at all" (Harry Darbee with Austin Mac Francis, *Catskill Flytier*, 1977).

THE THORAX-WING DUN (Marinaro)

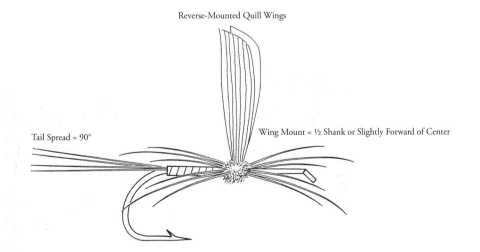

Reverse-Mounted Quill Wings

The Thorax-Wing Dun

Tail Spread = 90°

Wing Mount = ½ Shank or Slightly Forward of Center

Tail: Tail, split at right angles to shank, equals shank length. Casting invariably reduces the angle. Vincent Marinaro used one tail barb per side on hook size 22 and 24, two barbs per side on sizes 16 and 14. A turn or two of thread behind the tail barbs and a drop of cement at the base secures the angles. For maximum support, the tails mount 90° from each other.

Body: No body, only a small thoracic dubbing ball at the wing base. The thoracic ball anchors the figure eight turns of hackle.

Wing: Wings mounted at shank center (Marinaro) or slightly forward of shank center. Compare the Catskill-style wing-mount point. The thoracic wing may also occur as far forward as ¼ hook shank. Marinaro reverse-mounted quill wings for greater durability (Vincent Marinaro, *A Modern Dry-Fly Code*, 1970).

Hackle: When mounted, the hackle barbs should cloak the bottom of the hook. Wrap hackle on the thoracic ball with three crossing turns (figure eights).

THE COMPARA-DUN (Caucci and Nastasi)

The Compara-Dun

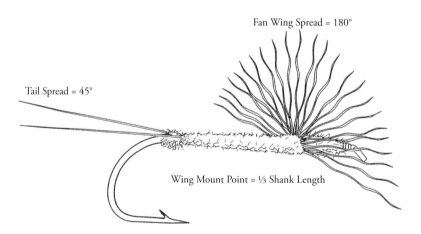

Fan Wing Spread = 180°

Tail Spread = 45°

Wing Mount Point = ⅓ Shank Length

Tail: Stiff hackle barbs tied outrigger, divided by a small dubbing ball.

Body: To support wings, dubbed body continues to wing front.

Wing: Mount wing ⅓ shank length behind eye. Hair wing fans or radiates 180° on each side to support the pattern on the surface (Al Caucci and Bob Nastasi, *Hatches II*, 1986).

THE HAIR-WING DRY FLY

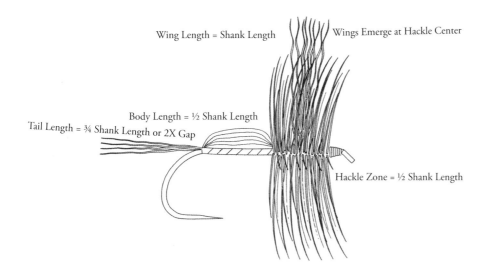

Wing Length = Shank Length   Wings Emerge at Hackle Center

Body Length = ½ Shank Length

Tail Length = ¾ Shank Length or 2X Gap

Hackle Zone = ½ Shank Length

The Hair-Wing Dry Fly: The Humpy

Tail: Hair or hackle-barb tail equals ¾ shank length or 2 times hook gap. The tail may equal the traditional tail length, especially hackle barbs. Some flared hair tails, however, may be slightly shorter. Although shorter, the flared or offset tails may actually intercept the hypothetical float line before the traditional, straight hackle-barb fibers.

Body: Body begins directly over the rear of the hook barb and terminates at wing mount point.

Wing: Wing length equals the shank length. Wing mount point may be at the front ¼ shank length, i.e., the Humpy pattern. There is a unique tying method to the traditional hair-wing Humpy. Having long, soft hairs for tying makes this pattern much easier to tie. The number of hairs will determine, to a significant extent, the total deer-hair bundle length used in tying the pattern. And the more body hairs that are used, the wider the body bends will be; hence, more length will be required for those bends at the rear and at the wing base. Fewer hairs, of course, bend more abruptly. The length of the deer hair will constitute the underbody, the overbody, and the wings. Therefore, the correct amount and length of the hair bundle are critical.

Hackle: Hackle barb length equals ¾ shank length. A dry-fly hackle with multiple wraps may occupy ½ of the total shank length.

THE FOLDED-WING WET FLY

The Woodcock and Harelug, an elegant-winged Tummel, circa 1890.

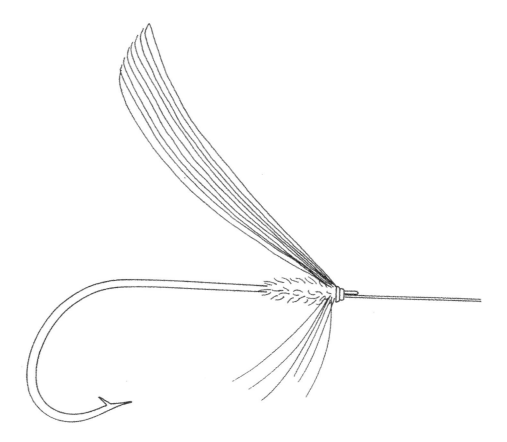

Tail: The tail equals 1½ shank length, or tail extends to rear extremity of the overwing. The tail should not "exceed a total length of more than twice the gape of the hook, and preferable [sic] not more than one and a half" (William B. Sturgis and Eric Taverner, *New Lines for Fly-Fishers*, 1946). On some patterns, tail length may equal shank length.

Body: Body begins directly above the rear of the barb and ends at the rear of the hackle mount point. Body length may also conform to Scottish tying tradition (W. H. Lawrie, *Scottish Trout Flies*, 1966). The rationale behind the abbreviated body and naked hook shank is based on sink rate. Evidently, the Clyde fishermen required quicker sinking patterns than those required for the larger Tweed, while the early Tummel anglers went for instantaneous sink. The naked shank section defines the submergibility and the rate of river flow. The hook itself is the sinker. Since these traditional wets—or teams of wets—are fished upstream in fast water, the drifts are short. Rapid and frequent false casting would dry a fuller fly pattern, delaying the sink. The naked shank, however, absorbs no water and sinks the pattern quickly. Fast waters gave trout scant scrutiny of a passing pattern. In such waters, perhaps, thick and naked shanks made no difference. These Scotch wets require a pinch of dubbing and a pile of skill.

Tweed Style: Body ends midway above hook point and hook barb.

Clyde Style: Body ends mid-shank.

Tummel Style: Body ends at front ¼ shank.

Wings: Quill-wing length varies. Wing length may be "just proud [beyond] of the hook bend," equal to the shank length, or 1¼ to 1½ shank length. Wet-fly wing width is approximately ¾ hook gap. Wing-mount point, slightly beyond a head length from the eye, is forward of the dry-fly wing-mount point. "The length of wings made from slips of web, cut or torn from the primary or from secondary feathers, is in most flies equal to that of the hook" (William B. Sturgis and Eric Taverner, *New Lines for Fly-Fishers*,1946). The following illustration depicts the so-called sedge-mount wings that partially enclose the body on each side.

The Quill-Wing Wet

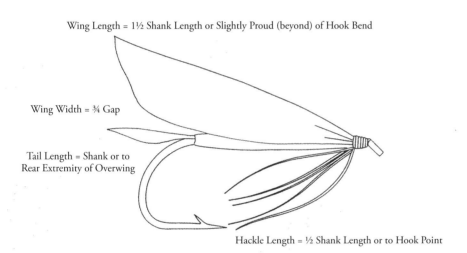

Wing Length = 1½ Shank Length or Slightly Proud (beyond) of Hook Bend

Wing Width = ¾ Gap

Tail Length = Shank or to
Rear Extremity of Overwing

Hackle Length = ½ Shank Length or to Hook Point

Wings may be mounted, after hackling, directly on top of the shank. Although some wet patterns may imitate ovipositing insects with extended wings, Sturgis asserts that "the wings of the wet fly are . . . *immature* and lie closely along the body" (*Fly-Tying*, 1940). E. M. Tod, in *Wet-Fly Fishing* (1914), claims that "the wings of a [wet] fly should never be longer than the hook" and tails, if included, should match the design—sparse and moderately long. Folded wings may be mounted slanting back (downstream wet), erect (upstream wet), or forward (upstream wet). The forward wing, and perhaps even the up wing, may quiver or tremble seductively in the current.

Hackle: The soft-hackle barbs may extend to the hook point, may equal hook gap, or may equal ½ hook-shank length. Sturgis and Taverner, in *New Lines for Fly-Fishers*, recommend that "hackles selected for wet flies are a little longer [than 1½ times the hook gap] in the fibre."

THE SOFT-HACKLE FLY

The Tweed-Style Soft-Hackle Fly

Tweed Body Length = Shank Length

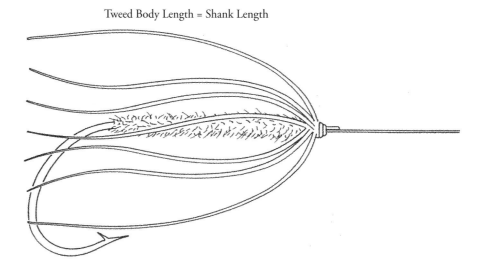

The Clyde-Style Soft-Hackle Fly

Clyde Body Length = ½ Shank Length

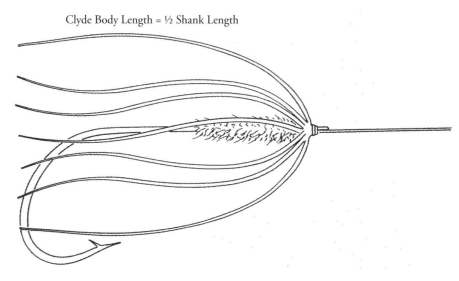

The Tummel-Style Soft-Hackle Fly

Tummel Body Length = ¼ Shank Length

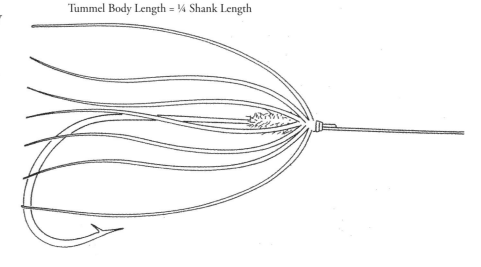

Tail: None.

Body: Body length variable. Body may imitate the standard hook-shank lengths of dry and wet patterns. The soft-hackle fly may wear Tweed, Clyde, or Tummel body lengths.

Hackle: The soft-hackle barb length equals the shank length or rear extremity of hook. Often 2 or 3 wraps of hackle only.

The Soft-Hackle with Thorax

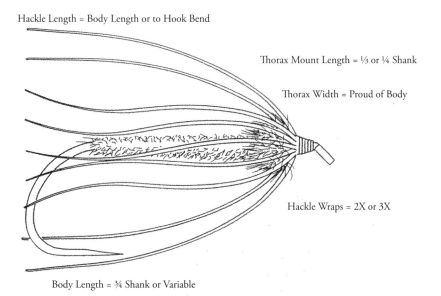

Hackle Length = Body Length or to Hook Bend

Thorax Mount Length = ⅓ or ¼ Shank

Thorax Width = Proud of Body

Hackle Wraps = 2X or 3X

Body Length = ¾ Shank or Variable

Thorax: Traditionally none. According to Sylvester Nemes in *The Soft-Hackled Fly* (1975), the addition of the thorax was a later development. If present, the thoracic segment (slightly fuller than the body to encourage the hackle barbs to spread and pulsate during the retrieve) is approximately ⅓ to ¼ hook-shank length. Nemes also notes that the term "soft hackle" first appeared in E. M. Tod's *Wet-Fly Fishing* (1914): "The only objection to the soft hackle that I can see, is, that it does not last long…"

THE PARACHUTE DRY FLY

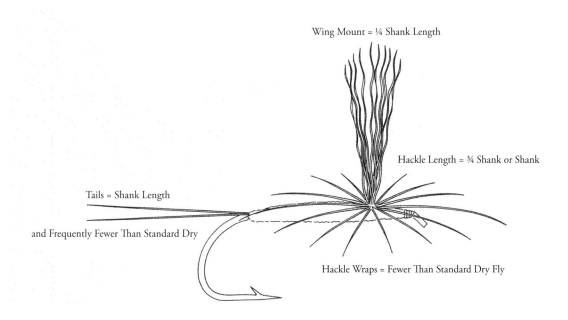

Wing Mount = ¼ Shank Length

Hackle Length = ¾ Shank or Shank

Tails = Shank Length

and Frequently Fewer Than Standard Dry

Hackle Wraps = Fewer Than Standard Dry Fly

Tail: Standard shank length.

Wing: Wing mounting point is ¼ shank length from hook eye (Dick Talleur, *The Versatile Fly Tyer*, 1990) at standard wing mount point, approximately 2 or 3 hook-eye lengths behind the eye. Wing materials include calf tail, calf-body hair, goat hair, and various synthetic yarns.

Hackle: For increased flotation, hackle barbs may be slightly longer than the standard ¾ hook-shank length. Because of increased floatation of longer horizontal barbs, some tyers use fewer hackle wraps.

NO-HACKLE DUN

(Swisher and Richards)

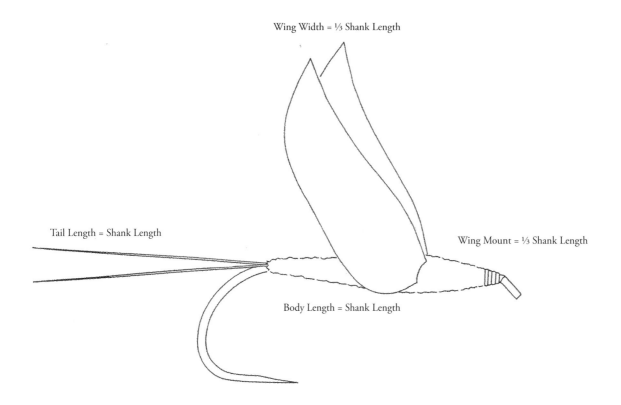

Wing Width = ⅓ Shank Length

Tail Length = Shank Length

Wing Mount = ⅓ Shank Length

Body Length = Shank Length

Tail: Tail, split 45° with dubbing ball, equals shank length.

Body: Body equals shank length.

Wing: Wing length equals shank length. Wing width equals approximately ⅓ shank length. Wing mount point equals ⅓ shank. The lower edge of the wing acts like an outrigger supporting the pattern. (Doug Swisher and Carl Richards, *Selective Trout*, 1971).

HEN-SPINNER DRY FLY

(Swisher and Richards)

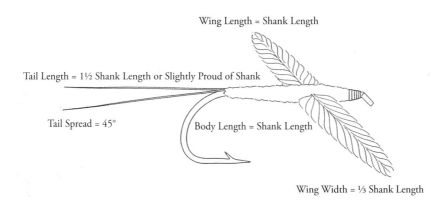

Wing Length = Shank Length

Tail Length = 1½ Shank Length or Slightly Proud of Shank

Tail Spread = 45°

Body Length = Shank Length

Wing Width = ⅓ Shank Length

Tail: Tail equals 1½ shank length. Tail split angle equals 45°.
Body: Body equals shank length.
Wing: Wing length equals shank length. Wing width equals approximately ⅓ shank length (Swisher and Richards, 1971).

THE STREAMER

The Gray Ghost: In creating the Gray Ghost, Carrie Stevens (1882–1970) glued the cheek-shoulder wing assembly together for later attachment to the rest of the fly. Mike Martinek, a nationally recognized streamer scholar, ascribes this assembly to her vocation as a milliner— building and gluing feather combinations to hats and hatbands.

Streamer proportions may vary significantly by tyer and region. Various streamer types encourage different proportions. There are damp streamers (muddlers), marabou streamers, bucktail streamers, hackle streamers, miniature streamers (dace patterns), pulsating splayed-wing streamers (Northwest Spruce-fly streamers), and saltwater streamers. Proportions may be partly based on the aquatic creature or forage fish imitated. To prevent short strikes, the tail may be shorter than ⅓ shank length and the over-wing may extend only to the bend. "The tail of a streamer fly on a regular length hook should be approximately the length of the hook shank." (A. J. McClane, *McClane's Standard Fishing Encyclopedia*, 1965).

The Streamer

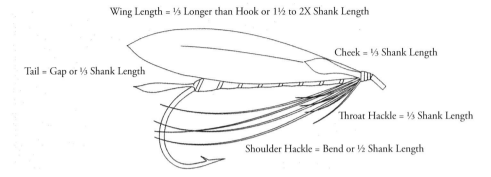

Tail: The tail is variable. If present, the tail equals hook gap, ⅓ shank length, or length of hook shank.

Body: The body, usually ribbed, equals shank length and terminates directly above the rear of the barb. Ribbing turns are variable, depending on shank length and ribbing width. Ribbing width and number of wraps are based on the particular hook. Mustad 9575 (forged Limerick, ½″ longer than regular) is a standard streamer hook. Streamer hooks also include Mustad 33957, Mustad 9674, and Thundercreek style Mustad 36620.

Cheek: If present, cheeks, such as jungle-cock eyes, extend ⅓ shank length from head.

Wing: Wings (such as saddle or schlappen feathers) are ⅓ longer than hook length or 1½ (John Merwin, *Stillwater Trout*, 1980) to 2 times longer than shank length. Hair wing should extend beyond the hook bend equal to the gap of the particular hook (William B. Sturgis, *Fly-Tying*, 1940). To prevent fouling or wrapping around the hook bend, an overwing (feather or bucktail) may extend only to the hook bend. The overwing may extend beyond the bend on trolled streamers that are not cast. Trolled streamers may also have an added stinger tail hook to pick up fish that nip at the tail (John Merwin). "The main difference between the 'Eastern' and 'Western' streamer is the angle at which the wing is set—The Eastern method dresses the wing low over the body of the fly, while the Western-style streamer wing is set at an approximate 40-degree angle above the body" (A. J. McClane, *McClane's Standard Fishing Encyclopedia*, 1965). Contemporary Western streamer wings may also match the Eastern wing set.

Shoulder Hackle: When wrapped, the shoulder hackle points just touch the hook bend or extend ½ shank length. Shoulder hackle may also equal ⅔ overwing length (John Merwin).

Throat Hackle: Throat hackle (the beard) equals 1½ gap (John Merwin) or ⅓ shank length from the head. On trolling patterns, the throat hackle may extend to the hook bend or wing extremity.

THE LARVA, PUPA, AND SHRIMP

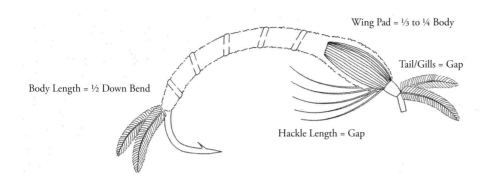

Wing Pad = ⅓ to ¼ Body

Tail/Gills = Gap

Hackle Length = Gap

Body Length = ½ Down Bend

The Larva and Pupa

Like streamer and nymph proportions, larva, pupa, and shrimp proportions are variable.

Tail: Short tail or gills, approximately equal to hook gap.

Body: Body length may vary depending on the particular hook bend. With a York or round-bend hook, the body generally extends halfway down the bend to take advantage of the circular form.

Wing pad: If present, the wing pad is ¼ to ⅓ body length.

Hackle legs: Leg hackle equals hook gap.

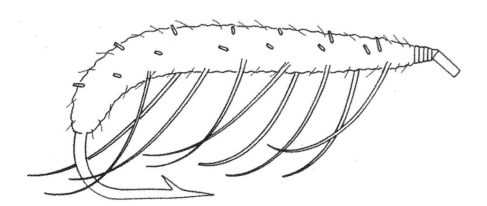

The Skues-Style Shrimp

Note: *Larva and shrimp patterns often vary in proportions depending on the natural and the hook shape.* Some tyers use the standard nymph proportions for larva and shrimp. Tyers also believe that shrimp patterns should be tied on straight-shanked hooks, using ½ of the bend for body curvature. "Body—Seal's fur mixed with pale orange and olive, tied to below the bend of the hook to suggest the curve of the shrimp's back" (G.E.M. Skues, *Side-Lights & Reflections*, undated).

THE NYMPH

The Nymph

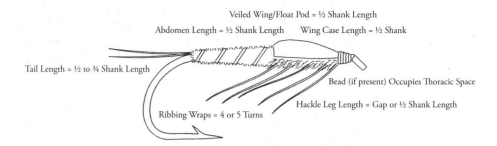

Veiled Wing/Float Pod = ½ Shank Length
Abdomen Length = ½ Shank Length   Wing Case Length = ½ Shank
Tail Length = ½ to ¾ Shank Length
Bead (if present) Occupies Thoracic Space
Hackle Leg Length = Gap or ½ Shank Length
Ribbing Wraps = 4 or 5 Turns

Proportions: Nymph proportions vary depending on the insect imitated or the whims of the tyer.

Tail: Tail equals ½ hook shank. Stonefly tail equals ¾ hook shank (William B. Sturgis, *Fly Tying*, 1940).

Body: Abdomen equals ½ hook shank. Head and thorax equal ½ hook shank. Head and thorax on natural stonefly and mayfly nymphs equal approximately ½ their total respective body lengths.

Ribbing: Four or five equally spaced turns. Total ribbing wraps depend on shank length, especially extended-shank lengths.

Wing case: Wing case equals thorax (½ shank length) minus the head space.

Hackle legs: Hackle equals hook gap or ½ hook shank.

THE FLOATING EMERGER

The Floating Emerger

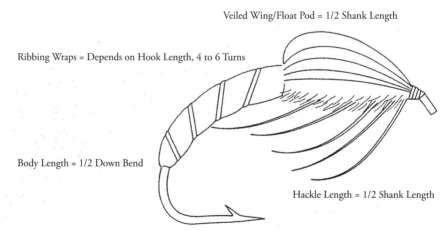

Veiled Wing/Float Pod = 1/2 Shank Length
Ribbing Wraps = Depends on Hook Length, 4 to 6 Turns
Body Length = 1/2 Down Bend
Hackle Length = 1/2 Shank Length

When tied on standard hooks, floating emergers usually assume the proportions of a dry fly. When tied on circular hooks, floating emergers usually adopt the proportions of a pupa or larva. To support the pattern, the float pod or veiled wings may be ½ shank length. The hackle legs of an emerging dun pattern should be "not more than two-thirds the length of the body" (Doug Swisher and Carl Richards, *Emergers*, 1991). Swisher and Richards also advocated the shuck, if present, to be ½ shank length. This assumes that half of the insect is still attached. Shank-length shucks may also be used for dry-fly emergers.

THE SALMON FLY: NOMENCLATURE, PROPORTIONS, AND TYPES

Trout fishers may wish a description of all pattern proportions, including the salmon fly. Salmon fly nomenclature is variable. Past and present tyers often tangle the terms for side and cheek feathers or designate one of them shoulder feathers. Perhaps the earliest and most universal approach appears in T. E. Pryce-Tannatt's *How to Dress Salmon Flies* (1914). The traditional fully-dressed salmon fly, such as the Jock Scott, has a built-wing and jointed-floss body. Much of the grace of a salmon fly lies in the wing and body work. The wing architecture may consist of three sections (strip, upper wing, and under wing) covered by three feathers (overwing, side, and cheek). Sometimes the overwing is omitted, and sometimes the wing widths are regular—main wing is ½ hook gap, outer wing is ½ main wing width, and the roof or upper wing is ½ the width of the outer wing. All feathers should have the correct arc and length. The soft, sheathy feathers and fibers should allow the various under-colors to show through. More for the historian than the modern angler, all references, unless otherwise indicated, are to Pryce-Tannatt's *How to Dress Salmon Flies* (1914). For historic completeness only, the following includes some rare or endangered materials. *Note: Modern substitutes are now used in place of restricted materials, and most modern patterns are often severely truncated or significantly simplified.*

The Fully-Dressed Salmon Fly

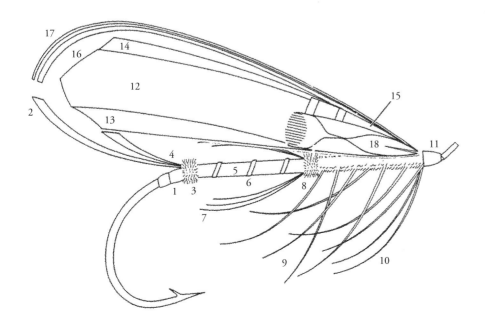

COMPOSITE SALMON-FLY NOMENCLATURE

1. *Tag* is the first dressed section, which consists of 2 or 3 turns directly above the barb. The tag may be divided into two sections, such as silver twist and light blue silk or gold twist and light orange silk. The second section of the tag, which has been called the *tip*, is equal to the length of the barb and directly above it. Tag materials include tinsel, wire, wool, fur, and floss.

2. *Tail* length is usually 1½ hook gap. Traditionally, tail materials include golden pheasant crest, Indian crow, blue chatterer, blue kingfisher, teal, or wood duck. Other feathers may be combined with the tail, such as a golden pheasant tippet, red-dyed breast feather, cock of the rock, and red ibis.

3. *Butt* is 3 or 4 wraps depending on the particular pattern. Butt materials include ostrich or peacock herl, yarn, or dubbing.

4. *Tail Topping* (sometimes called tag) is ½ tail length. Compound tails have "either a feather laid above the topping or tied on each side of the topping, forming thereby cheeks to the tail" (Eric Taverner, *Fly Tying for Salmon*, 1942). Tail topping may be hackle, herl, floss, or complete feathers.

5. *Body Length* is dependent on style:
    a. Standard length—the tag is directly above the barb.
    b. Low-water length—the tag mounts at midshank.
    c. Extended low-water length—the tag mounts ⅔ down the shank from the hook eye.
    d. If the tag mounts in the middle, the tail and hackle length should be about ¾ hook gap. If the tag mounts ⅔ down the shank, the tail and hackle should equal 1 hook gap. The wing tips always stand directly inside the tail tip. Silk and tinsel bodies are often jointed. Body materials include flat and oval tinsel, dubbing, chenille, floss, fur, and peacock or ostrich herl.

6. Traditional *ribbing* is 5 shank spirals only. Some of the earlier patterns used 3 to 4 spirals for each body section. Poul Jorgensen advocates 5 turns for a complete shank length, and on bodies broken up by butts, from 2 to 5 turns depending on the body-section length. Jorgensen also suggests a possible rationale for 5 turns. "If there were more than five turns of tinsel, the hackle would be too dense and thus adversely affect the performance of the fly" (Poul Jorgensen, *Salmon Flies*, 1978). "In flies ribbed with flat tinsel and possessing a body hackle, twist is used as well, and is wound behind the tinsel as a protection to the hackle" (T. E. Tannatt, *How to Dress Salmon Flies*, 1914).

7. *Trailers* or *joint trailers*, also called *veiling*, usually equal the length between the joints. Materials include Indian crow, toucan breast feathers, or floss.

8. The *joint* occurs directly at the mid-shank point. Joints may also occur anywhere on the shank. Materials are same as a butt.

9. *Palmered hackle* length at mount point equals hook gap. Various wet hackles create palmered hackles, also called *body* or *ribbing hackle*. Throat hackles may be totally different from the palmered hackle. Pryce-Tannatt regards the tail coverts as an exception both in character and mounting manner.

10. *Throat* or *beard* should be slightly longer than the hackle barbs or 1½ the particular hook gap. Traditional body hackles derive from teal, jay, and guinea fowl.

11. *Head* space equals the eye length of the particular hook.

12. *Main wing* is slightly short of the tail tip, and the width should be about ½ hook gap. Main wings include various natural and dyed strip or married feathers. Pryce-Tannatt classifies salmon flies according to their wing structure: ordinary or simple strip wings, whole feather wings, mixed wings, built wings, topping wings, and herl wings.

13. *Under wing* matches the length and taper of the main wing. The under-wing is often made with tippet strands, turkey panels, or jungle cock feathers.

14. *Upper wing strip* or *roof* matches the main wing length and is "normally half the width of the outer wing unless otherwise specified," according to *Salmon Flies* (1978), Poul Jorgensen. On some patterns, an *outer wing* sits on the outside and in the middle of the main wing. The outer wing is ½ the width of the main wing. Upper wing materials include brown mallard shoulder or bronze mallard.

15. *Side feather* or *shoulder feather*, located on the outside of the main wing, is usually ⅓ to ½ the main wing length and other feathers, often longer. Pryce-Tannatt notes that the side feather may extend as far back as the butt. Side feathers include jungle cock, starling, teal, or black-barred wood duck.

16. *Topping*, which follows the outer perimeter and can with the tail tip. According to Pryce-Tannatt, the topping is invariably from the golden pheasant's crest and creates "a glistening transparence to the upper edge of the wings," while keeping them together.

17. *Horns*, if present, normally extend to the end of the wing. Traditionally, single strands of the tail feather of the macaw are used. Pryce-Tannatt claims that the horns "constitute an element of mobility in a fly, and mechanically are used in protecting brittle, delicate feathers, such as jungle cock, when the latter are as cheeks or sides."

18. The *cheek*, also called *side* or *shoulder* feathers, is usually ½ to 1 gap width in length unless otherwise stated (Jorgensen). It sits on the out-side of the side feather. "Cheeks, that is, the last pair of feathers put on close to the head" (Taverner). Cheek feathers include Indian crow, blue

chatterer, or jungle cock. Pryce-Tannatt adds that in some patterns, such as the Akroyd, the cheeks are droop mounted.

SALMON FLY TYPES

There are several types (classifications) of salmon-fly patterns based on proportions, materials, methods, and angling conditions. The traditional fly types, principally based on wing classification, include: (1) Built Wing, (2) Mixed Wing, (3) Whole-Feather Wing, (4) Simple-Strip Wing (5) Herl Wing, (6) Topping Wing, (7) Dee, (8) Spey, (9) Grub, and (10) Low Water. Other types of salmon flies not included here are hair wings, tube flies, dry flies, and Irish flies. Pryce-Tannatt defines Irish flies as "general patterns, possessing as a rule rather more wing. . . . They have a very special feature in the shape of the mallard strips partly veiling the mixed-wing underneath, and very few of them have the adornment of a topping over the wing." *Special note*: *All excerpts and descriptions are from Pryce-Tannatt's* How to Dress Salmon Flies, *1914*. He offers a consistent though somewhat dated nomenclature. The illustrated patterns were tied by tying historian Marvin Nolte, a recognized international authority on salmon flies.

The Built-Wing Salmon Fly

The Butcher, married wing and seal body

"These have as a foundation either a plain wing of paired upright strips or a whole-feather wing. Over this, 'married' fibres of several sorts of feathers are imposed in batches of two or more."

The Mixed-Wing Salmon Fly

The Gordon, married wing and floss body

"Mixed wings . . . are made up of a number of single strands of various feathers 'married' to each other in one continuous 'sheath'" Moreover, "Strictly speaking, a mixed wing is composed of a number of single strips of several different kinds of feathers. Not uncommonly these are tied on as a bunch anyhow, but usually all the fibres are carefully 'married' one to another in a certain definite order. The appearance of a carefully mixed wing gives one the impression of a Persian carpet, a conglomeration of a multitude of colours. A built-wing, on the other hand, is constructed in bolder lines, and the essential thing about it is, that instead of being tied in all at once, it is built in stages, one portion over another, but in such a manner that, like the tiles of a roof, the portions underneath are left exposed by those immediately above them. Very often the first portion is made up of broad paired strips of some feather . . . over which 'married' strips of different feathers are built, but always in such a way as to leave a portion of the first pair visible."

The Whole-Feather Wing Salmon Fly

The Durham Ranger, tippet and jungle-cock wing

Whole-feather wings "are composed of entire feathers (*e.g.,* Golden Pheasant tippet and sword feather, Jungle Cock neck) set on upright in pairs, back to back." Back to back means "the direct opposition of the under or inner surfaces, *i.e.,* the outer or 'best' surfaces showing on each side."

The Simple Strip-Wing Salmon Fly

The Blue Charm, turkey wing with teal roof

"These may be set on (a) with a slight upright inclination, or (b) more or less on a slant. The kind of feather used as well as the manner in which it is put on will influence the set of this variety of wing."

The Herl-Wing Salmon Fly

The Beauly Snow Fly, peacock herl-strand wings

Herl wings "are composed of strands or strips from either the tail or the sword feathers of the Peacock."

The Topping-Wing Salmon Fly

The Variegated Sun Fly, tricolor body and six wing toppings

"Golden Pheasant crest feathers form the entire wing."

The Dee Strip-Wing Salmon Fly

The Akroyd, white turkey-tail strip wings

The Dee Strip-Wings are:

> "A very distinct group, being peculiar in their appearance and geographical application. They originate from . . . the Aberdeenshire Dee, and are the oldest types of patterns still surviving."

According to Pryce-Tannatt, these are large, early-spring or late-summer patterns with sparse dressing and somber colours.

> They possess "the extreme mobility of hackle and wings, which impart a very life-like appearance of the fly as it works in the water."

The Spey Salmon Fly

The Purple King, bronze mallard wings, Spey hackle, and three ribs, one counter-wrapped

"The bodies are short, and have no adornments in the shape of tag, tail or butt: and are usually composed of crewels or Berlin wools of various and varying colours, put on as sparingly as possible. The ribbing tinsel is individually broad and collectively plentiful, and, as often as not, besides thread and twist, gold and silver tinsel are used on one and the same body. The hackles are long and very mobile. Both grey and black Heron hackles are used, but the hackles of a typical Spey fly are obtained from the lateral tail feathers of a certain breed of domestic fowl, known as a 'Spey-cock' [a tyer's misnomer]. The method of putting them on is contrary to the general rule, as they are tied in base first instead of tip first—*i.e.*, the longest fibres are at the tail end of the fly—and they are sometimes wound round the body in the reverse way to the tinsel, a piece of twist or fine oval tinsel being used wound on last over the hackle, to prevent it from getting torn by the fishes' teeth. As a matter of fact, the direction in which the hackle is wound will depend upon which side of it is stripped, for only one side is used, and accordingly it may go with or against the body tinsel . . . ."

The Grub Fly

The Tippet Grub, tippets wound as hackles

"These are merely glorified palmers, glorified in the sense that they are as a rule much larger and almost invariably more ornamented than the trouting editions."

According to Pryce-Tannatt, grubs are used in warm weather and resemble, though remotely, the "caterpillars prevalent in summer and early autumn."

The Small Summer Fly (Low Water)

The Logie, yellow swan strips
faintly covered by brown
mallard strips

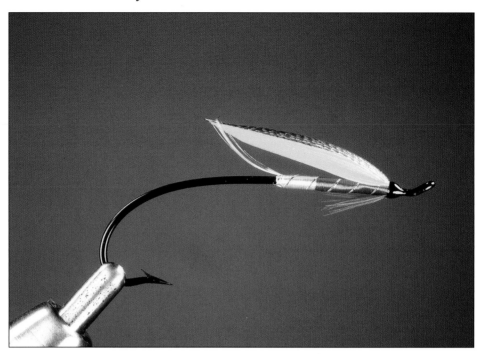

"These are . . . in the main small editions of the regular salmon flies. They
are very often dressed on small double hooks, and the materials are sparingly
used."

Pryce-Tannatt concludes that they are late-spring, summer, and early-
autumn patterns when settled weather and clear, low waters are present.

9

THE PATTERNS:
A TOUCH OF TYING

T HESE PATTERNS GATHER A SIGNIFICANT VARIETY OF BASIC TYING skills in a concise text. By blending these skills with different materials, a larger variety of patterns can be created. Thomas Barker, in *The Art of Angling* (1651), proclaimed, "Now I will shew you how to make flyes. Learn to make two flyes and make all. . . . These are the ground of all flyes." I do not claim that the following five patterns will allow you to tie all other possible patterns, but they certainly are the ground, or foundation, for many patterns. Let this be the beginning of a pleasurable pursuit.

All patterns require consideration of proportions, material selection, and threadwork. They also require the basic techniques of dubbing, winging, tailing, stacking, hackling, and more. Tie slowly and thoughtfully; after all, you will cast and fish these patterns far longer than it takes to tie them. Tying speed, if desired, can come later. Enjoy the process as much as the pattern. Here are effective dries and wets. These patterns require a modicum of skill, while others require more. Some patterns are moderately simple (The Poly-Humpy) while others may test your tying (The CDC Spent Spinner). The CDC Spent Spinner also includes directions for creating wing burners. The instructional detail is comprehensive enough so that even the more complex patterns should be clear. Nevertheless, these patterns are best done with an instructor. No tyer should become lost in a maze of methods and materials. In any case, these patterns teach in fine detail the methods for many other patterns. They help to develop fine motor skills, spatial considerations, color harmony, and proportioning. Tying teaches frugality of materials and methods. *A complex pattern is merely a series of simple wraps.* For improvement, tie two or more of the same pattern each session. These patterns are not without difficulties. Each pattern has its challenge: the Poly-Humpy (proportions), the Woolly Bugger (spun body), the Damsel Nymph (split thread), the Panel Wing (matched wings), the BWO Puff Dun, and the CDC Spent Spinner (burnt wings). A few may require substitute materials, and some will require special tools and techniques, but all will improve your proficiency.

Proportion is important, but it does not demand that all patterns must conform to an absolute paradigm. Creative tyers will experiment and change patterns. The best tying variations, nevertheless, are those with a purpose or rationale for that change. At the outset, attention should be given to the twelve basic tying faults:

1. Improper hook mounting. Traditionally, the vise should firmly grip the hook heel while exposing the spear and barb. The hook shank should be horizontal.

2. Improper proportioning of tail, wings, and hackle. Consult the section of fly-tying proportions.

3. Fraying the tying thread. Avoid snagging the hook point with the tying thread.

4. Cutting the natural fiber tips of hackle, tails, and wings. Generally, such trimming is unaesthetic, unnatural, and encourages surface penetration and water absorption.

5. Failure to maintain appropriate thread tension during tying. A substantial bobbin and hackle pliers can maintain tension during tying. Do not create slack by allowing the bobbin to touch the tying table. Use a short length of tying thread between bobbin and pattern.

6. An excessive amount of thread wraps, dubbing, or other materials. Tying parsimony requires that each wrap and each fiber do its duty. For delicacy, materials should be mounted sparingly and firmly with the fewest number of wraps.

7. Cramming the components. Tyro tyers often compress the space for wings, hackle, and head. Allow sufficient tying space for each pattern component. Avoid the tendency to mount body parts slightly forward of the proper position. At first, it may be beneficial to use a fine-point felt marker to indicate the major mounting points on the hook shank for head space, tail, wing, and mid-shank prior to tying. Although the marks are covered during tying, they do offer a sense of position.

8. Uneven or stroppy stacking or mismatching of fibers, barbs, or components. Take time to properly stack and match materials before mounting.

9. Lack of appropriate materials or colors. Substitute materials are often possible, while others may not be appropriate.

10. Failure to keep the working thread advanced for the tie-off.

11. Failure to use clean materials. Some tying materials should be cleaned, which makes them more manageable and attractive. Feathers may be washed in a mild detergent, such as Woolite, and crushed chenilles and peacock eyes may be plumped by steaming. Do not, however, saturate them with steam. Completely dry all materials before tying.

12. Failure to correct an error before continuing. Wrapping in an error does not mean that it must stay. Be satisfied with each thread wrap as you travel down the hook shank. Correct faults as they occur for the best possible pattern. Do not tolerate tying mediocrity.

THE POLY-HUMPY

The Poly-Humpy, a buoyant and insectile pattern, is simple and unpretentious. It seems to imitate anything that a trout desires, including mayfly, caddis, and terrestrials. This variation on the traditional deer-hair Humpy is a humble wrap, yet effective in streams and lakes. It uses polypropylene yarn (with a specific gravity lighter than water) for underbody, overbody, and wing. Moreover, with material and color variations in tail, yarn, and hackle, a pile of delicate and practical patterns hatch. When tying any Humpy, proper body and wing proportions are paramount. Even a minor error in proportions makes a gauche Humpy. The body-wing material, the polypropylene yarn, must account for underbody, overbody, and wing length. If the tail and wing equals shank length, then the body-wing yarn will be slightly more than twice the shank length, about 2¼ shank length. Once the body loop, which constitutes ½ shank length, is completed, it is wrapped down and emerges ¼ shank length from the hook eye to form the wing. It may then be trimmed to proper wing length.

The underbody may be dubbed or threaded down. Merely use thread color for the underbody on small patterns. Thread or dubbing may be used on size 12 and larger patterns. With a cinnamon brown yarn, a pale yellow tying thread creates contrast and an attractive underbody and head.

Hook: Standard dry-fly hook, size 16-10, Daiichi 1190BL and Tiemco 100BL, 101, or similar hook

Thread: Pale yellow, 6/0 or 3/0 Uni-thread

Body and Wing: Polypropylene yarn, various colors

Hackle: Grizzly and brown or any appropriate multicolored hackles

The Poly-Humpy Architecture

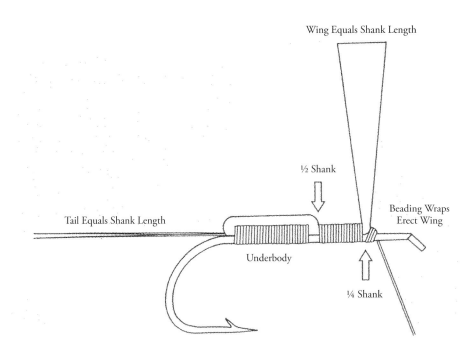

Wing Equals Shank Length

½ Shank

Tail Equals Shank Length

Beading Wraps
Erect Wing

Underbody

¼ Shank

1. Precise mounting is critical for proper proportions. For a standard tail, stack and mount a slender, stiff hackle barb bundle at mid-shank. Any straight, stiff hackle barbs will work. The vibrantly mottled *gallo de Leon* barbs are excellent. The tail should mount on the rear half of the shank and extend a full shank length beyond the hook bend.

2. Then select the appropriate color of poly yarn, approximately 3″ long. Three-ply poly yarn may be thinned for the smaller patterns. Two ply or a 1½ ply may be appropriate for smaller patterns. After thinning, mount the tip of the poly yarn at mid-shank or slightly short of mid-shank. Smoothly overwrap the mounted butt with the tying thread to create the underbody color. Spread and flatten the tying thread (with a fingernail) to create the underbody color.

Tying The Poly-Humpy

3. Now fold the yarn forward to mid-shank and secure. Then overwrap the yarn to ¼ shank length from the hook eye, and erect the yarn (to become the wings) with a thread bead in front.

4. *Note that the hackle or hackles fill the front half of the shank.* Select and mount the hackles. For a clean head, strip the barbs from the hackle tip first so that when whipping off, the thread captures only the hackle stem. This avoids trimming the trapped hackle barbs at the head. Wrap the hackle as many times behind the wings as in front of the wings. For large patterns, this may require an additional forward hackle, mounted, wrapped, and whip-finished.

5. For a standard shank-length wing, fold the wing yarn beyond the rear extremity of the hook or slightly proud of (beyond) the hook bend and trim, taking care to avoid cutting any hackle barbs. Do not merely trim the wing at the end of the hook shank. Because the wings are mounted ¼ shank length from the hook eye, the wings should be trimmed ¼ shank length beyond the shank. This creates shank-length wings. Otherwise the wings may be trimmed to any desired length. Finally, fluff the wing.

THE SPUN WOOLLY BUGGER

The original Woolly Bugger is usually credited to Russell Blessing of Pennsylvania, dating about 1967. It is, fundamentally, a Woolly Worm with a marabou tail. And the woolly worm or palmer worm dates back to the days of Isaac Walton and Charles Cotton of the mid-17th Century. This ancient pattern originally imitated "the rough and woolly caterpillar sometimes called 'wool-beds'" (James Chetham's *The Angler's Vade Mecum,* 1689). A palmer hackle is a forward spiraling or running hackle lapped around the hook shank to resemble the palmer worm, a hairy caterpillar. Since then, it has evolved into a plethora of patterns. The modern Woolly Bugger has as many variations as there are tyers. Some patterns wear beads for sink, some add flash for attraction, and some even have dangling rubber legs. And all catch fish. The tying materials may be basic: a black marabou tail, an olive chenille body, and a grizzly palmer. Select materials with complementary colors or those materials that meld into an attractive pattern. The popular Woolly Bugger is often the first pattern taught and tied. Although it frequently ranks low as an imitative pattern, it ranks high in productivity. This durable, buried-stem method conceals the hackle stem within the chenille body, where it is less likely to be torn by trout teeth.

Hook: Tiemco 300, 5262 and 5263, size 12 to 6, Daiichi 1760 and the 1720, or similar hooks. The Daiichi 1720, 3X long accepts Spirit River's Brite Bead, Real Gold in size 5/32. A firm shove should slide the bead over a hook barb.

Thread: 3/0 thread to match or contrast with body color.

Tail: Marabou strands, often with added flash. Perhaps tail length should be ¾ hook length or hook length. Some commercial patterns have protracted tails that may generate short strikes. Try to select marabou strands that are fluffy rather than the thin, thread-like strands. The plump tail becomes slender and mobile when wet. To prevent a butt bump and uneven body, extend the marabou base fully along the hook shank to the bead.

Hackle: Some are tied with a soft, webby saddle hackle for increased barb motion; others are tied with a stiffer, dry saddle hackle. Soft hackle may merely cling to the chenille body rather than extend. The extended hackle barb length should match the hook gap or beyond.

Flash: Any type of sparse, fine flash strands, such as Flashabou, Flashabou Mirage, or crinkled Krystal Flash. Match the flash strand colors to the pattern. Flash strands, trapped by the standard palmer hackle, may also be added to the sides or top of the body. This spun-body, however, does not allow longitudinal strands laid along the side. Instead, use chenille with added flash if desired.

Bead: Bright, double-drilled gold or silver beads, such as Spirit River's "Brite Beads, real gold." Check to make certain that the bead cannot slip past the hook eye.

Body: Variegated chenilles with integrated flash are desirable, such as Speckled Crystal Chenille. Packaging often compresses or flattens chenille: to plump chenille, pass a length of chenille through steam. Dry before tying. Other Bugger bodies are possible, such as dubbed strands and spun peacock-tail barbs. *Note: This ingenious Bugger wears a unique spun body hackle.*

Tying the Spun Woolly Bugger

1. Place the smaller hole of a double-drilled bead onto the hook point. Slide the bead over the point and barb to the hook eye. To allow bead entry, it may be necessary to pinch the barb down. The bead should not slip over the hook eye. Now, mount the thread and add a plump tail bundle of marabou above the barb. Some tyers lightly dampen the marabou strands for control. When sunk and retrieved, the plump marabou tail becomes slender and undulating. Traditionally, tail length equals shank length. Though rarely possible, the marabou should be fine and fluffy all the way to the tips.

2. Now, at the end of the chenille strand, remove ¼″ fuzz or nap to expose the twisted center threads. Avoid using a short thread-mount over the chenille thread ends: the spinning tension should not pull the chenille out. Mount the chenille by its exposed end-threads on the hook shank directly above the barb. Then firmly mount the palmer hackle by the tip directly over the chenille mount point. This places the shorter barbs at the rear and the longer barbs behind the bead at the front. To securely mount the tail flash strands, select about three or four long strands. Then figure eight them at shank middle and extend them back with an equal number of strands on each side of the tail. Trim the strands to tail length. This method firmly locks down the tail flash strands. Now, caress the hackle barbs from tip to base so that they stand at right angles to the hackle stem.

3. Next, lay the mounted hackle stem directly over the extended chenille and firmly spin both tightly together.

4. Now, spiral the spun chenille hackle as a single-body unit forward. If need be, caress the barbs back to avoid trapping them while spiraling forward. Finish the body with added thread wraps behind the bead and then separate the chenille and hackle. Trap the chenille and trim excess.

5. If desired, add two or more hackle wraps behind the bead before securing and trimming the excess. For a secure whip-finish, apply a short smear of cyanoacrylate glue gel (super glue) to the thread close to the hook shank. Finally, wrap the glued section tightly down behind the bead while forcing a firm whip-finish into the bead's rear cavity.

THE DAMSELFLY NYMPH

Dave Whitlock's *Guide to Aquatic Trout Foods* (1982) taught me the imitative value of Swiss straw. Wet Swiss has a spongy, almost gelatinous texture, similar to the natural nymph. The damsel's gills (the feather-like caudal lamellae, or paddles at the rear of the body) are well-developed and appear as an extension of the body and should be part of any damsel pattern. These nymphs swim by body whips and undulations with the gills functioning as sculling oars. No pattern can match the rippling writhes of the natural, but with a rhythmic retrieve, this pattern travels with a trouting tease. Damsel nymphs vary in color, but they usually reflect their habitat: pale olives, browns, tans, and pale yellows. The high-visibility of pale yellow, the color of this pattern, may attract trout from a distance. When transforming to the adult stage, the damsel nymph usually crawls out of the water onto plants or rocks for the final molt. Once out of the final nymphal husk, the newly hatched adult (the teneral) lacks full pigmentation and may be soft and pale yellow for the first few hours or so.

This pattern is a mild variation of the Whitlock damsel nymph. The primary differences are the eyes and the zonker sections for tail and legs. *Do not overdress this slender and sparse pattern.* Remember, this pattern swims on the retrieve so that every rod twitch translates into a wave of the banner tail. Select a medium- or heavy-wire hook for adequate sink. Weight may be added to the selected hook. Depending on size and color, this pattern may also imitate large burrowing mayfly nymphs.

Hook: Various 1X to 3X long, medium- and heavy-wire hooks, size 6 to 10, Tiemco 5262 and 200R, Daiichi 1260 (2X long, curved shank), or 1720 (3X long).

Thread: 6/0 Pale yellow.

Body: Pale yellow Swiss straw and matching dubbing.

Dubbing: Pale yellow rabbit or synthetic dubbing with or without added synthetic flash fibers.

Thorax and legs: A short, pale yellow rabbit Zonker strip.

Ribbing: Depending on hook size, medium or fine, gold oval ribbing.

Eyes: Small bird eyes (glass on wire) offer appropriate weight but are prohibitively expensive. Though lacking weight, an attractive alternative is Spirit River's Glassy Eyes, size small in various colors. Select eye color for contrast or congruency.

Tying The Damsel Nymph

1. Color match the Swiss straw, tying thread, dubbing, and rabbit fur. Mount the matched eyes. Trim the eye stems to ¾ shank length and mount them on shank top. The stem length will add some weight. Depending upon the hook size and diameter of the hook wire, the eyes should be about 1 to 2 millimeters apart. Secure and divide the eyes with figure eights, then wrap along the eye stems, returning the thread to the rear.

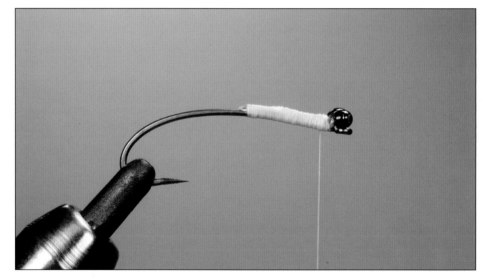

2. Mount and secure a tapered tuft of rabbit fur for the banner tail, approximately ¾ to 1 shank length.

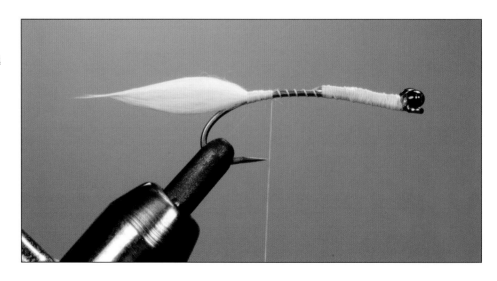

3. Before mounting the Swiss straw, fold the edges under, doubling the straw and creating a clean overbody line. Then mount the Swiss straw and oval gold ribbing. The width of the Swiss straw, which extends about halfway down on each side of the body, should be trimmed for small patterns.

4. Now, dub a slender body forward over the eye stems to the eyes.

5. Next, split the thread. Then insert a short zonker section (rabbit fur with a narrow hide-strip attached) into the waxed, split thread. Use only a meager amount of rabbit fur. Adjust the hair overlap length to ½ shank length.

6. Next, eliminate the hide strip and all guard hairs.

7. Now tightly spin the trapped zonker fur collar.

8. Wrap the spun fur behind the eyes to suggest the thorax and legs.

9. Next, firmly fold the Swiss straw forward over the abdomen and secure behind and in front of the eyes.

10. To complete the overbody, spiral the oval ribbing forward over the Swiss straw and secure behind the eyes. Trim excess ribbing. After securing the ribbing and Swiss straw, fold the Swiss Straw back between the eyes and secure with thread directly behind the eyes 2 or 3 times. If desired, the thread may be lightly dubbed for concealment. Now, trim the Swiss Straw to create the ½ body length wing pad. Finally, advance the thread to the hook eye and firmly whip-finish.

The Completed Damsel Nymph

THE PANEL-WING MAYFLY

This dry fly requires judicious material selection and wing making. By changing the thread, tails, dubbing, and hackle, the panel wing may be adapted to create various dry patterns.

Rather than the traditional rolled wing, this pattern uses two center sections from lemon barred wood duck flank feathers. A center section is sized and removed from the center of two flank feathers. Each section tip should be the same width. Although the sections may be longer than they should be, they can be mounted to proper length proportions with a soft loop. Lay one section on the other, concave side to concave side (dull side to dull side) with tips matching. The matched center sections—the panel wing—create a delicate flat wing with a clean silhouette.

Hook: Any standard dry hook, such as Daiichi 1190, Tiemco 100, or 102, size 12.

Thread: Color match the selected dubbing, 6/0 Danville, Unithread or similar.

Wing: Two lemon barred wood duck flank feathers. Small feathers are best.

Tail: Any fine, stiff, and straight hackle barbs.

Body: Fine denier synthetic or natural dubbing, such as Nature Spirit's preen oil dry dubbing.

Hackle: Any color dry hackle of appropriate barb length.

Tying the Panel-Wing Mayfly

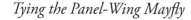

1. Begin with a thread foundation at the hook-shank wing space. Use finely spaced wraps for sufficient wing grip. *Note the tying sequence.* If the wing is mounted first, the thread can then spiral back to mount the tail and body. Before advancing the body, the thread must spiral to the base of the wings for securing the body wraps. After completing the body, the thread can then attach the hackle stem.

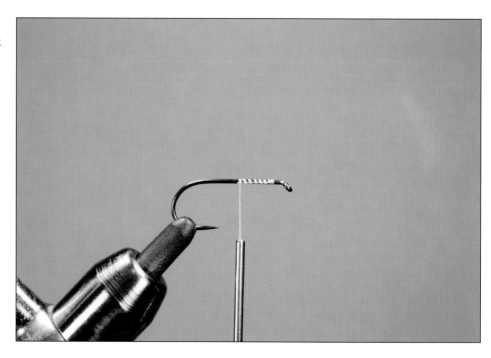

2. Next, select and stack the center sections of two wood duck flank feathers.

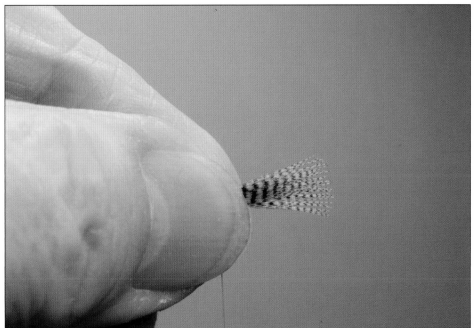

3. Now, with a soft loop firmly mount the base of the wings directly on top of the hook shank. Do not allow the feather to twist. Position the wing length so that it matches the hook shank length. The wing may be rather wide at the mount point. Merely compress the wing base and firmly stack all fibers vertically together.

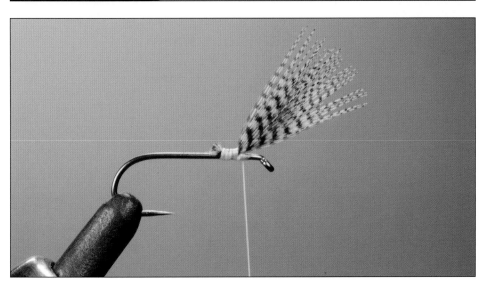

4. Over-wrap the wing base and bead in front of the wings with tightly twisted thread to erect them.

5. Then spiral the thread to the rear and mount the tail barbs.

6. Now, mount the selected dubbing and wrap the body forward to wing base. Remove any excess dubbing before continuing.

7. Firmly mount the hackle stem with slight freebore both behind and in front of the wings.

8. Finally, spiral the hackle forward with equal wraps on each side of the wing, whip-finish, and trim excess thread.

THE CDC SPENT SPINNER (A SOFT VARIANT)

William Lunn's legendary Particular, an imitation of the ubiquitous spent olive, may mimic a variety of small mayfly spent spinners. The original 1917 pattern—dressed on a small offset Limerick hook—had a stripped Rhode Island hackle stem body, medium-blue hackle point wings, four Rhode Island hackle barb tails, and a medium Rhode Island cock hackle. Although Lunn's original tie cannot be improved, this pattern is a soft offspring or variant that uses (1) shaped CDC feathers for the wings, (2) stiff, straight barbs, such as glassy *gallo de Léon* barbs for the tail, (3) spun CDC barbs for hackle, and (4) a dubbed body. John Waller Hills, in *River Keeper: The Life of William James Lunn* (1934), records that Lunn was well aware of the singular benefit of softness.

> "Trout, especially as the season gets on and they become fat and lazy, hardly open their mouths when taking a fly, either real or unreal. They draw in a thread of water, the fly with it, expelling the water through their gills and retaining the fly. Once, watching a trout being fished for on a hot day in slow water, Lunn saw it attempt to suck in the angler's artificial, but failed to get it into its mouth, as the fly did not pass its hardly opened lips." Hills found that "far too little attention is paid to the softness of fibre and general collapsibility of a fly."

The imprint of all insects produces a telltale spoor. The CDC Particular has a realistic imprint and profile in clear water. Furthermore, the fluffy CDC wing barbs trap air bubbles, creating the "star burst of light" that Brian Clark and John Goddard identify as the "first trigger" to provoke a rise. These sparkles may mimic those emanating from a spent spinner's wing.

Additionally, by changing the body, wing, and CDC colors, a myriad of small and large mayfly spents are produced. The imprint and profile of this pattern on clear water is an enticement to many reluctant trout. The CDC wings and hackle effectively float the pattern flush in the surface.

Hook: Size 18 to 10, Daiichi 1220, 1180, and 1190, Tiemco 101, or similar hook. On small hooks, this pattern does require attentiveness.

Thread: 6/0 thread matched to dubbing color.

Tail: For still or slow water, three or four *gallo de Léon* barbs or various straight, stiff hackle barbs. Heavy water may require more tail barbs.

Body: A slender dubbed body. For smaller patterns, use an ultrafine and soft dubbing, such as Nature's Spirit preen oil processed fine natural dubbing.

Wings: White or pale gray CDC feathers shaped with wing burners. Commercial wing burners may be used for this pattern. A wing burner is a metal template that holds the feather so that a flame, usually from a butane lighter, can burn the surplus, thereby forming a shaped wing. I make my wing burners from brass strips—½″ or ¼″ wide, at least 8″ long, and .032″ thick—with metal shears and a small hand grinder. Thinner strips form more easily but deform readily. Brass strips are available at many hobby shops, hardware stores, and catalogs. *Note: Always use a dust mask and protective eyewear when shaping metal.* First, draw the wing shape at the end of the brass strip and trim excess metal with metal shears. With files and grinders, take the metal down to within a couple of millimeters. A small rotary Minimite Dremel tool, mounted with ¼″, ⅜″, and ½″ sander/grinder caps or drums, works well for close shaping. Once the shape is close, fold and match the ends together. Then firmly tape the folded strip to match the ends for final shaping. Now rough cut and trim the other matched end, and bring the template down to final shape with the Dremel and a disk grinder. Water cools the metal if heated by grinding. Polish all edges with fine emery when done. Once made, the wing burner will last a lifetime of tying.

Hackle: Spun medium or light dun CDC barbs in split thread.

Tying The CDC Spent Spinner

1. First, make two matched wings. Use a wing burner to shape each CDC wing. When burning each wing, match the position and angle of the wing stems.

2. After burning, prune surplus stem length, overlap the stem bases, and place a droplet of super glue gel (cyanoacrylate glue) to join the wings before mounting.

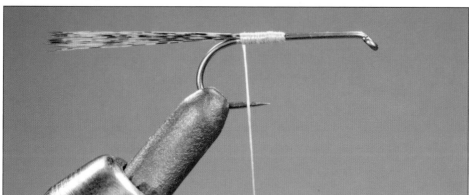

3. For the tail, stack and mount several shank-length barbs, such as *gallo de Léon* or Rhode Island cock hackle barbs. If desired, match tail barbs to the particular insect tail color. Spinners may have tails longer than their dun stage.

4. Next, mount the selected dubbing and tightly wrap a slender body.

5. After drying the wings, secure them with figure eight wraps on the hook shank. If desired, add a final bead of super glue gel to lock them down onto the hook shank.

6. After mounting the wings, flatten the thread over a fingernail and split the thread with a needle. Capture the barbs in a bulldog clip from one side of two or three stacked CDC feathers, and trim away the stems. Insert the barbs into the split thread and release the bulldog clip. Now adjust the overlap barbs to match the pattern size.

7. Next, spin thread firmly to create a CDC hackle.

8. Wrap the spun barbs over the wing base and figure eight fore and aft to create the thorax, legs, and hackle. Finally, remove any excess or skewed CDC barbs and whip-finish.

THE BWO PUFF DUN

The ubiquitous Blue-Winged Olive (BWO), a member of the genus *Baetis*, appears in ponds, chalk streams, freestones, and quiet tail waters. Hatching on waters throughout the year, BWOs are diverse and prolific. Some species even produce two or more separate broods a year. Frank Sawyer's classic Pheasant Tail Nymph and the modern Flash-Back Pheasant Tail Nymph effectively imitate many *Baetis* nymphs. Although the nymphs may be the primary prey for trout, drifting duns can also create enchantment for the dry-fly angler. The small emerging duns struggle to penetrate the surface film and often become stillborn or crippled as they drift long distances. Such behavior makes them readily available for fish. With mild modifications in color and size, this puff dun can imitate a true tribe of pond olives, iron blues, little olives, small blue duns, and, in effect, many other diminutive duns. Use one puff for the wings and one for the hackle. Depending upon the puff size, a size 14 dry hook may require more puffs. Do not, however, over-puff the pattern. Hareline Dubbin Inc. of Oregon distributes exceptional natural and dyed CDC oiler puffs that may be used for the wing or the hackle. Along with their slate grays and natural duns, their dyed colors include Blue Winged Olive, olive, pale olive, and gray olive. Check your local fishing shops. With proper CDC selection and application, this puff dun is a slender, wispy pattern for fastidious trout.

Hook: Various small hooks are appropriate. Hook sizes range from 20 to 14, most commonly from 16 to 20. Any small hook should have an adequate gap to hold fish. A slight uplift of the forward shank can increase capture. I use Daiichi 1220 (turned up foreshank), Daiichi 1100 (wide gap), Tiemco 102Y (wide gap, 1x fine), Tiemco 100BL (barbless, 1x fine, wide gap), and Tiemco 900BL (1x fine, 1x wide). Other hooks may be suitable, especially when you slightly raise (by bending) the foreshank. Although this does not increase the gap, it does create a somewhat searching spear. The raised foreshank also realistically slants the dun wings astern.

Thread: 6/0 pale olive, olive dun, or dun. At times, a dull-red thread may suggest some dun eyes.

Tails: Although *Baetis* have two tails, more fibers are usually necessary to float a pattern. Mount only the number of barbs that will float the pattern on a particular water, usually two barbs on mute ponds to six barbs on bubbling freestones.

Body: Pale olive, dark olive, and olive-brown dubbing, pale olive-dyed hackle stem, or stripped peacock herl.

Wings: The wings are made from one or more CDC oiler puffs, nipple plumes, or CDC tufts. These terms describe the small stemless CDC feathers, ranging from white to dark dun, that cap the duck's uropygial gland. They form a wick at the base of the upper tail feathers that transfers oil to the duck's bill during preening. These puffs, plumes, or tufts are not the traditional large stemmed CDC feathers. All the puff barbs extend from of a small single bud base. Because of the embedded oils, these barbs are remarkably water-repellant and buoyant. For the wings and hackle, select the fluffy rather than the supersaturated and matted barbs.

Hackle: Stripped light-gray or olive-gray CDC puff barbs spun in a split-thread and sparingly wrapped fore and aft of the wing. Merely place one to two puffs in the split-thread and prune the base buds to spread the barbs. Usually one hackle puff is sufficient even for quick water.

Tying the BWO Puff

1. Mount the thread base and tail barbs.

2. Mount and wrap slender body.

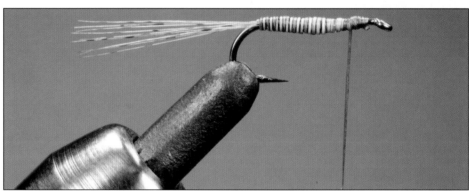

3. Mount and secure the wings. Use 1 or 2 puffs for the wings but avoid excessive winging. Once you have overlapped the puff with a thread, slide it to the proper length, and then remove the base bud. Secure the wings with additional thread wraps.

4. The short, fuzzy CDC puff barbs make superior hackle. Split the thread and insert the puff so that the thread traps the middle of the puff. Then trim the bud base to spread the barbs.

5. Spin the split-thread hackle.

6. Wrap the hackle fore and aft and then remove residual barbs and whip-finish.

10

THE BASIC INSECTS

THE ANGLER'S *BASIC INSECTS* IS A BRIEF GUIDE TO IDENTIFYING SOME common aquatic insects. It is only a beginning. Matching the hatch is the traditional method of capturing an insect and selecting a fly pattern to match it. It is direct and simple, requiring minimal insect knowledge. In time, however, most anglers want to know more about the insects that trout consume and that tyers imitate. Insect knowledge—the insect's appearance, life cycle, and movement—is a fascinating study that often results in greater angling success. When sampling insects, select the most active and prevalent. Check the aquatic plants, the submerged rocks, the tree leaves, and the bushes along the bank. What flies in the air or floats on the water or clings to the leaves? It is certain that when you fly fish, you will eventually come to admire a few selected insects. They are, after all, one of the exquisite charms of fly fishing.

THE CADDIS, THE SEDGE

The tailless adult caddis or sedge is dressed in dull motley. It has four membranous wings with the forewings slightly longer than the hind wings. These tent wings, which completely cover the body of the insect when at rest, are commonly covered with minute hairs or, in some species, scales. *Cul de canard* (CDC) barbs effectively imitate the fuzzy, floating adult caddis. The order designation, *Trichoptera*, means "hair-wings" (Greek *tricho* = hair and *ptera* = wing). The term caddis may derive from the Old French, *cadis*, meaning "silk floss" in reference to the caddis case construction. Another possible origin is the Greek *cadus*, meaning case or vessel, perhaps in reference to the cylindrical larva case. The Middle English *cadas* or *cadace* may also refer to the case. "Both the caddis or artificial fly and the caddis fly (the caddis worm) derive from caddis, caddice, floss silk, cotton wool, worsted yarn, especially ribbon. . . ." Eric Partridge, *Origins* (1983). The term sedge most likely refers to the insect's appearance on riparian sedge grass.

Caddis have a flopping, fluttering flight. The adults feed upon liquid foods—moisture is the most important factor for insect longevity—and will live about one month. They may be found in calm (static) waters—these may be reared in a home aquarium—as well as moving (lotic) waters. The larva is called, in the promiscuous angler's argot, such names as rockworm, caseworm, periwinkle, and strawworm. In a manner of speaking, the caddis or sedge is an aquatic silkworm moth. The adult sedge has fine wing hairs or scales. At dusk, the sedge is attracted to light like a moth. The extended wings of an adult sedge pattern conceal the hook bend and spear, thereby increasing its effectiveness.

They have a complete metamorphosis, and the aquatic larva, after a year, will pupate. Pupation lasts about two weeks after the insect seals the case, allowing water entry. The pharate adult (the adult immediately prior to emergence still enclosed in the pupal husk) then cuts the case open with mandibles and swims to the surface (in swift water) or crawls out on objects (in calm water) to emerge. The midlegs, or mesotarsus, of the pharate adult are free and formed for subsurface emergence. The larval cases, which are cemented together with sticky, silk-like saliva, possess a slight negative suspension that helps the larva pull the case along the bottom as it grazes upon algae and plant debris. The heavier case constructions, of course, occur in flowing water, while the lighter construction occurs in calm water. The majority of caddis larvae consume various plants and perform a significant act in the biosystem by converting plants into protein.

Characteristics of the Sedge

The Caddis Larva

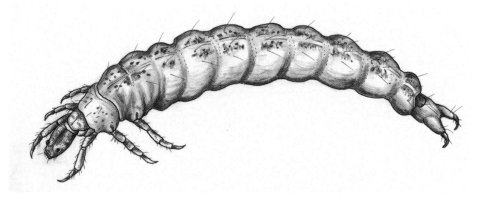

The Caddis Larva

1.   Minute antennae
2.   Caterpillar-like without wing pads
3.   Filamentous gills, if present, only on abdominal segments
4.   Anal hooks on the last abdomen segment
5.   Cased (a mineral or plant shelter) and uncased (campodeiform) species

The Caddis Pupa

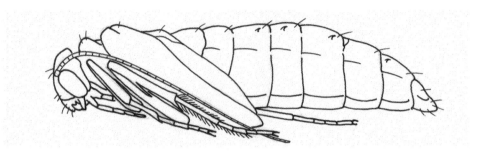

The Caddis Pupa

1.   Subsurface emergence upon pupation
2.   Antennae nearly body length
3.   No anal hook or tail
4.   Immediately prior to emergence, housed in a silk cocoon usually encased in mineral or plant debris

The Caddis Adult

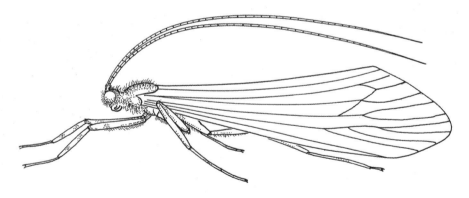

The Caddis Adult

1.   Four wings covered with fine scales or hairs; many adults have slate-brown wings and antennae that are two to three times longer than the body length
2.   Wings swept back and held tent-like over the abdomen
3.   Antennae body length or longer
4.   A fluttering, floppy flier
5.   Attracted to light at night

Pupation lasts about two weeks after the insect seals the case, allowing water entry. The pharate adult then cuts the case open with mandibles and swims to the surface (in swift water) or crawls out on objects (in calm water) to emerge. The midlegs (the mesotarsus) of the pharate adult are free and formed for subsurface sculling emergence.

The ova are usually laid *en masse* in the water or on objects; some species enter the water to deposit the eggs. The larval cases, which are cemented with a sticky silk-like saliva, possess a slight negative suspension that helps the larva pull its case along the bottom as it grazes upon algae and plant debris. The heavier case construction, of course, occurs in flowing water, while the lighter construction occurs in calm water. While it appears that most species hatch during early or late hours of the day, a few species evidently are purely nocturnal in their emergence.

Most adults have lackluster wings and antennae that are two or three times the body length. It is important to note that some species are transformed immediately into fliers as soon as they surface. Others swim and struggle a considerable distance before flight. The struggle of an emerging caddis is perhaps due to the difficulty in breaking the pupal cuticle or increasing wing strength. It is not the act of wing drying. The fine hairs or scales make caddis wings water repellant, thereby eliminating the need for drying prior to flight. On still waters, this flight struggle is quite evident and encourages trout feeding.

Much has been written concerning the caddis's toleration for adverse water conditions and pollution. The importance of pollution toleration of particular insects may favor the needs of one insect over another. For example, if water enrichment occurs, the algae increase may favor the existence of the net-spinning caddis, which feeds on drifting algae in the water column. Since productive space is limited, other insects may decrease, thereby drastically altering or decreasing the fauna. Caddis patterns—larva, pupa, and adult—are remarkably effective. A larva pattern is wormlike; a pupa pattern typically has an enclosing body sheath; an adult pattern usually includes appropriate body color, folded tent wings, and long antennae.

The Cased Caddis

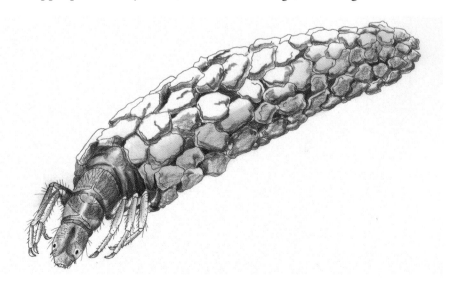

General classification includes the following five categories:

1. Casebuilders: This embraces the majority of caddis; they are herbaceous and, based on their case construction, are called carpenters or masons.
2. Campodeiform: This includes the caseless free-livers or hunters.
3. Net Spinners: This comprises the silk-tube makers and the herbaceous weavers.
4. Purse-Makers: These larvae are extremely small and free living until the final instar (stage), when they make a portable purse case.
5. Saddle-Makers: These larvae construct a portable saddle case.

THE MIDGE, THE CHIRONOMID

The Chironomid (Greek: *chronom*, *-us*, "one who moves the hands") is a nonbiting midge. They take their name either from the plumose or palmated hand-like male antennae or from "one who gestures with the hands," referring to the upraised waving forelegs of the adult. Anglers call the Chironomids, midges, gnats, bloodworms, and, in England, buzzers. The English term buzzer describes its circular dance on the water surface prior to flight. Emergence differs in species; there is typically a spring and summer maxima (the period of greatest hatching) in March and April and later in about July. Otherwise, they will emerge throughout the year. Winter midging can be excellent due to the multi-brooded midge and lack of competing hatches. It is claimed that midges or Chironomids inhabit half of all available waters and, when present, there will be 50 or more different species. There are more than 100 genera and more than 2,500 species in North America. Larval density of 50,000 per square meter is not unusual and may be exceeded. The larval stage, with four instars (the nymphal period between molts), usually lasts from two weeks to six months depending upon species, temperature, and food. Those that inhabit the deep Northern lakes may require up to seven years before maturing. They have one or more generations per year and are the most prolific and widespread of all aquatic insects. Other species of *Diptera* (two-winged insects) are often confused with midges: the Reed Smut or Black Fly (*Simulium spp.*) and the Black Gnat, a common title for a myriad of insects including the Black Dance Fly (*Hilara femorata*) and Dixa Midge (*Dixa minuta*).

The Larvae

It is of interest that larval coloration is often associated with a particular habitat. In general, the olive and brown larvae occur in high-alkalinity and high-oxygenated waters. The red and purple larvae appear in high-acid and low-oxygenated waters. The olives are most common in moderate or high-oxygenated waters. Consequently, an angler may base the pattern color, with modest accuracy, on habitat alone.

The red larvae, sometimes called bloodworms, live in lake mud, in oxygen-poor bogs, or lake depths, as well as rivers and streams. The bloodworm, a title granted to all red larvae, may be prolific and constitute the principal food for certain fish. The blood is hemoglobin. John Goddard, in *Trout Flies of Still Water* (1966), states that the hemoglobin assists the blood by storing oxygen and providing it when required. Thus the insect is able to live in low-oxygenated or deep waters. Also, in specimens that he had studied, it appeared that the more mature the larva, the brighter or denser the hemoglobin as pupation approached. The larvae feed upon diatoms, bacteria, periphyton, and algae. Periodically, some larvae swim about with a whipping action, often going to the surface. Such ramblings are probably due to a lack of oxygen. The angler's sink and draw retrieve imitates this descent-ascent behavior.

Chironomid Larva Characteristics

The Chironomid Larva

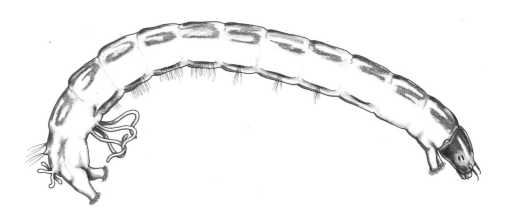

1. Larval body length 1–20 mm (most 1–10 mm).
2. Segmented maggot-like body with no distinctive thorax or abdomen.
3. A small, round head and olive, black, gray, yellow, tan, and red body colors.
4. Usually the larvae have 11 or 12 soft abdominal segments with the last segment ending in a conspicuous tuft of hair.
5. Many species live in slender silk tubes attached to the bottom (substrata) of a stream or lake.
6. Some species have fine, scattered body hairs or individual tufts or fringes.

7. Small, fleshy projections (called tubercles), may be present on one or more body segments.
8. No distinctive gills, legs, or wing pads, but in many species, the tubercles form a pair of short, ventral prolegs with crotchets (small curved hooks) on the first thoracic and last abdominal segments.
9. Larvae have a sclerotized (hardened cuticle) head capsule or retracted head capsule.
10. The worm-like larvae prefer slow streams with heavy plant growth and soft silt but can survive in a wide span of temperatures and habitats.

The Pupa

Pupation usually occurs in the last larval skin. Prior to emergence, the pupa, provided with respiratory filaments or horns, may hang vertically in the surface film. After ecdysis (the actual shedding of the larval skin), the pupa may hide until emergence. Although fish actively pursue the larvae on the bottom, they feed principally on the active pharate adult (the developed adult in the pupal case). Although the pharate adult is often the main trout food, all stages may be effectively imitated and are taken by trout.

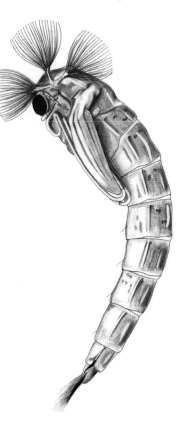

The Chironomid Pupa

Chironomid Pupa Characteristics

1. In the pupa, the appendages are sealed to the body surface. Otherwise, pupation occurs in the puparium or last larval skin. Some pupate in cocoons or in gelatinous purses.
2. Head, thorax, and wings are concentrated and clustered together.
3. They may have distinct filamentous gills, commonly imitated in pupal patterns, on top of the thorax.
4. The pupae lack tails.

The Adult

The male adult midge has a distinctive plumose or feather-like antenna, often longer than the head, and mating forceps. Beyond fishing the major and sporadic midge hatches, winter midging can be excellent due to the multi-brooded midge and the lack of competing hatches. The gnat-like adults have scaleless, simply veined, flat-lying wings, which are usually shorter than the body. The male has mating forceps, but neither sex has tails. The wings are either clear or dun, whereas the body is often black, olive, greenish-gray, or gray. They have one pair of minute halteres (halters, balancing knobs, or vestigial wings) in place of the rear wings, a thickened thorax, and long slender legs.

The midges are one of the few insects to emerge in abundance from the deepest areas of a lake. When so doing, the midge creates a soft, slowly-expanding rise ring known as a smut rise. However, some species may be found in the shallow and moderate margin areas of lakes. Most emerge at dusk, a few emerge at dawn, others during the day. Populations in rivers may undergo enormous fluctuations that are rapidly repopulated from a small residual colony. If there are adults on the water, the pupa will be commonly active in the water column. The adult Chironomid characteristics are as follows:

The Adult Male Chironomid

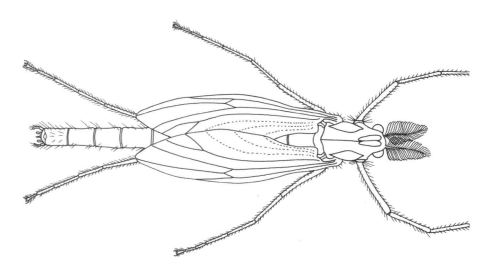

1. The adult has an enlarged thorax, which measures from 1–15 mm and lacks tails.
2. The slender adult body has the same color range as the larva.
3. The adult has long slender legs with the forelegs the longest.
4. The antennae with more than five segments are less than half the body length.
5. Males have bushy or feathered antennae (plumose antennae) and mating forceps.
6. The wings are either gray or transparent while the body is often gray-green, green, or black.

The typical hook size of the larvae ranges from about 16 to 20 or larger. Imitative patterns of the pupa, the stage commonly fished, are tied in hook sizes 14 to 20, and the adult from about 14 to 18. Such hooks should be strong with an adequate gap. Larger patterns, such as a size 6 or 12 Red San

Juan Worm, may mimic the bloodworm. A sinking line, a long leader, and an ultraslow retrieve are the hallmarks of pupa fishing. In fly-tying, the imitative elements of the pupa include size, color, body shape, and filamentous gills. The adult requires two small flat wings slightly shorter than body. The distinctly segmented body is often imitated with stripped peacock herl. The Chironomid, by sheer volume and distribution, are important inhabitants of streams and lakes.

THE CORIXA (THE WATER BOATMAN)

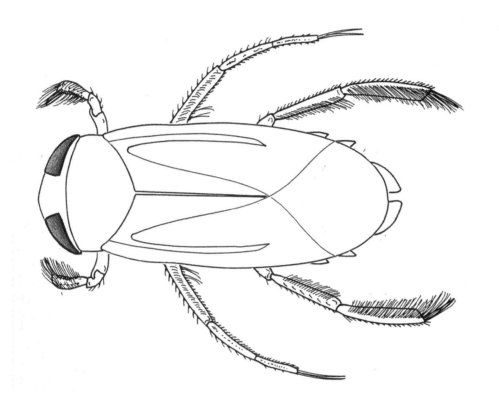

The Corixa

Many years ago, when trout were large and the summer days long, I scooped up a corixa, the water boatman, to examine it. As I admired its glistening wing case and long oar legs, it startled me with an abrupt flight. Stunned, I stared as it flew away and splatted back into the water. I had never seen a corixa on the wing before. They filled the shallows of the lake, resting at the surface and then diving down among the weeds. Underwater, their bodies shimmered in a silver sheath of air.

With well more than one hundred species, they constitute the largest group of water bugs and are a principal fish food in late summer, fall, and winter. The corixa, the water boatman (family *Corixidae*), is often confused with the similar backswimmer (family *Notonectidae*). As the name implies, backswimmers swim backside down. Both insects occupy the shallows and have a jerky, sculling motion. And both usually have oval bodies with white or pale abdomens, though the abdomen of some corixa may be pale tan, brown, or yellow. Corixa and backswimmers have four wings, tightly folded, resembling the leathery wing case of beetles. The wing case of the backswimmer is sometimes paler than a corixa case. Unlike the corixa, the highly predacious backswimmer can inflict a stinging bite if handled roughly.

Backswimmers often rest at the surface with their bodies at an angle, head down, and swimming legs extended. Both insects are active in the shallows, rising and diving to replenish their oxygen. Fine hydrofuge hairs hold an air bubble in place along the abdomen. When submerged, corixa cling to plants, often for some time. Mating and migration may be the cause for most flights. They splat into the water like hail. Though I have not been privy to their music, the curious corixa even sing to each other. Due to the similarities of boatman and backswimmers, a single pattern usually suffices.

The elements of imitation include the simple oval body, the conspicuous oar legs, and a body bubble of tinsel, glass, or silver bead. Bright dubbing, a synthetic or feather wing case, and oar legs complete the pattern. A shallow pattern requires little weight; often a proper weight hook, a 1X or 2X heavy, is sufficient. A floating or sink-tip line is regularly used for these shallow running bugs. Patterns, either in hook size 12 or 10, may be unweighted for shallow running or weighted for deeper running. A short staccato retrieve imitates the sculling motion of the insect. Cast near aquatic plants while varying the retrieve speed. Unfortunately, the corixa is better known by trout than by anglers.

THE DAMSELFLY

The damselfly—order *Odonata*, suborder *zygoptera* (Greek *zygo* = yoke, *ptera* = wings, hence "yoke-winged")—has gills that appear like three feathered paddles at the end of a slender abdomen. The nymph swims by body undulations, the gills functioning much like sculling oars. The nymph travels with minnow-like whipping motions. Most damselfly nymphs are somewhat transparent pale yellow, tan, olive, or brown. Immediately before hatching (usually in June or July), the nymphs migrate to shore in numbers. Such migrations during the morning hours will boil the water with slashing and rolling trout as they feed on the struggling nymphs. When at rest, the wings of the adult damselfly are folded parallel on top of the body with the edge up. The base width of the forewing and hind wing is nearly the same; the hind wings of the adult dragonfly are wider than the forewings.

Damselfly patterns, unlike dragonfly patterns, are a rather recent development. According to Marvin Nolte, damselfly patterns did not reach importance until after the late 1940's. In the 1950's, both William F. Blades and C. F. Walker tied adult damsel patterns.

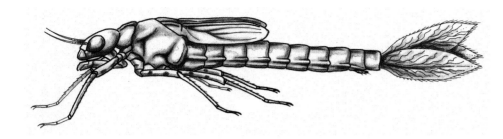

Typical Damselfly Nymph

Characteristics of the Damselfly Nymph

1. Three paddle-like tails (actually, caudal gill lamellae)
2. Large eyes
3. Modified and extendable capture lobes (the labium). As with the dragonfly, the prehensile labium masks the lower head and mouthparts.
4. Long, slender body
5. Two pairs of wing pads
6. Whipping undulations of body when swimming
7. Inconspicuous bristle-like antennae

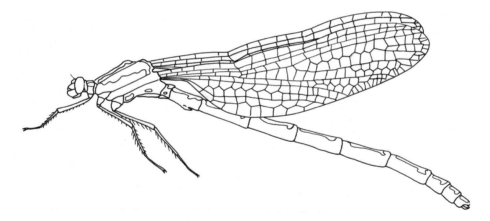

Adult Damselfly, Lateral View

Characteristics of the Adult Damselfly

1. Four wings yoked or narrow at the base
2. When at rest, wings held together (often edge up and extended above and parallel to the body)
3. Large eyes separated by more than their width
4. Inconspicuous bristle-like antennae
5. Unusual male sexual organ (accessory genitalia) on the ventral surface of the second abdominal segment

In fly-tying, the imitative elements of nymph and adults include size, slender body, and colors. The brightly colored adults with parallel wings are often imitated. The dragonfly nymph is common in lakes and slow streams. Retrieve the sunken nymph with slow to medium 10″ line strips near water plants and cruising or rising fish.

THE DRAGONFLY

The dragonfly, suborder *anisoptera* (from Greek *anis* = unequal, plus *ptera*=wings, hence "unequal wings"). The adult dragonfly holds its wings at right angles to the body while in flight or repose. The nymphs appear in still or slow waters and, although not as abundant as insects such as the mayfly, can attain a length of more than 30 millimeters before emergence. Their size alone is enough to support large trout. The order *Odonata*, which the dragonfly shares with the delicate damselfly, refers to the toothed labium or "lower lip" that extends nearly ⅓ the body length and functions as a capture lobe. They are predaceous in their nymphal stages, particularly in the stages near emergence (the senior instars). They devour nymphs, larvae, and even small fish. Leonard West, in *The Natural Trout Fly and Its Imitation* (1921), calls the dragonfly nymph the *bête noire* of caddis larvae, "The long spear, with which they are armed, proving a capital weapon for poking the Caddis-worm out of the protecting sheath."

When ready for transformation to the adult stage, the nymph usually crawls out of the water onto rocks or plant stems for the final molt. Once out of the final nymphal husk, the newly hatched (teneral) adult is soft and a pale yellow for a few hours. The adult will expand its wings to full size in about a half-hour. Male and female adults are usually similar in color, although the male may be brighter.

Characteristics of the Dragonfly Nymph

The Dragonfly Nymph (*Aeshnidae*)

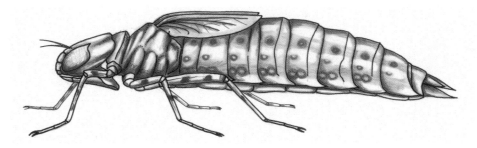

1. Large compound eyes
2. Inconspicuous bristle-like antennae
3. Modified and extendable capture lobes (the labia)
4. Internal rectal gills
5. Usually a compact, corpulent body, often oval or triangular in cross section
6. Locomotion by rectal expulsion of water
7. Six clustered legs moved forward on the thorax

Characteristics of the Adult Dragonfly

1. Large compound eyes
2. Inconspicuous bristle-like antennae
3. Lacks tail
4. Two pairs of large wings held horizontally, often tilted up or down, when at rest
5. Eyes never separated by more than their own width
6. Superb fliers that capture insects with their "net" legs during flight
7. Unusual sexual organ (*penis vesicle*) on the ventral surface of the second abdominal segment

Unlike the fabled dragons of yore, the dragonfly breathes water. Nymphal movement is the result of the rapid expelling of water from its anal cavity, which functions as a rectal gill due to the thin-walled lower intestine. This anal respiration produces an unusual swimming pattern. The common expulsive attitude consists of a slightly arched body with the legs relaxed and folded beneath the thorax. The abdomen dilates and contracts both in length and diameter during propulsion. The movement is a fast-slow sequence, followed by a momentary sink before another expulsion of water propels it up and forward. Once I filmed the swimming nymph in slow motion. Although the film results were inconclusive due to the limited study and abnormal environment of the filming tank, they were suggestive. The dragonfly nymphs averaged 22 mm in length and 7 mm in abdominal width. The glide length was only a few inches. Slowly retrieve the sunken pattern with 3″ to 5″ line strips. The nymphs seldom travel long distances through open water; they live a furtive existence among the plants and debris. The length of the explosive glide depends on speciation and maturation of the nymphs.

For the fly fisher, the dragonfly nymphs may be classified according to two habitat types: the plant clingers (such as the *Aeshnidae*), which actively pursue their prey, and the burrowers or silters (such as the *Libellulidae* and the western riffle-dwelling *Gomphidae*), which either camouflage themselves with silt and algae or burrow into the marl and mud. The more predaceous clingers usually have an ovoid cross section. There are distinctions between the borrowers and silters, but for practical purposes, both may be considered bottom dwellers. The silters have minute hairs or horns that assist in camouflage, whereas the burrowers have somewhat flattened or shovel-shaped body parts for digging. The burrowers and silters normally strike only when their prey is within close range. The clingers inhabit the marginal epilimnion of the lake, the moderately shallow shore zone. Their general coloration tends toward the mottled deep olives, bright greens, and dark browns with often intricate, cryptic stippling and delicate runic etchings along the abdominal plates. The nymphs that conceal themselves in the silt and mud appear, for the most part, dull and mottled; those that inhabit the plant mats are olive and brown.

Fly-tyers imitate nymphs and, to a lesser degree, adults. In fly-tying, the imitative elements of the dragonfly nymph include size, spindle shape, and mottled coloration. This, along with the retrieve, are probably essential imitative elements. Adult patterns with stiff, extended wings usually defy casting; soft, collapsible wings are preferred. The dragonfly nymph, rather than the adult, is the customary stage imitated and fished. To replicate the blotched body colors, some nymphal patterns have woven bodies. Casts are made near aquatic plants, rises, or cruising fish. Use a short staccato retrieve with periodic pauses.

THE MAYFLY

The mayfly (order Ephemeroptera, *ephemero* = "short lived" and *ptera* = "winged," hence "lasting but a day," the day fly) is most important to the fly fisher. The English term mayfly was so given because the major appearance of this particular insect occurs during the month of May. A few larger mayflies are called drakes, such as the Green Drake, Brown Drake, and Gray Drake. The term drake is cognate with dragon. The mayfly develops from egg (ova) to nymph to dun (subimago) to spinner (imago) to spent spinner (dead upon the water with spread wings). Nymphal growth progresses through a series of twenty to thirty molts. Each growth phase between molts is called an instar. The mayfly is the only insect to molt again with wings (from dun to spinner) after emergence. This final molt is sometimes known by the angler as the bush hatch. Mayflies are often uniquely named by anglers according to their habitat adaptation as swimmers, burrowers, clingers, and crawlers. This generic classification is the first step in identification, imitation, and presentation. Mayflies display a remarkable variety of body shapes and sizes. The adult male *Hexagenia limbata* is 28 mm excluding tails; the adult male *Caenis amica* (earlier *simulans*) is 4 mm long excluding tails. The non-feeding adults spend their brief time swarming, mating, and egg-laying (ovipositing). The mayfly is a principal insect for fish, fly-tyers, and fly fishers. It is the icon of angling with a fly.

Mayfly Nymphal Characteristics (junior and senior instars)

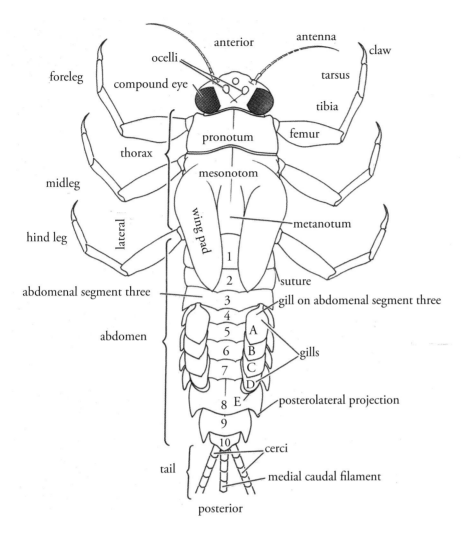

Although mayfly nymphs vary greatly in shape and size, this illustration offers basic terminology.

1. Three distinct body parts: head, thorax, and abdomen
2. Three tails, with some exceptions, e.g, clinger genus *Epeorus*, swimmer genus *Acentrella*, and the species *Baetis bicaudatus* (*bi* = two, *cauda* = tail)
3. Two short antennae
4. One obvious pair of wing pads. Near emergence, the wing pads darken.
5. Plate-like or leaf-like gills on the top or sides of abdomen
6. Ten abdominal segments
7. Six legs, each with a single claw
8. Significant variety in body shape and size

A Mayfly Nymph

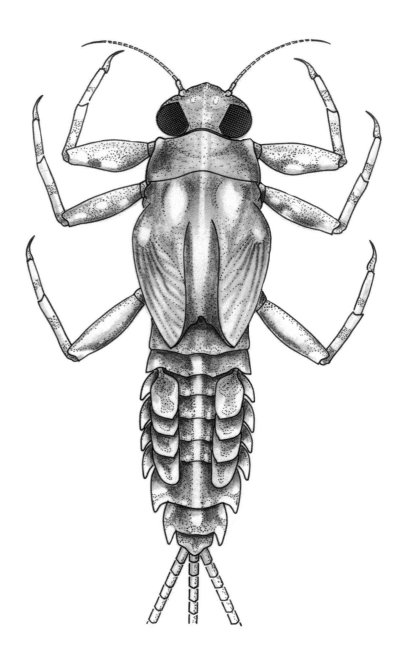

Dun Characteristics (the subimago)

1. The sexually immature adult
2. Opaque wings (gray or gray-brown, pale yellow, etc.) with or without contrasting markings
3. Lack of mature coloration of body and wings
4. Two or three thread-like tails
5. Large front wings held erect or sail-like and smaller or absent hind wings
6. Small bristle-like antennae

Spinner Characteristics (the imago)

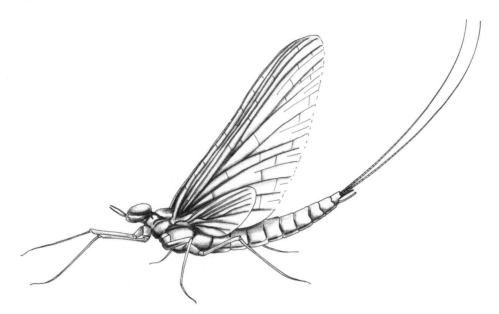

A Mayfly Adult

1. The sexually mature adult
2. Male with elongated front legs and much larger eyes than the female
3. Glassy hyaline (transparent) wings with or without contrasting markings
4. Terminal mating claspers on males
5. Tails may equal body length or longer
6. Development of complete mature coloration after six to eight hours

In fly-tying, the imitative elements of the mayfly include wing and body shape, size, and color. Nymph, emerger, dun, drifting adult, and spent spinner (exhausted or lifeless spinner upon the water) are all imitated. More realistic patterns may match tail color and accurate length. Some insects have a dominant eye color that tyers match with the head threads. Traditionally, the shoulder hackle imitates either the wing or the leg color of the insect. A nymph pattern usually requires a slow retrieve; a dun or spinner needs a drag-free drift on slack tippet.

The Basic Mayfly Nymphs

There is parsimony in nature. Nature often simplifies or eliminates what it cannot use. It should not surprise us, then, that in the insect world, form follows function. The shape of an insect comments on its habits and habitat. Nature's economy, the simplicity expressed in the form of a nymph, actually allows us to casually classify mayfly nymphs according to the four fundamental groups: the Clingers, the Swimmers, the Burrowers, and the Crawlers.

The Clingers: The compressed clingers (such as *Heptageniidae*) with flat head and body hug the stones in fast flowing waters. The clinger has a wide head—wider than the thorax and abdomen—and two or three tails. The body appears compressed and somewhat horizontally flattened. Dorsal eyes may appear on a horizontal head. Duns and spinners have only two tails.

The Swimmers: The swimmer body is cylindrical, slender, and streamlined often with three interlocking fringed tails. A few have two tails. Some have long antennae of more than three times the head width and long slender legs. The slender, small swimmers (such as *Baetidae*) with fringed tails scurry about like micro-minnows while the duns and spinners have only two tails.

The Burrowers: The large tusked burrowers (such as *Ephemeridae*) bury themselves in silt, mud, or marl of lake and streambeds. The burrow body varies but is often rectangular and flattened with a head narrower than the thorax. Gills are often forked. They have tusks (mandibles) and flanged, turned-out front legs for burrowing. Duns and spinners have two or three tails.

The Crawlers: The crawlers (such as *Ephemerellidae*) with oval gills on top of the abdomen clamber sluggishly among the stones and debris on the bottom. They are generally stout and more rectangular than swimmers, though with significant exceptions. Unlike the dorsal eyes of clingers, the crawlers have eyes on the side of the head. The duns and spinners have three tails. Crawlers include some of the angler's best friends: the genera *Ephemerella*, *Paraleptophlebia*, *Leptophlebia*, *Tricorythodes*, and *Caenis*.

THE STONEFLY

The stonefly (the *plecoptera* or "folded or twisted wing" fly, from Greek *plektos*=twisted) has a head and thorax with a combined length that nearly equals that of the abdomen. The abdomen has ten segments with nine clearly discernible. Each thoracic section has a pair of legs terminating in a two-clawed tarsus. A pair of wings is rooted in each of the two rear thoracic sections. The ventral thoracic area carries the filamentous gills. The placement of the hair gills is one index to speciation. The nymphs have two whiplike tails that are segmented and slightly shorter than the abdomen. However, in some genera, the tails are noticeably longer than the abdomen.

The nymphs are primarily herbivorous, living on riparian plant matter, but depending on species and available food, predacious activity is found among some senior instars (the nymph prior to emergence). The nymphs are easily distinguished by the absence of abdominal gills; only the two-inch *Pteronarcys* will have minor strand gills on the first few abdominal segments. The nymphs usually have one subaquatic year; the large species, however, such as *Pteronarcys californica*, may have three. With minimal swimming ability, the nymphs crawl and clamber among the rocks. They are best imitated with an upstream or cross-stream tension drift or teasing dead drifts.

The notable hatch of the salmon fly (*P. californica*) on the Madison River in Montana begins about the first week in June at Three Forks and moves upstream. The hatch arrives about the Fourth of July at Ennis, appears about the fourteenth of July at McAtee Bridge, and finishes during the last week of the month at Slide Inn. The three-year-old *P. californica* develops rapidly in the warm waters of spring and migrates to the slack shallows, where it crawls out on rocks and other objects. The cranial suture splits, and the adult emerges. The nymphs will emerge for a couple of days on any particular stream section as the hatch slowly moves upstream. Such mass hatching provokes active rises from cruising trout.

Stonefly Nymph Characteristics

The Stonefly Nymph

1. A distinct head, thorax, and abdomen
2. Six legs, each terminated by two claws
3. Two distinct and separated whiplike tails
4. Distinct, segmented antennae
5. Gills absent or filamentous gills beneath the thorax and between the legs
6. Ten distinct abdominal segments, usually oval or circular in cross section
7. Inferior swimmers that either arch the body or assume a fetal position when adrift

8. Instars (the stage or periods between molts) vary from 22 to 33 days with a nymphal period from one to three years
9. Two pair of wing pads

Stonefly Adult Characteristics

The Stonefly Adult

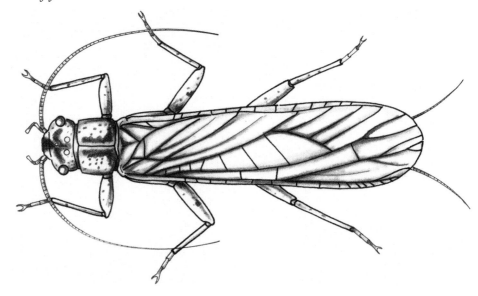

1. The general appearance of a squat aquatic cockroach with wings tight and flat above the abdomen
2. Four equal-length, strongly veined wings
3. When airborne, a near-vertical body attitude and a heavy, fluttering flight
4. Three tarsal leg segments, the leg segments next to the claw

In fly-tying, the imitative elements of the nymph include size, color, and drift attitude. Drift attitude is sometimes imitated with particular hook bends, such as the York bend with a mildly arched hook shank. Most adult patterns emphasize size, color, and large flat wings over the body.

Stonefly

BIBLIOGRAPHY

Ashley, Clifford W. *The Ashley Book of Knots*. New York: Doubleday, corrected reprint of 1944 edition, undated.

Bainbridge, George C. *The Fly-Fisher's Guide to Aquatic Flies and Their Imitation*. London: A&C Black Ltd., 1936.

Baird, R.D. *A Trout Rose*. Norwich, England: Jarrolds Publishing, 1948.

Berners, Dame Juliana (attributed author). *The Book of Saint Albans*: includes facsimile reprint of *The Treatyse of Fysshynge Wyth an Angle*, (1496). New York: Abercrombie & Fitch, 1966.

Brooks, Joe. *Complete Book of Fly Fishing*. Outdoor Life, 1958.

Caucci, Al and Bob Nastasi. *Hatches II*. Revised edition. New York: Lyons & Burford, 1986.

Chouinard, Yvon with Craig Mathews and Mauro Mazzo. *Simple Fly Fishing: Techniques for Tenkara and Rod & Reel*. Ventura, California: Patagonia Books, 2014.

Clarke, Brian and John Goddard. *The Trout and the Fly*. London: Ernest Benn, Ltd., 1980.

Darbee, Harry with Austin Mac Francis. *Catskill Flytier*. New York: J.B. Lippincott Company, 1977.

Halford, Frederic. *The Dry Fly Man's Handbook*. London: George Routledge & Sons, Ltd., 1913.

————, ————. *Floating Flies and How to Dress Them*. London: Sampson Low, Marston, Searle and Rivington, 1886.

Harding, Col. E.W. *The Fly Fisher & the Trout's Point of View*. London: Seeley, Service, & Company, Ltd. 1931.

Hills, John Waller. *River Keeper: The Life of William James Lunn*. London: Geoffrey Bles, Two Manchester Square. 1934.

Jorgensen, Poul. *Salmon Flies*. Harrisburg, Pennsylvania: Stackpole Books, 1978.

Kelleher, Kevin, MD with Misako Ishimura. *Tenkara*. Guilford, CT: Lyons Press, an imprint of Globe Pequot Press, 2011.

Knight, John Alden and Richard Alden Knight. *The Complete Book of Fly Casting*. New York: G.P. Putnam's Sons, 1963.

Kreh, Lefty and Mark Sosin. *Practical Fishing Knots II*. New York: Lyons & Burford, 1991.

Kreh, Lefty. *Ultimate Guide to Fly Fishing*. Guilford, CT: The Lyons Press, 2003.

Lawrie, W.H. *Scottish Trout Flies: An Analysis and Compendium*. London: Frederick Muller, Ltd. 1966.

Leiser, Eric. *The Book of Fly Patterns*. New York: Alfred A. Knopf, 1987.

Leonard, J. Edson. *Flies*. New York: A.S. Barnes, 1960.

Maclean, Norman. *A River Runs Through It*. Chicago: University of Chicago Press, 1976.

Marinaro, Vincent. *A Modern Dry-Fly Code*. New York: Crown Publishers, Inc., 1970.

Marinaro, Vincent. *In the Ring of the Rise*. New York: Crown Publishers, Inc., 1976.

Martin, Darrel. *Fly-Tying Methods*. New York: Lyons & Burford, Publishers, 1987.

———, ———. *Micropatterns*. New York: The Lyons Press, 1994.

———, ———. *The Fly-Fisher's Craft*. Guilford, CT: The Lyons Press, an imprint of Globe Pequot Press, 2006.

———, ———. *The Fly Fisher's Illustrated Dictionary*. New York: The Lyons Press, 2000.

McClane, A.J., editor. *McClane's Standard Fishing Encyclopedia*. New York: Holt, Rinehart, and Winston, 1965.

Nemes, Sylvester. *The Soft-Hackled Fly*. Old Greenwich, CT: The Chatham Press, 1975.

Nichols, Jay, editor. *1001 Fly Fishing Tips*. New Cumberland, Pennsylvania: Headwater Books, 2008.

O'Gorman, James. *The Practice of Angling, Particularly as Regards Ireland*. reprint of first 1845 edition, in two volumes. The Fly Fisher's Classic Library Edition. Bath, England: Bath Press, Ltd. 1993.

Owen, Peter. *The Book of Outdoor Knots*. New York: Lyons & Burford, 1993.

Partridge, Eric. *Origins*. New York: Greenwich House, distributed by Crown Publishers, Inc., 1983.

Pryce-Tannatt, T.E. *How to Dress Salmon Flies*. London: Adam & Charles Black, first edition, 1914.

Pulman, G.P.R. *The Vade Mecum of Fly-Fishing for Trout*. London: Longman, Brown, Green, and Longmans, third edition, 1851.

Ronalds, Alfred. *The Fly-Fisher's Entomology.* London: London: Longman, Brown, Green and Longmans, third edition, 1844.

Schwiebert, Ernest. *Trout.* New York: E.P. Dutton, two volumes, 1978.

Skues, G.E.M. *Side-Lines, Side lights, & Reflections.* Philadelphia: J.B. Lippincott Co., first American edition, undated.

Stewart, W.C. *The Practical Angler.* Edinburgh: Adam & Charles Black, 1857.

Sturgis, William B. *Fly Tying.* New York: Charles Scribner's Sons, 1940.

Sturgis, William B. and Eric Taverner. *New Lines for Fly-Fishers.* London: Seeley, Service, & Company, Ltd. 1946.

Swisher, Doug and Carl Richards. *Emerger.* New York: Lyons & Burford, 1991.

Swisher, Doug and Carl Richards. *Selective Trout.* New York: Crown Publishers, Inc., 1971.

Talleur, Dick. *The Versatile Fly Tyer.* New York: Lyons & Burford, 1990

Taverner, Eric. *Fly Tying for Salmon.* London: Seeley, Service & Company, Ltd., 1942.

Taverner, Eric. *Trout Fishing from All Angles.* London: Seeley, Service & Company, Ltd., 1933.

Tod, E.M. *Wet-Fly Fishing.* London: Sampson, Low, Marston & Company, Ltd. third edition, 1914.

Venables, Col. Robert. *The Experienced Angler.* London: T. Gosden, 1827, reprint of Richard Marriot 1662 edition, 1827.

Walton, Izaak and Charles Cotton. *The Complete Angler.* London: John Hawkins of Twickenham, second Hawkins edition, 1766.

Whitlock, Dave. *Guide to Aquatic Trout Foods.* New York: Nick Lyons Books/Winchester Press Books, 1982.

Willers, W. B. *Trout Biology.* Madison, Wisconsin: The University of Wisconsin Press, Ltd., 1981.

Wright, Leonard M. Jr. *The Ways of Trout.* New York: Nick Lyons Books/Winchester Press Books, 1985.